Live to Be Forgotten

Dixon Edward Hoste, China Inland Mission,
and the Indigenous Chinese Church in
Early Twentieth-Century China

Patrick Fung

ACADEMIC

© 2024 Patrick Fung

Published 2024 by Langham Academic
An imprint of Langham Publishing
www.langhampublishing.org

Langham Publishing and its imprints are a ministry of Langham Partnership

Langham Partnership
PO Box 296, Carlisle, Cumbria, CA3 9WZ, UK
www.langham.org

ISBNs:
978-1-83973-917-0 Print
978-1-78641-030-6 ePub
978-1-78641-031-3 PDF

Patrick Fung has asserted his right under the Copyright, Designs and Patents Act, 1988 to be identified as the Author of this work.

All rights reserved. No part of this publication may be reproduced, stored in a retrieval system or transmitted, in any form or by any means, electronic, mechanical, photocopying, recording or otherwise, without the prior written permission of the publisher or the Copyright Licensing Agency.

Requests to reuse content from Langham Publishing are processed through PLSclear. Please visit www.plsclear.com to complete your request.

Scriptures taken from the Holy Bible, New International Version®, NIV®. Copyright © 1973, 1978, 1984, 2011 by Biblica, Inc.™ Used by permission of Zondervan.

British Library Cataloguing-in-Publication Data
A catalogue record for this book is available from the British Library

ISBN: 978-1-83973-917-0

Cover & Book Design: projectluz.com

Langham Partnership actively supports theological dialogue and an author's right to publish but does not necessarily endorse the views and opinions set forth here or in works referenced within this publication, nor can we guarantee technical and grammatical correctness. Langham Partnership does not accept any responsibility or liability to persons or property as a consequence of the reading, use or interpretation of its published content.

In Chinese historiography and Christian biography, there is a striking contrast between the justifiable attention given to James Hudson Taylor, the founder of the China Inland Mission (CIM), and the relative neglect of his successor, Dixon Edward Hoste. This lacuna has been ably filled by Dr. Patrick Fung in his landmark study of Hoste. One of the Cambridge Seven, and Hudson Taylor's successor, Hoste led the CIM during momentous events in China – including the Boxer Uprising in 1900, the 1911 Revolution and its aftermath, and the Anti-Christian Movement. Hoste guided the CIM through these turbulent waters, which included persecutions and martyrdoms. Dr. Fung gives us important and fresh insights into the shaping of this man of God in the context of his times and his significance for God's missional purposes. May this work have the wide and attentive readership in a new generation that it deserves.

Ernest C. T. Chew, PhD
Vice-Chairman, The Evangelical Alliance of Singapore
Associate Senior Fellow, ISEAS - Yusof Ishak Institute, Singapore

Dr. Patrick Fung's fine account goes a long way to fill a longstanding gap in our understanding of the work of the China Inland Mission (CIM), which is the crucial role played by Dixon Edward Hoste, who succeeded Hudson Taylor as general director. Dr. Fung's meticulous analysis, much of it based on primary sources, clearly demonstrates that Hoste not only built on Taylor's vision of planting a fully indigenous church in China, but put in place the essential steps needed to bring about its fulfilment. How Hoste handled taking over from Taylor in the aftermath of the Boxer Uprising, arguably the most difficult period of CIM's history, gives us the true measure of the man. This is altogether a penetrating and invaluable study!

Hwa Yung
Bishop Emeritus, The Methodist Church in Malaysia

Contents

Acknowledgements ix

Foreword xi

Introduction 1
    1. From Taylor to Hoste: The China Inland Mission towards a
        New Era 1
    2. Objective of the Research 4
    3. Literature Review 7
        3.1. Archival and Biographical Writings on Hoste 8
        3.2. Studies on the CIM with Reference to Hoste 11
        3.3. Studies on Christian Missions in China during the
            Period of Hoste's CIM Leadership 14
        3.4. Studies on Hoste's Legacy and the CIM's
            Organizational Transition to OMF 17
    4. Methodology and Sources 19
    5. Scope of the Research 21
    6. Outline of Chapters 22

Chapter 1 25
Hoste's Early Works under a Chinese Leader
    1. Introduction: When West Meets East 25
    2. Young Life: Military Training and Religious Conversion 27
    3. Applying to the China Inland Mission 31
    4. Becoming a Member of the Cambridge Seven 34
    5. Pastor Hsi's Initial Contact with Hoste 36
    6. Hoste Learning the Chinese Language 43
    7. Hoste's Support for Pastor Hsi in a Time of Crisis 45
    8. Hsi's Involvement in Hoste's Family 47
    9. Hoste Helping Western Readership Appreciate Hsi 51
    10. Building the Indigenous Church Together 53
    11. Hoste Getting Ready to Lead 57

Chapter 2 59
Hoste Taking the Lead in Responding to the Boxer Crisis
    1. Introduction 59
    2. Christian Missions in the Turmoil of the Boxer Uprising 60
    3. The CIM's Work in Shanxi and the Boxers 65

    4. The CIM in Severe Crisis 68
    5. Hoste Appointed as the New Leader of the CIM 71
    6. The Decision on the Boxer Indemnity 76
    7. Hoste's Negotiation for the Chinese Church 79
    8. Insisting on Integrity on the Matter of Indemnity 83
    9. Conclusion 86

Chapter 3 89
  Hoste's Vision of the Indigenous Chinese Church
    1. Introduction 89
    2. Early Ideas on the Indigenous Principles before Hoste 90
    3. An Early CIM Example of Developing an Indigenous Church 92
    4. Hoste's Claim for Implementing the Indigenous Principles 95
    5. Defence of the CIM's Stance on the Boxer Indemnity 98
    6. The Start of Change in Organization and Cooperation 102
    7. Hoste's Warning against Denominationalism 106
    8. Creating an Indigenous Model in Shanxi 109
    9. Hoste's Resolution of Financial Problems 112
    10. Hoste and Women's Leadership in the CIM 115
    11. Conclusion 118

Chapter 4 119
  Hoste Launching the Statement of Policy and the Forward Movement
    1. Introduction: CIM and the
       Anti-Christian Movement 119
    2. Dilemma concerning the National Christian Council 124
    3. Hoste and the Groundbreaking "Statement of Policy" 128
    4. Concerns of the Chinese Church 135
    5. Hoste and the Forward Movement 138
    6. Emphasis on "Brotherly" Cooperation with the Chinese
       Church 144
    7. Conclusion 145

Chapter 5 149
  Hoste's Legacy to the CIM and the Chinese Church
    1. Introduction 149
    2. Hoste Handing Over the Directorship 150
    3. Continual Growth of the Indigenous Churches after Hoste 155
    4. Further Development of Hoste's Indigenous Principles by
       Houghton 159
    5. Hoste's Indigenous Principles and the "CIM" Name Puzzle 163

  6. Evolving Relationship between the Chinese Church and the
    CIM 166
  7. The "Reluctant Exodus" of CIM missionaries 170
  8. From CIM to Overseas Missionary Fellowship.............................174
  9. Conclusion..176

Conclusion 179
  1. Overview..179
  2. Hoste and His Leadership 180
    2.1. A Visionary Leader Bringing the CIM through Crises
      and Changes 181
    2.2. A Faithful Friend Journeying with the Indigenous
      Chinese Church 183
    2.3. An Unassuming Character..188
  3. Lessons for Today 194
  4. Concluding Remarks...198

Bibliography 199

Dixon Edward Hoste with a local Chinese[1]
**Source: Phyllis Thompson, *D. E. Hoste: A Prince with God*
(London: China Inland Mission, 1947), 64.**

---

1. Source: Phyllis Thompson, *D. E. Hoste: A Prince with God* (London: China Inland Mission, 1947), 64.

Acknowledgements

First, I offer my deepest thanks to my research supervisor, Dr. Song Gang. I am grateful to him for his professional dedication, academic insight, and unceasingly gracious character. I have benefitted immensely from his guidance and encouragement. I also want to thank the University of Hong Kong for allowing me to "go back to school" again.

I wish to thank my wife, Jennie, and my two children, Elaine and Samuel, for their ongoing support for me in this research work. The gentle, affirming manner in which they offered constructive criticism meant a lot to me.

I also acknowledge the tremendous help I received from colleagues of OMF International, particularly Mr. Au Ka-Neng, the chief archivist, for his generous assistance in helping me search for archival materials.

Above all, I am grateful to God for the life of Dixon Edward Hoste – a man who demonstrated to me what it means to live and be forgotten, to let go of controlling hands while, at the same time, offering helping hands when needed.

Foreword

This is an assiduously researched, carefully presented, and captivating piece of work. Patrick Fung has done us a great service in recounting the impact of one of God's great servants, Dixon Edward Hoste, who served as the general director of the China Inland Mission (CIM) from 1900 to 1935, following on from its founder, James Hudson Taylor. Fung provides an example of how to trace and draw out lessons from the life of one God's choicest servants and I believe his findings are important for at least three reasons.

Firstly, this research demonstrates the great importance of Christians having an historical awareness. Martin Luther once remarked that there is nothing so short as a Christian's memory. Christians, as are all people, are impoverished if they lack a historical perspective. I remember when visiting universities in Israel, I was being shown around a museum with a student who was obviously not interested in history. I asked him if he had visited the museum before. "No", he said, "I think history is pointless. We should only be concerned about the present and the future." I was surprised, as we were visiting a museum focused on the Holocaust!

In his book *The Age of Extremes,* historian Eric Hobsbawm referred to the loss of a sense of history as "one of the most eerie phenomena of the late twentieth-century." A progressive disconnection from the past has given rise to a profound sense of disorientation. We live in an age consumed by a quest for identity, and much of the debate is a clear product of an absence of historical perspective. This has serious implications for Christians as Scripture is full of stories of God's acts in history. Without an awareness of them our lives can become very shallow.

Why then is it important for all Christians to have historical perspective? I suggest three reasons:

- History reminds us of what God has done in the past – of significant answers to prayer, evidence of his supernatural power, and ways in which he has intervened. This provokes a spirit of praise. In the Psalms, time and time again the exaltation to "Praise the Lord!" came after a reminder of God's acts in history. The Psalmist constantly refrains "remember how God led us out of Egypt, remember how he led us through the wilderness, remember how He led us across the Jordan, therefore praise the Lord…" An historical awareness is central to praise in the Christian tradition. The phrase "Praise the Lord!" is repeated over 500 times in the Bible, making it the most common command and is almost always an exhortation rather than an exclamation.
- History reminds us of who we are – our identity and our roots. Seeing ourselves as God's servants in the long line of history helps us to remain humble. It is important, for Christian leaders especially, to be reminded of those who have gone before, and of the baton being passed down the generations. Mature Christians usually see themselves as part of a long line of saints from time past. One of the best marks of the work of God is that it continues to grow after the leader is taken out of the way. To grasp that fact, we need to have some awareness of Christian history. If we are unaware of God's work in the lives of individuals in time past, we will have an insufficiently clear sense of our own heritage. Theologian Samuel Escobar once said that a movement is often renewed if it has three types of people involved in leadership: the storyteller who reminds people of past events; the teacher who reminds people of the values and convictions which shaped the ministry; and the prophet or visionary who points towards the future. The challenge is to keep all three emphases in balance.
- We also need a historical awareness as we formulate a vision for the future. Often when we are reminded of the great things God has done, the daring attempts people have made to serve him, and audacious acts of testimony, not mention wise decisions, it gives us fresh determination. We see that God has often used fragile, broken, and even inadequate or dysfunctional people in the past, so perhaps he can even use us. This can give us a solid foundation

from which to dream. It is true that we should not dwell in the past, but we must start from a reminder of what God has done, through previous believers and leaders, such as Hoste.

Secondly, this groundbreaking piece of research teaches us much about the nature of Christian leadership. Transitions can be difficult in the life of Christian ministries, especially when moving from a period when a work is being shaped by a dynamic visionary leader or founder of a great ministry to the second or third generation. This is therefore a wonderful piece of historical research, tracing the development of CIM from its early years under the great Hudson Taylor through the transition to his successor Hoste, and beyond. There are many lessons to be learned from Hoste's style of leadership and character. These lessons include:

First, the fact that great leaders are not always dynamic extroverts. Hoste was apparently a shy introvert without a charismatic gift of oratory. At his initial interview for CIM, the interviewer was uncertain as to whether he had much to offer as a cross-cultural missionary. What he did possess, however, was a careful, orderly mind with an attention to detail, in part shaped by his military training. Tacitus, the famous Roman historian, once argued that "calm judgement and reason are the qualities of a leader." Hoste seems to have possessed these in abundance.

Second, despite being a shy introvert, he was nevertheless a visionary. Hoste was able to articulate a vision which, like his predecessor, galvanised and mobilised many thousands of workers, including both cross-cultural missionaries and Chinese leaders.

Third, he was the possessor of an unimpeachable character, demonstrating a life of great integrity. This was especially evident in the aftermath of the Boxer Uprising in 1900 which resulted in the deaths of many missionaries and Chinese leaders. After the uprising, many took the line that the Chinese government should remunerate those agencies and individuals churches who had lost fellow workers or property. Hoste, however, believed that the cause of the gospel and the indigenous Chinese church would be best served by refusing to request reparations for the loss of life and property owned by CIM. He recognised that it if the government was forced to pay reparations, this would probably be paid for by an increase in taxes which would have created hardship for the very people that CIM was trying to reach. The local governor was impressed by this, and it may well be that other Chinese political leaders and members of the populace were similarly impressed that a Western mission agency was not interested in playing politics. It may have contributed to a softening of hearts and opened the door to gospel advance, since the next 20 years came to be called the "Golden Age" when there was a large turning of Chinese people to the gospel.

In addition, where reparations were sought by Chinese churches, Hoste insisted that there should be careful analysis of the costs incurred and that the Chinese authorities should not be overcharged in the demand for reparations. At his heart, Hoste was a man of great integrity.

Furthermore, Hoste was gentle in his demeanour, always seeking a peaceful solution to thorny problems or an explosive situation. Some might see this as a weakness, but it is the gentleness of the strong whose strength is under control. He was meek, but not weak. It is the quality of a strong personality who is nevertheless master of himself and the servant of others. He led by humble and loving service, emulating the example of his Lord. The emphasis of Jesus was not on the authority of a ruler-leader but on the humility of a servant-leader. The authority by which the Christian leader leads is not power but love, not force but example, not coercion but reasoned persuasion.

He was willing to learn from others. Hoste's 10 years of service alongside and under Pastor Hsi helped to develop his convictions and convinced him of the importance of western missionaries working alongside and under Chinese nationals. His convictions regarding the effective capacity of indigenous leadership were thus undoubtedly shaped before he came into a position of senior leadership.

Hoste's leadership style was consultative. Previously CIM had operated something of a pyramidal style of leadership with many decisions being made at the top by Hudson Taylor. Hoste, copied incidentally by his successors, developed a much more consultative approach, keeping everyone informed, avoiding cliques, and giving attention to people. This was especially evident when faced with major crises or challenges, including the response to the Boxer Uprising; the Statement of Policy, which was preceded by nine months of consultation and led to a decision to focus on developing Chinese churches that were self-supporting, self-governing, and self-propagating, with missionaries having a role as advisors and servants of local indigenous leaders; and in the formation of the Forward Movement, which was born out of the conviction the Chinese leadership should take control "with immediate effect" of indigenous churches, with CIM missionaries ceding control, working alongside and in partnership with them, as well as taking responsibility for pioneering new work in the unevangelized interior. The call went out to let go of controlling hands, but to instead offer helping hands with an emphasis on partnership. He was convinced that the purpose of the gospel would be best served if the leadership of the churches could be handed to nationals with foreign missionaries in a supportive role.

He espoused a vision of brotherly cooperation. This emphasis on the three-self ministry had been posited by earlier missionary figures like Henry Venn and Hudson Taylor but Hoste codified or clarified what this would mean. It became part of the life blood of gospel ministry in China, contributing to its accelerated growth, and prepared the church for a future when all western missionaries were forced to leave China in the early 1950s. It had far-reaching consequences. It would do many contemporary mission agencies much good if we were to reflect on these policies and review our own practices in the twenty-first century.

Hoste was not afraid to make courageous decisions. Even though he was committed to visible unity, when the National Christian Council began to demonstrate liberalising tendencies on key doctrines, he removed CIM from the council. This was done, again, after consultation with other leaders. It was regrettable, but necessary. His actions in this respect may have contributed to CIM maintaining its doctrinal clarity and robustness over the long haul. Guarding the gospel remains a key role for all mission leaders.

Thirdly and finally, it is possible to see in this groundbreaking study how CIM (now OMF International) has thrived as a mission agency for over 150 years. Hudson Taylor and Hoste, his successor, built strong doctrinal foundations, shaped a clear and captivating vision, modelled servant leadership, ceding control early to indigenous leadership, with a continued strong focus on pioneering and evangelism. This has entered the lifeblood of the mission agency. It is clear that taking time to establish strong foundations, developing a clear vision, trusting indigenous leaders, together with the careful selection of successive leaders who embody this vision have enabled this mission agency to maintain its focussed efforts on advancing the cause of Christ across Asia, long may it continue.

Reading and reflecting on Hoste's style of ministry can only prompt mission leaders like myself to ask what we can learn from this approach to leadership, and whether our style of ministry should change. This unsung hero and modest mission leader never sought to accumulate plaudits for himself but saw himself as a servant who was prepared to live to be forgotten. Such an approach would probably revolutionise the leadership style in many Christian fields today.

Readers of this text, therefore, have cause to be grateful to Patrick Fung for his careful research. He has unearthed and polished a gemstone which may well challenge the leadership style of many, myself included. There are many lessons to be learned here which, if applied, could have significant and beneficial outcomes for how we engage in cross-cultural mission in the contemporary world. I wish I had learned more of these lessons earlier but many current and future leaders, and consequentially, the ministries they lead, could benefit enormously by heeding and applying these lessons today.

Lindsay Brown
December 2023
General Secretary, IFES (1991–2007)
International Director, Lausanne Movement (2008–16)

Introduction

1. From Taylor to Hoste: The China Inland Mission towards a New Era

The China Inland Mission (CIM) has been one of the most researched topics in the history of Christian missions in modern China. Kenneth S. Latourette (1884–1968) comments that "this society was in time to have in China more missionaries than any other single agency, Protestant or Roman Catholic. Its beginnings and its development are in some respect the most remarkable chapter in all the history of Christian missions in China."[1] Indeed, as one of the most established and organized mission societies from among over one hundred Christian agencies, the CIM never failed to attract the attention of people of its time as well as the interest of historians in later times.[2] More significantly, modern scholars have done extensive research on Hudson Taylor (1832–1905) – the prominent founder and the first general director of the CIM – and his key role in leading the CIM to great success within just a few decades. It is, therefore, commonly accepted that Taylor's pioneering work laid the foundation of the CIM enterprise in late Qing China until 1900, when a paradigmatic shift for further developments was called upon as China underwent a series of drastic changes.

---

1. Latourette, *History of Christian Missions*, 382.
2. Tao Feiya 陶飛亞 and Dai Wanqi 戴婉琦, "Jinnianlai Dalu Zhonghua Neidihui yanjiu zongshu" 近年來大陸中華內地會研究綜述 (Recent Survey of Studies in Mainland China on the China Inland Mission) in *Kuayue sange shiji de chuanjiao yundong, 1865–2015: Neidihui laihua yibaiwushinian xuanjiao lunwenji* 跨越三個世紀的傳教運動, 1865–2015: 内地會來華一百五十年宣教論文集 (Christian Missions Spanning Three Centuries 1865–2015: Essays on the 150th Anniversary of CIM-OMF Work in China), ed. Lin Zhiping 林治平 and Wu Yoxing 吳昶興 (Taiwan: Yuzhouguang, 2016), 48–87.

Taylor's legacy, as has been frequently discussed in previous studies, is of particular importance in several aspects. First, Taylor's vision to spread the Christian faith to the vast inland regions in China was an unprecedented task that had once been considered impossible.[3] Before 1865, the missionary work of most Protestant societies had concentrated on the coastal provinces, with few missionaries adventuring to the inland regions of China.[4] The primary purpose of the CIM was not so much to win converts as to "diffuse as quickly as possible a knowledge of the Gospel throughout the Empire."[5] Second, Taylor's insistence on being a faith mission became a hallmark of the CIM. No personal solicitation of funds was to be made, no collections were to be taken at meetings, and fixed salaries for missionaries were not guaranteed. As a pioneer, Taylor had no backing from established denominations or any prominent ecclesiastical system. Third, the CIM was to be non-denominational, and both "people of education" and those "without much learning," as well as single women missionaries, were welcomed.[6] Before the establishment of the CIM, single woman missionaries had rarely stepped into the inland provinces of China.[7] Moreover, Taylor was innovative in his methods, insisting on missionaries wearing Chinese clothes and conforming as nearly as possible to the social and living conditions of the Chinese.[8] In addition, the CIM was to be governed from China, rather than by a council in England.[9]

Taylor repeatedly appealed for new workers – eighteen men for nine unreached provinces in 1874, seventy for further expansion in 1882, one hundred in 1887, and, together with other mission agencies, one thousand workers at the General Missionary Conference in 1890.[10]

By the time of Taylor's death in 1905, the CIM had become an international "corporation," with eight hundred men and women at sixty stations in fifteen of China's eighteen provinces.[11] It was the largest and most influential

---

3. Latourette, *History of Christian Missions*, 382–390.
4. Latourette, 382–390.
5. Latourette, 386.
6. Latourette, 386.
7. Latourette, 390.
8. Taylor and Taylor, *Growth of a Work of God*, 43, 54, 89.
9. Broomhall, *Shaping of Modern China*,:448, 470. See also *Principles and Practice*, 14.
10. Broomhall, *Shaping of Modern China*, ix.
11. Broomhall, *China's Open Century*, 6:23; quoted in Austin, *China's Millions*, preface.

Protestant mission, constituting a quarter of the entire Protestant mission force in China.

Taylor was a pioneer at heart, and his focus was the speedy spreading of the Christian faith. Though Taylor did not write extensively about the indigenous principle "though a thoroughly indigenous Chinese Church was always his declared aim."[12]

However, the Boxer Uprising in 1900 and the Anti-Christian Movement in the 1920s forced the CIM to rethink its mode of operation and its relationship with the Chinese church. It was in this context that Dixon Edward Hoste (1861–1946), who succeeded Taylor, played a key role in guiding the CIM to remain relevant in a changing mission landscape by not only advocating but also implementing the indigenous principles to the full.

With Taylor serving as an admirable model of leadership in the heyday of the CIM, the appointment of Hoste as the second general director in 1900 was unexpected. When Taylor, due to illness, was no longer able to effectively direct the CIM, it became imperative that a capable successor be appointed to lead the members to face the devastating Boxer crisis. William Cooper (1858–1900), a promising and capable CIM missionary, was expected to succeed Taylor, but he was murdered by the Boxers in June 1900. In a surprising move, Hoste – a quiet character, barely forty years old – was entrusted with this important leadership position. His previous work experience had been mainly in Shanxi, where he had spent ten years working with a local Chinese leader called Pastor Hsi (Xi Shengmo, c. 1836–1896). Undoubtedly, it would have been a great challenge for Hoste to take charge of the CIM's macroscale mission across China.

Hoste, who came from an elite military family in England, was very different from Taylor in personality and communication skills. He spoke and behaved with great precision and clarity, though always in a low-key manner. In the decades that followed, his leadership, though largely overshadowed by that of Taylor, proved successful. Hoste led the CIM to effectively respond to several major crises, including the Boxer Uprising in 1900 and the Anti-Christian Movement in the 1920s. If Taylor is regarded as the person who laid the foundation for the work of evangelism in China, Hoste should be seen as his competent successor who made continuous efforts to further expand

---

12. Broomhall, *China's Open Century*, Appendix XXIX, 79.

the mission and build up the indigenous Chinese church.[13] Hoste's insight and determination to foster the growth of the Chinese church went beyond Taylor's work. As discussed later in this book, Hoste successfully led a major reform in the operations of the CIM to ensure that its missionaries let go of power and control so that the Chinese church could be truly indigenous and independent.

A brief statistical survey demonstrates the impressive advancement of the CIM under Hoste's leadership. In 1899, the CIM had 730 missionaries, with 624 paid local workers and relatively few unpaid, self-supporting workers.[14] In 1935, three decades later, when Hoste completed his long period of service and stepped down from the post of general director, there were a total of 1,313 missionaries serving in 333 centres across nineteen provinces in China.[15] Even more striking, by that time, there were 3,900 Chinese workers serving with the CIM, of which 2,350 were full-time workers or part-time volunteers, meaning that they were mostly self-funded and received no financial support from the CIM.[16] These numbers clearly suggest a great shift in the CIM's relations with the emerging Chinese church in a new age.

In previous research, attention was focused on Taylor and his leadership during the early decades of the CIM, overshadowing the work of Hoste. One only finds scattered and incomplete information about Hoste. Much like his quiet and discreet character, his life story is buried in the historical archives that have remained largely unnoticed in past decades, and there has been no substantial analysis of the importance of his leadership during the post-Taylor period.

2. Objective of the Research

This thesis presents a comprehensive study of Hoste's life and work, highlighting his leadership of the CIM during the post-Taylor period, his contribution to the emerging Chinese church in the first half of the twentieth century, and his legacy in modern Chinese Christianity. While there has already been

---

13. So, "Passion for a Greater Vision," 19–27.

14. *China's Millions* (1899): 165–168. Unless otherwise stated *China's Millions* refers to the British edition.

15. *China's Millions* (1935): 2.

16. *China's Millions* (1935): 2.

extensive scholarly research on the first-generation leadership of the CIM – namely, its founder, Hudson Taylor – not much attention has been given to the leadership of the CIM in the post-Taylor period. This research looks at the second-generation leadership of the CIM under Hoste and his unique contribution to the CIM, considering the changes implemented during the thirty years following the Boxer crisis in 1900 and the development of the indigenous Chinese church to become self-supporting and self-governing.

First, the thesis examines how Hoste was trained in leadership during his early years in China when working under Pastor Hsi, the well-known Chinese Christian leader. The key issues discussed include the following: How did Pastor Hsi influence Hoste and his perception of the Chinese? What did Hoste learn from this Chinese leader? How did Hoste first begin to understand the importance of the indigenous church? These issues are important because they help in understanding how Hoste was shaped and prepared for his leadership role in the CIM. Hoste's deep friendship with Hsi and their close working relationship may shed light on why and how Hoste worked closely with the Chinese church in their negotiation process with the Qing authorities on the indemnity issue. The analysis of the relationship between Hoste and Hsi is also important to our understanding of Hoste's confidence in the ability of the Chinese church to rise to the challenge of leadership without foreign missionary control.

Second, this book aims to reveal how Hoste led the CIM to respond to the Boxer crisis after Taylor fell ill. Leadership is seen not only in the growth of an organization but also in the manner in which times of crisis are handled. It is also worth knowing how Hoste engaged in complicated negotiations with the Qing authorities regarding compensation for the atrocities suffered by the missionaries. How was Hoste different from the leaders of other missionary organizations? How did his responses affect the way the Chinese church and wider Chinese society viewed the CIM in comparison to these other organizations? How was Hoste recognized as a leader not just by the CIM missionaries but also by members of the Chinese church? In what ways, directly or indirectly, did the Boxer crisis facilitate the early development of the indigenous Chinese church? The answers to these questions may help us understand Hoste's different view of the Chinese church, particularly given that many mission societies demanded compensation based on the rationale that the Chinese who suffered at the hands of the Boxers were "in the service of foreigners."[17]

The third aim of this research is to explore what lessons Hoste had learned from the great evacuation of the CIM from China in the late 1920s. Like other missionary societies, the CIM enjoyed a twenty-year period of further growth and freedom to evangelize after the Boxer Uprising. Yet Hoste had to face another major crisis when, in the midst of anti-foreign sentiments, there were increasing attacks on missionaries and missionary premises. Several key issues need to be clarified to better understand this critical moment: What was Hoste's view on the Anti-Christian Movement in the 1920s? How did the Chinese church respond to the withdrawal of foreign missionaries? Was there any change in the relationship between the CIM and the Chinese church because of the evacuation? In what ways did the change have an impact, if any, on the development of the indigenous church? The answers to these questions will help us understand the reasons behind Hoste's introduction of the "Statement of Policy," with its emphasis on the CIM giving up control while encouraging the Chinese church to take up leadership. This analysis will also reveal Hoste's leadership and his ability to see beyond the immediate crisis with his long-term vision of the Chinese church becoming indigenous and totally self-governing.

Another aim of this study is to explore the major reforms at an institutional level – within and without the CIM – especially the Statement of Policy implemented by Hoste to facilitate the process of developing the Chinese church so that it would be self-supporting, self-governing, and self-propagating. I will examine a group of lesser-known sources from the CIM archives to reveal the main reasons for the reforms, the positive and negative effects of these reforms on the CIM, and the ways these reforms facilitated the growth of the Chinese church. These new findings will help us to understand why the Chinese churches associated with the CIM were better able to stand on their own when all the missionaries had to leave China by 1951. This fresh information also reveals Hoste's gentle but determined leadership when dealing with doubts and hesitations on the part of his followers.

Finally, the study aims to rehearse Hoste's legacy, with particular attention to how his earlier indigenous principles prepared the CIM and Chinese

---

17. Broomhall, *China's Open Century*, 7:724.

Christians for the shaping of a truly indigenous Chinese church, free from foreign influence, after the People's Republic of China was founded in 1949. The reluctant exodus of all missionaries in 1951 brought the CIM's work in China to an abrupt end. The CIM had to change the scope and focus of its missionary work from China to other parts of East Asia. Moreover, after a vigorous debate among CIM leaders, the name of the society was later changed to the Overseas Missionary Fellowship (OMF). Taking these drastic changes into consideration, I will emphasize the long-term impact of Hoste's vision and principles, which can only be understood in the larger historical context and which are still not given due recognition in many recent studies on the indigenous church in China.

Based on a full-fledged study of Hoste's life and work, this book aims to rediscover a long-neglected episode in the history of the CIM. Hoste played a pivotal role in the CIM's developments during a new age. His careful but unyielding character was shown in response to the severe crises and his strategic turn to a new pattern of relationship with the Chinese church, constituted the core of his second-generation leadership. As the next section will show, these key aspects have remained unnoticed or underexplored by previous scholarship. Only by a thorough analysis of all relevant sources, including newly discovered ones, can researchers truly recognize Hoste as a decisive figure who led the continual expansion of the CIM and facilitated the final shaping of the indigenous Chinese church during the first half of the twentieth century.

3. Literature Review

There have been extensive studies on the history of the CIM, placing a great deal of emphasis on its founder, Hudson Taylor. In sharp contrast, there are few studies focusing on Hoste and his work. However, the CIM archival collections at the OMF Archive Department – in particular, the China Council minutes recorded during Hoste's leadership period (1900–1935) and the full collection of CIM's regular news publication *China's Millions* – provide abundant valuable information about Hoste, which has so far remained largely unnoticed.

The literature review below consists of four major categories. First, the archival and biographical writings on Hoste, which are key primary sources that lead to a better understanding of Hoste's life, his character, and particularly his leadership. Second, the review covers studies on the CIM that make reference to Hoste. For instance, although CIM writers like Alfred. J. Broomhall (1911–1994) and Geraldine Guinness (1862–1949) wrote extensively about Hoste's contribution to the CIM, these writings seem relatively insignificant compared to the substantial coverage given to Taylor. Third, the review examines studies on the Christian missions in China during the period of Hoste's leadership. This will help us to understand the historical context of the Chinese church, the CIM, and China during Hoste's leadership and to better appreciate his contribution, which has not been given due attention by previous scholarship. Finally, the review reflects on studies of the CIM's organizational transition from the China Inland Mission (CIM) to the Overseas Missionary Fellowship (OMF) to find out the impact, if any, of Hoste's legacy, particularly his emphasis on the importance of indigenous principles for the Chinese church.

3.1. Archival and Biographical Writings on Hoste

One of the most valuable archival resources is *China's Millions* – which has yet to be fully utilized by scholars studying the life of Hoste – which brings to light the life and work of many CIM leaders. In the case of Hoste, *China's Millions* covers the period from his first arrival in China in 1885, at the age of twenty-four, up to the time he left China for Britain in 1945 from the Japanese internment at the age of eighty-four – a total of sixty years of close relationship with the CIM in China. There are more than 460 references related to Hoste in the issues of *China's Millions* between 1885 and 1946. These include at least ten articles written by Hoste himself or by others about Hoste, covering important topics such as the CIM's response to the Boxer Uprising,[18] the future role of missionaries in the post-Boxer period,[19] the need to expand the educational work of the CIM to prepare the next Chinese Christian generation with the long-term goal of establishing indigenous churches,[20] and Hoste's views on the life and leadership of Hudson Taylor, his predecessor.[21] Some

---

18. *China's Millions* (1901): 141.
19. *China's Millions* (1909): 99.
20. *China's Millions* (1922): 115.
21. *China's Millions* (1932): 86–87.

important decisions made by the CIM while Hoste was its general director are also revealed in *China's Millions*. Understandably, since this publication was geared towards the Christian public, some of the more complex reasons behind the major policy changes in the CIM, particularly the Statement of Policy in relationship to establishing indigenous Chinese churches, are given in much more detail in the China Council minutes than in *China's Millions*. Therefore, while *China's Millions* is a valuable primary source that helps in understanding Hoste's leadership in general, it is the China Council minutes – which were previously not readily available – that reveal, in much greater depth, why and how Hoste made some of the difficult decisions that resulted in changes to the CIM as well as Hoste's view on the CIM's relationship to the Chinese church.

Among the books published by the CIM, only *D. E. Hoste: A Prince with God* by Phyllis Thompson (1906–2000) presents a detailed account of Hoste as the leader of the CIM during the first few decades of the twentieth century. Her book is the only one with an exclusive focus on Hoste. Thompson adopts a biographical approach – with an emphasis on Hoste's spirituality – combined with selected extracts from some of his letters, mainly those dealing with spiritual matters. Information on Hoste's leadership remains sketchy and, despite the brief chapter on Hoste as the "Leader of the Mission,"[22] the focus is on Hudson Taylor, who decided to appoint Hoste to succeed him. As no diaries of Hoste were available, Thompson depended heavily on others who had known Hoste.[23] Thompson pays far more attention to Hoste's personal character than to his role as the leader of the CIM. The selected extracts of Hoste's correspondences are mainly sermons for biblical instruction and offer little first-hand information about how Hoste managed to cope with the more difficult challenges in his position as the top CIM leader. Partly due to its religious stance, almost one-third of the book relates to the devotional writings of Hoste with Thompson's highly positive comments.

Geraldine Guinness (1862–1949) – a CIM missionary and Taylor's daughter-in-law – writes about Hoste's long-term friendship and collaboration with Pastor Hsi. In the first edition of her biography of Pastor Hsi, Guinness mentions that Hoste joined Hsi's work in May 1885 and accepted

---

22. Thompson, *Prince with God*, 88–102.
23. Thompson, 11.

the latter's guidance during the next ten years.[24] Since the focus of the book is Hsi, Guinness does not go into the details of the friendship between the two men, except to record that Hoste supported Hsi when the latter faced criticism and was even attacked by his own co-worker, Fan.[25] In the 1903 edition of the work, a new introduction, written by Hoste himself, was added. In it, Hoste addressed Hsi as his "elder brother" and a friend "who was intimately associated with him for ten years."[26]

In a more recent study, Wu Yaqun 吳亞群 discusses the life and work of Hoste and the CIM.[27] However, this research has only one reference drawn directly from *China's Millions*, with the rest depending heavily on the books by Thompson, Guinness, Broomhall, and others who often provide indirect references to Hoste. However, one important point raised by Wu, which is not mentioned by Thompson, is that Hoste worked mainly among the lower social classes and the poor. Wu points out that Hoste did not adequately understand the culture of the intellectuals and did not have any significant influence among them.[28] Yet, according to Wu, compared to CIM missionaries like W. W. Cassels (1858–1925) and Stanley Smith (1861–1931), Hoste's attitude towards the traditional Chinese culture was much more measured. Wu mentions that Hoste never resorted to extreme methods in handling problems related to ancestral or idol worship and emphasizes that Hoste held to a principle of meeting hostility and opposition with meekness and quietness.[29] However, Wu's analysis, which reveals Hoste's gentle character, fails to highlight another aspect of Hoste – namely, his courage and determination, qualities that were revealed in his negotiations with the Qing authorities on the indemnity issue in the aftermath of the Boxer Uprising. Wu's coverage of Hoste's handling of the Boxer crisis is very brief.

---

24. Taylor, *Pastor Hsi*, 166.
25. Taylor, 222–223.
26. Mrs Howard Taylor, *Pastor His- One of China's Christians*, p19–20
27. Wu Yaqun 吳亞群, "A Study on Dixon Edward Hoste, the Second General Director of the CIM" (中國內地會第二代總主任何斯德研究).
28. Wu, 32.
29. Wu, 39.

3.2. Studies on the CIM with Reference to Hoste

Alongside the biographical studies, Hoste is also mentioned in some more focused studies of the CIM, including the voluminous 4000-page series, *Hudson Taylor and China's Open Century* (1981) by A. J. Broomhall. This particularly well-researched work is based on CIM records, archives, and Council minutes and has become a key reference on the history of the CIM and missionary activities in China in the nineteenth and early twentieth centuries. Though some significant references are made to Hoste's role in handling the Boxer crisis, Broomhall gives most attention to Taylor and his work, with a fairly sketchy account on the new age of the CIM after Hoste assumed leadership. On the subject of the indigenous Chinese church, Broomhall compares Taylor to Hoste in their approach to establishing the indigenous church: "A thoroughly Chinese Church was [always] his [Taylor's] declared aim. His indigenous principle was practiced but he did not formulate it until later [under Hoste's leadership]." In his book, he discusses several Chinese Christian leaders, including the great evangelist John Sung (宋尚節, 1901–1944), Wang Mingdao (王明道, 1900–1991), and Ni Tuosheng (倪柝聲, 1903–1972), together with other Chinese colleagues working alongside the CIM at that time.[30] However, Broomhall does not specifically examine the major causes for the remarkable growth of Chinese workers associated with the CIM in the post-Taylor period. His research apparently overlooked Hoste's key role in implementing the indigenous church principles in a new historical context.

An earlier CIM writer, Marshall Broomhall (1866–1937), provides a detailed analysis of the first fifty years of the CIM, in chronological order, covering major aspects such as its organization, ethos, operations, and strategies.[31] While Marshall Broomhall gives a detailed record of the Boxer Uprising, he only briefly mentioned Hoste "assisting Mr. Stevenson, [the CIM China Director] with the heavy burden of responsibility."[32] Little attention is given to Hoste's leadership in helping the CIM and the Chinese church respond to

---

30. Broomhall, *China's Open Century,* 7:548.

31. Broomhall, *Jubilee Story*. Marshall Broomhall was A. J. Broomhall's uncle. All three generations – Benjamin Broomhall, Marshall Broomhall, and A. J. Broomhall – were prolific writers of CIM history.

32. Broomhall, 247. John Stevenson (1844–1918), who was the China director at that time, was based in Shanghai at the CIM Headquarters.

the crisis and beyond. Broomhall's analysis does not extend to Hoste's commitment and achievements beyond Taylor's leadership.

The more recent work by Alvyn Austin (1945-) contains a more critical evaluation of the China Inland Mission and Hudson Taylor[33] but also falls short in terms of describing the history of the CIM after Taylor. Not much detail is given about Hoste's leadership, but Austin shares a sharp observation about Hoste and his relationship to Pastor Hsi. Austin comments that Hoste, as a man of military background, loved order and might, and remained distant and unemotional.[34] Thus, Hoste's commitment to serving under Pastor Hsi was seen as one borne out of obligation and regulation. However, this analysis by Austin seems incomplete as very little is mentioned regarding the deep friendship between Hoste and Pastor Hsi, and how the latter had influenced Hoste and his future leadership on a personal level. However, Austin rightly points out that Hoste, like his predecessor, was a visionary who was an entire generation ahead of his time and who believed that missionaries were building the "scaffolding" of a Chinese church, which, under Chinese leadership, should be self-governing, self-supporting and self-propagating.[35]

Before the 1980s, studies on the CIM were mostly done by Western scholars, but there has been a notable increase of interest in the CIM among Chinese scholars during the recent decades. According to Tao Feiya (陶飛亞) and Dai Wanqi (戴婉琦), more than sixty theses in Chinese were completed between 2001 and 2015 on various subjects related to the CIM.[36] The topics that received the most attention include, among others, Hudson Taylor and political power, Chinese workers and the CIM, medical missions, women missionaries, and mission and education. These reviews present a panoramic picture of the history of the CIM, including the period under Hoste's leadership. Although some of the listed studies focus on the work of individual missionaries, little attention has been paid to the life and the work of Hoste.

---

33. Austin, *China's Millions*.
34. Austin, 383.
35. Austin, 383.
36. Tao Feiya 陶飛亞 and Dai Wanqi 戴婉琦, "Jinianlai Dalu Zhonghua Neidihui yanjiu zongshu" 近年來大陸來華內地會研究綜述 in *Christian Missions Spanning Three Centuries: Essays on the 150th Anniversary of CIM-OMF Work in China*, 跨越三個世紀的傳教運動 (Christian Missions Spanning Three Centuries 1865–2015: Essays on the 150th Anniversary of CIM-OMF Work in China), ed. Lin Zhiping 林治平 and Wu Yoxing 吳昶興, 48–87.

Interestingly, the lack of attention to Hoste may be related to another important yet still greatly underexplored subject – the relationships and collaborations between the CIM leaders and local Chinese workers. Only in recent decades have scholars begun to pay more attention to the role of local Chinese workers in the CIM organization. In her study, Zhang Liang 張靚 examines two types of Chinese workers. First, itinerant workers travelling with the CIM missionaries and, second, those who worked at the CIM stations.[37] However, her study still lacks some of the key primary sources required to present a full picture of their relationship. Zhang also points out that the Chinese workers associated with the CIM were the "silent group" (默默無語的群體) as little was written about them.[38] Zhang attributes this to the fact that since most readers of *China's Millions* or other CIM publications were from the West, it seems that they would have been more interested in the lives and the work of missionaries rather than of the Chinese. However, Zhang does pay special attention to the work of Pastor Hsi, discussing the friendship between Hoste and Pastor Hsi and describing how Hoste offered his support to Pastor Hsi during times of crisis.

Apart from Phyllis Thompson's book focusing on Hoste, research is scarce, especially about the relationship between Hoste and the Chinese church. One possible reason is that very little information is available in Chinese on this subject. Archives at OMF, the School of Oriental and African Studies (SOAS) in London, and the Billy Graham Center at Wheaton, Illinois, did not contain any collection of such Chinese materials.[39] While *China's Millions* often published names of Chinese church leaders who were associated with the CIM, this was primarily in romanized script and hardly any names were recorded in Chinese. Among Chinese scholars, Li Nan (李楠), in his research on the CIM, indicates that most of the important documents of the CIM were

---

37. Zhang Liang 張靚, "Zhonguo Neidihui zaoqi xuanjiao shiyeli de Zhongguo tonggong" 中國內地會早期宣教事業裏的中國同工 (Chinese workers of early China Inland Mission), *Shilin* 史林 4 (2015), 119–126.

38. Zhang Liang 張靚, 119–126.

39. CIM London Archives, School of Oriental and African Studies, University of London; Collection #215, CIM Philadelphia Archives, Archives of the Billy Graham Center, Wheaton College; Collection AR 6.1.4, Box 1, CIM Singapore Archives, OMF International, Singapore.

lost during the evacuation period in 1950 and that anything left was mostly destroyed during the cultural revolution.[40]

3.3. Studies on Christian Missions in China during the Period of Hoste's CIM Leadership

Beyond studies specifically on Hoste and the CIM, Andrew Kaiser, in his latest book – *The Rushing On of the Purposes of God* – studies Christian missions in Shanxi from 1876. This book contains a historical review of the Boxer Uprising and its aftermath. Kaiser only briefly mentions Hoste, even though Hoste spent a significant amount of time in Shanxi, especially with Pastor Hsi. However, Kaiser acknowledges that Hoste, together with Pastor Hsi, "curbed the previous policy of taking legal troubles involving believers to the provincial officials and claiming treaty protection for the Christians." From the start, Hoste, like Taylor, was against the idea of relying on the British authorities to protect Christians.

Though both Kaiser and Austin acknowledge that Hoste was a key negotiator with the Qing authorities regarding indemnity, little research has been done on Hoste's view of the Chinese church in the negotiation process.[41] Nor is there solid analysis on how Hoste saw beyond the initial trauma of the Boxer Uprising and turned his attention to the opportunities for the establishment of the indigenous Chinese church. Hoste challenged his fellow missionaries to change their mindset and let go of authoritative power and control over the Chinese. Although his position on how the CIM should enhance the establishment of the indigenous Chinese church was clearly articulated and published in the *Chinese Recorder* in 1900, this fact has rarely been referred to in previous studies.[42] As will be discussed below, Hoste's determined stance on this matter made a deep impression on his colleagues and other missionary agencies of the time.

Kenneth Scott Latourette, in his monumental work, surveys the history of Christianity in China up to the 1920s, a period that covers Hoste's heyday

---

40. Li Nan 李楠, "Huigu yu qianzhan: Sanshi nianlai Zhongguo Neiduhui shiyanjiu" 回顧與前瞻：三十年來中國內地會史研究 (Retrospect and Prospect: Research on the China Inland Mission in the Past Thirty Years), *Religious Studies* 宗教學研究 2 (2015): 212–219.

41. Kaiser, *Rushing On*, 106.

42. *Chinese Recorder* (1900): 509.

as leader of the CIM.⁴³ Yet Latourette acknowledges the limitation of his book in stressing the "part of the foreigner [perspective]" and not paying enough attention to the part of the Chinese in the life of the church.⁴⁴ As a church and mission history scholar, Latourette focuses his attention on the contributions of Christian missions to China, including education, medical work, and social reforms by the CIM and other mission societies. Within such a macrohistorical approach, he has only one reference to Hoste joining the CIM in 1885 and another dealing with the transfer of leadership from Taylor to Hoste.⁴⁵ Latourette does observe that the CIM slowed down in its numerical growth of new stations between 1901 and 1910 – that is, the first ten years of Hoste's work as the leader of the CIM – in comparison with the previous decade under Taylor's leadership.⁴⁶ The reason for this lies in a different kind of growth under Hoste's leadership that put more weight on the development of the indigenous church than on the expansion of the CIM. This key point will be elaborated on in a later chapter.

John King Fairbank (1907–1991), in *The Cambridge History of China*, highlights that the CIM was the largest Protestant mission society in China in 1919, with 960 missionaries covering 246 stations when Hoste was the leader. Fairbank mentions in particular that the CIM employed a significant number of Chinese staff.⁴⁷ However, his research does not differentiate between those Chinese workers who were volunteers – that is, those who were self-supporting – and those who were employed by the CIM. It is important to note that by 1935, there were 3,900 Chinese workers in the CIM, including 2,350 men and women who were self-supporting.⁴⁸ This was a major achievement of Hoste, who had advocated the establishment of the indigenous Chinese church over the thirty-five years of his service. As he sketches a broad historical narrative, he talks about the CIM's relations with the Chinese church. First, while most Protestant missionaries shifted their focus after

---

43. Latourette, *History of Christian Missions*, viii.
44. Latourette, viii.
45. Latourette, 581.
46. Latourette, 581.
47. Fairbank and Twitchett, *Republican China*, 168–172. Although Fairbank and Twitchett do not give the exact number of Chinese workers, he gives the ratio as being 66 percent in evangelistic work, 30 percent in education, and 4 percent in medical work.
48. *China's Millions* (January 1935): introduction.

1900 to "Christianizing China," the CIM, under Hoste, remained adamant that its priority was to establish the Chinese church.[49] Second, the CIM had a significantly higher number of Chinese workers directly involved in evangelism compared to other organizations.[50] However, no further analysis was provided on the growth of the indigenous Chinese church, its indigenization process, or the leadership and influence of Hoste.

Various studies have been done on the contributions of Christian missions to Chinese society. I have already alluded to the work of Latourette in an earlier section. In addition, A. J. Broomhall records, in particular, the CIM's famine relief and opium refuge work in Shanxi. During one of the worst famines (1878–1879), there were at least ten million deaths according to the official figure, and Shanxi was the worst hit in China.[51] It was very much against this backdrop that Hoste was sent to Shanxi in 1885. However, these records also reveal that Hsi was already successful in running opium refuges in an indigenous manner, without the help of missionaries, even before Hoste's arrival. Hoste worked under the supervision of Pastor Hsi in opium refuge work for more than ten years.

Though Hoste was supportive of social service work – including education, famine relief, and medical work – his emphasis, due in part to his conservative theological and doctrinal stance, had always been on direct evangelism. Kevin Yao's *The Fundamentalist Movement among Protestant Missionaries in China, 1920–1937* is helpful in looking at how and why Hoste made the difficult decision that the CIM should withdraw from the National Christian Council (NCC) in 1926 because the NCC had become increasingly liberal.[52] The interdenominational nature of the CIM had allowed it to embrace other groups with different theological views since the days of Taylor, though a common doctrinal commitment was considered important. However, the NCC's pursuit of liberal theology forced Hoste and the CIM to finally break ties with it. This is just one of the many difficult decisions that Hoste had to make during his leadership as the general director of the CIM.

---

49. *China's Millions* (January 1935): 168.
50. *China's Millions* (January 1935): 172.
51. Broomhall, *Shaping of Modern China*, 331–338.
52. Yao, *Fundamentalist Movement*, 183–223.

3.4. Studies on Hoste's Legacy and the CIM's Organizational Transition to OMF

Even after Hoste stepped down from leadership in 1935, after more than thirty years of being the general director of the CIM, his convictions about the indigenous principles for the Chinese church continued to reverberate throughout the Mission in subsequent years. Furthermore, the exodus of all the missionaries by 1951 made the practice of indigenous principles even more relevant and necessary. The CIM changed its focus from China to other parts of East Asia and became the OMF (Overseas Missionary Fellowship). However, the core value of promoting indigenous principles that had been advocated by Hoste remained.

Sylvia Y. Yuan studied the globalization of the CIM and the organizational transition of the CIM to OMF. She makes a the observation that before the reluctant exodus of all the CIM missionaries in 1951, most of the churches established by the CIM had already become "self-governing, self-supporting, [and] self-propagating."[53] The CIM did not control church finances or administration. What is even more important is Yuan's conclusion that the difficult exodus of the CIM from China in 1951 actually led to the realization of the true indigenization of the Chinese church via the "natural euthanasia" of mission organizations originally proposed by Henry Venn.[54] This illuminating point opens up a new understanding of Hoste's endeavour in this respect. Nevertheless, Yuan does not highlight Hoste's special contribution to the Chinese church becoming truly indigenous. Nor does she explore further whether the indigenous church principles may have influenced the CIM's own transition to becoming the new OMF.

With a focus on the writings of Leslie Lyall (1905–1996), one of the third-generation leaders of the CIM, So Wing Yui's thesis presents an extensive study on the major changes of the CIM up to the mid-twentieth century.[55] He discusses the four key stages in the development of the CIM, from the

---

53. Sylvia Y. Yuan 袁瑒, "Zhongguo Zhihou Hechuqu? Zhongguo Neidihui/ Haiwai Jidu Shituan (CIM/OMF) Guoji Chuanjiaoyundong Zhi Quanqiudiyuhua Jincheng" 中國之後何處去? 中國內地會/海外基督使團 (CIM/OMF) 國際傳教運動之全球地域化進程 (After China, what?: The Glocalization of the International Missionary Movement of the China Inland Mission/ Overseas Missionary Fellowship CIM/OMF) (PhD diss., Fudan University, 2012), 29.

54. Yuan, 49.

55. So, "Passion for a Greater Vision," 19–27.

leadership of Taylor focusing on evangelism in the inlands of China, to Hoste prioritizing building up the indigenous Chinese church, to the changing role of the CIM from leader to partner, and, finally, the extension of evangelistic work to intellectuals rather than just people at the grassroots level.

According to So, Lyall was the key architect who was particularly instrumental in the transition from the old CIM to the new OMF. So also pays special attention to Lyall's work among the intellectuals, particularly his association with the Chinese Inter-Varsity Christian Fellowship.[56] So makes an interesting remark about Hoste, indicating that he had a "prophetic" role,[57] as someone who was ahead of his time. So's research affirms that the ultimate goal of Hoste's "Forward Movement" was a "rapid transfer of CIM churches to Chinese leadership."[58] Though So makes references to Hoste in his study, his main focus is Leslie Lyall, who belonged to the third generation of leadership of the CIM, rather than Hoste, who belonged to the second generation of leadership.

From the above review, it is obvious that extensive efforts have been made to explore a number of interrelated topics on the history of the CIM, with a special focus on its founder, Hudson Taylor, and the heyday of the Mission under his leadership. The life and work of Hoste in the post-Taylor period receives scant attention, and no comprehensive study has been carried out in this respect. By using varied primary historical sources, some of which have been newly discovered, this thesis aims to present full-fledged research on Hoste and his role in the CIM. These findings will shed new light on how Hoste fulfilled his role as a capable leader in some of the most challenging periods of CIM history, especially the Boxer Uprising and the Anti-Christian Movement. This research not only recovers the missing link in the CIM's succession of leadership but also helps enrich our understanding of the complex shaping of the indigenous Chinese church during the first half of the twentieth century.

---

56. So, 14–25.
57. So, 16.
58. So, 331.

4. Methodology and Sources

Taking a historical approach, I will develop arguments that combine contextual and textual analysis. I will show how careful examination of a number of primary sources, including *China's Millions* and the CIM Council minutes, reveals the leading role played by Hoste in the CIM during the post-Taylor period.

First, I made use of relevant references in *China's Millions*, paying particular attention to those between the period 1885 – the year Hoste joined the CIM – and 1946 – the year Hoste died. I will also refer to issues of *China's Millions* that are linked with Hudson Taylor's leadership, looking at publications from 1875 – when the first edition of *China's Millions* was published – to 1900 – when Taylor stepped down from the post of general director. Some rare manuscripts – such as the Chinese letter written by Pastor Hsi to Hoste's father – will be discussed to shed light on a previously unnoticed part of Hoste's life and work. Moreover, I will examine Hoste's own writings, including his letters and articles published in *China's Millions*.[59] Since Hoste was a low-key person, it is difficult to locate all relevant records on his major achievements. However, his own writings provide valuable information about his vision, thoughts, and convictions about the CIM as well as about the Chinese church.

Second, I will examine the records of the China Council minutes of the CIM from 1897–1947, the fifty-year period during which Council minutes were maintained.[60] These minutes record some of the difficult decisions that Hoste had to make on complex matters such as the response of the CIM to the Boxer crisis, the decision to reduce financial support for Chinese workers in order to foster the development of the indigenous Chinese church, the CIM's withdrawal from the National Christian Council (NCC), the changing relationship between the CIM and the Chinese church, and the "Statement of Policy" that articulated the indigenous church principles to be adopted by the whole CIM.[61] As the China Council minutes were archived by the OMF and were previously not readily available, the information newly found from

---

59. *China's Millions* (1928): 190; (1931): 39–40.

60. The China Council minutes are currently kept at the archives of OMF International, Singapore, AR 6.1.4, Box 1.

61. "China Council Minutes" (December 1918): 6–7; (March 1926): 6–7; (July 1927): 6–7; (September 1928): 6.

these records is invaluable for our understanding of those discussions on leadership at the highest level of the CIM. According to the constitution of the CIM, Hoste, as general director, had to chair all China Council meetings. Thus, the China Council minutes provide further insights into the ways Hoste handled various challenging issues.

Third, another important source is the *Chinese Recorder*, published by the Presbyterian Mission Press and covering an extensive period of mission work in China from 1870 to 1935. These contain at least twelve articles written by Hoste himself between 1900 and 1932, as well as articles by other authors commenting on Hoste.[62] One key article – entitled "Possible Changes and Developments in the Native Churches Arising out of the Present Crisis" – was written by Hoste immediately after the Boxer Uprising and published in the *Chinese Recorder* in 1900. This article, which reveals Hoste's revolutionary thinking, may be seen as an exemplary piece that points to Hoste's influence beyond the CIM.[63] For the first time in his leadership role as CIM's general director, Hoste articulated his clear vision about the importance of Chinese church leaders taking on leadership roles. The *Chinese Recorder* provides important background information on Hoste and his leadership and on how the CIM differed from other mission agencies, both in its approach and in its views regarding claiming indemnities.[64]

Fourth, the CIM *Field Bulletins* – found today at the OMF Archives in Singapore – is another key source that has not been well examined in previous scholarship. As the China Council minutes were not maintained after 1947, the CIM *Field Bulletins* are an important source, providing precious supplementary information about the CIM during the transition period until its reluctant exodus from China in 1951. These records document how the CIM continued to uphold the indigenous church principles initially proposed by Hoste even after its relocation beyond China under a new name –Overseas Missionary Fellowship (OMF).

---

62. *Chinese Recorder* (1900): 509. Since 1909, Hoste was also on the Editorial Board of *Chinese Recorder*.

63. *Chinese Recorder* (1900): 509.

64. More than twelve articles written by Hoste during his period of leadership in the CIM were published in the *Chinese Recorder* between 1900 and 1932. See *Chinese Recorder* (1900, 1910, 1902, 1907, 1908, 1909, 1910, 1912, 1914, 1915, 1917, 1921, 1922, 1930, 1932).

Fifth, in terms of secondary sources, I will highlight two books that are particularly noteworthy. The first is A. J. Broomhall's seven-volume work, *Hudson Taylor and China's Open Century* (1981–1989), which provides valuable information on the China Inland Mission – particularly during the period of Hudson Taylor's leadership – as it is based on the CIM records, archives, and Council minutes. Broomhall's research was unique because of his extensive access to the CIM archive materials, many of which have now been disposed of and are no longer available. The second source is Andrew Kaiser's book *The Rushing On of the Purposes of God*, a more recent publication. This book has one particular chapter focusing on the "Golden Age of Mission" after the Boxer Uprising and examining the work in Shanxi, including the CIM's work during Hoste's leadership.[65] Since Hoste spent ten years there before becoming CIM's general director, Shanxi had special significance to him. Both books provide probably the most detailed information regarding Hoste's response in the aftermath of the Boxer crisis, particularly with regard to the issue of indemnity, which Hoste rejcted outright. These secondary sources provide crucial information about the context within which Hoste exercised his leadership and the situation of the CIM, the Chinese indigenous church, and China in those days.

5. Scope of the Research

With a clear focus on Hoste and his leadership, this thesis is different from a general survey on the history of the CIM. Thus, I have examined, in particular, the CIM archive materials that contain specific references to Hoste in light of leadership succession.

Another key concern is how Hoste developed his vision of the indigenous Chinese church. While there will be some references to how other mission organizations attempted to develop a vision similar to that of Hoste, these are mainly for the purpose of comparison and my focus will be primarily on the CIM.

The work of Hoste frequently overlapped with the work of other missionary societies in China – for example, the American Board of Commissioners for Foreign Missions, the London Missionary Society, the Church Missionary

---

65. Kaiser, *Rushing On*, 135–138.

Society, the American Presbyterian Mission, and the Wesleyan Methodist Missionary Society.[66] Given the central role of Hoste in this study, I will only refer to the activities of these societies where this is necessary to relate to or compare with Hoste's work.

While this thesis will refer to a number of key figures and major events related to Hoste in certain contexts, it does not expand into a macrohistorical narrative. Regarding the Boxer Uprising, for example, my primary interest is the response of the CIM, under the leadership of Hoste, to the massacre and damage done by the Boxers. Except for a comparison of the different responses of the CIM and other mission groups, the process and aftermath of the Boxer Uprising only provides some background information for my analysis.

6. Outline of Chapters

Introduction: *From Taylor to Hoste*. This section briefly traces the history of the China Inland Mission (CIM) from the founder, Hudson Taylor, to the young leader Hoste. A major part of this chapter is the literature review of four major categories in previous research: first, an investigation of archival and biographical studies on Hoste, especially those materials provided by the CIM archives; second, studies on the CIM that refer to Hoste, looking both to authors related to the CIM/OMF and to scholars with no direct connection; third, an examination of broader studies on Christian missions in China during Hoste's leadership period; and, finally, an exploration of studies on Hoste's legacy and his impact on the CIM's organizational transition from the CIM to the OMF. From this review, I have identified some valuable findings in recent scholarship and positioned my own research on the subject by pointing out the missing link of Hoste's leadership in the CIM during the post-Taylor period as well as his role – which is often neglected or ignored – in facilitating the shaping of the indigenous Chinese church in modern China.

Chapter One: *Hoste's Early Works under a Chinese Leader*. I will specifically look at Hoste's leadership preparation, focusing on his life and character as a military man in the period before he joined the CIM. I will also look at how Hoste, as a low-key person, was different from the rest of the Cambridge Seven who joined the CIM and went to China in 1885. I will then examine

---

66. Broomhall, *Martyred Missionaries*, 315.

how Hoste worked under the leadership of Pastor Hsi in Shanxi and how their friendship developed. I will also explore some of that affected Hoste's view on the Chinese, Chinese leadership, and the Chinese church.

Chapter Two: *Hoste Taking the Lead in Responding to the Boxer Crisis.* This chapter will present Hoste's leadership in response to the Boxer Uprising. I will first examine the details of the lesser-known internal selection process through which Hoste was appointed as Taylor's successor at a critical time during the Boxer crisis. Next, special attention will be given to the complex factors behind Hoste's bold decision not to accept compensation on behalf of the CIM. I will also examine how Hoste gained the trust of Chinese church leaders and officials during this crisis. Finally, I will look at how Hoste reflected on the longer-term implications, beyond the Boxer Uprising, with a strong conviction that the Chinese church should take on leadership and that the foreign missionaries should let go of their authoritative control.

Chapter Three: *Hoste's Vision of the Indigenous Chinese Church.* In this chapter, I will examine how Hoste developed a vision for the indigenous church. For the first time, in his article published in the *Chinese Recorder* in October 1900, Hoste clearly articulated the importance of the development of the indigenous church. Instead of focusing on the suffering of the missionary community, Hoste shifted his emphasis to the future of the Chinese church. I will also compare the way Hudson Taylor practised the indigenous church principle, with the way Hoste, his successor, articulated and implemented the principle in the CIM.

Chapter Four: *Hoste Launching the Statement of Policy and the Forward Movement.* I will investigate how Hoste boldly responded to the Anti-Christian Movement by introducing his "Statement of Policy" in 1928, calling for an unprecedented reform of the CIM through a transfer of church leadership from CIM missionaries to Chinese Christian leaders. I will also look at Hoste's call to recruit two hundred new missionaries in 1929, which is known as the "Forward Movement." Hoste's vision of the indigenous church was not that the missionaries should retreat but, rather, that they should actively cooperate with the Chinese church to spread the Christian faith, particularly in the inlands of China. I will look at the initial setbacks faced and the CIM's failure, up to this point, to prepare for a fully independent Chinese church. I will also describe Hoste's efforts to rectify these problems and eliminate the hindrances to the development of the indigenous Chinese churches, an aspect that has not been addressed in previous research.

Chapter Five: *Hoste's Legacy to the CIM and the Chinese Church*. This chapter focuses on Hoste's legacy. I will examine the evidence for the steady growth of the indigenous Chinese churches after Hoste. Houghton, the successor to Hoste, fine-tuned Hoste's vision by articulating a "New Emphasis" that CIM missionaries should "indeed remove the controlling hand, but that we may offer the helping hand. It is right that we should think of ourselves as "advisers" rather than "rulers" of the Church."[67] The key was cooperation with the Chinese church and Chinese co-workers. The organizational changes launched by Hoste in 1928 had prepared the Chinese church to face the challenges that would confront them in 1951. Hoste's vision of "self-supporting, self-governing and self-propagating churches" was fully realized when the People's Republic of China was founded in 1949. I will discuss the exodus of the CIM missionaries from China and the subsequent founding of the OMF. Finally, I will evaluate Hoste's lasting legacy through the transformation of the CIM into the OMF and leading Chinese Christianity into a new era.

Conclusion: Here, I will bring together the various findings and show how Hoste, succeeding Taylor, fulfilled his role as a capable leader for the CIM during some of the most challenging periods of CIM history, especially the Boxer Uprising and the Anti-Christian Movement. I will also draw the conclusion of Hoste's long-term commitment to develop and journey with the indigenous Chinese churches as a faithful friend over his thirty-five-year period of leadership for the CIM. Hoste's committed work should, therefore, be duly recognized as an integral part of the indigenous movement of modern Chinese Christianity.

---

67. *China's Millions* (1944): Appendix 2.

CHAPTER 1

Hoste's Early Works under a Chinese Leader

1. Introduction: When West Meets East

Imagine the initial encounter between a British aristocrat and a Chinese Confucian scholar in Ping-Yang Fu (平陽府, today Linfen 臨汾), Shanxi, in the summer of 1885. The British figure was Dixon Edward Hoste. Like his father, who was a major-general of the Royal Artillery, Hoste had joined the Royal Military Academy in Woolwich, England. The Chinese figure was Paster Hsi (Xi Zizhi 席子直, 1835–1896), who came from a noble family that had been destroyed by opium before he was converted to Christianity.[1] Hoste, a quiet and gentle figure, did not like to stand out; yet he was gifted with a disciplined mind of military precision. Hsi, in contrast, was charismatic, forceful, and hot-tempered.[2] It seems that there was nothing in common between these two men in terms of their background, culture, or language. Yet they were both devout Christians and shared the same goal of spreading the Christian faith in Shanxi.

---

1. Hsi's original Chinese name, Zi Zhi 子直, is not so well-known. But Geraldine Guinness (also known as Mrs. Howard Taylor) used the name "Pastor Hsi" in her two-volume biography: *One of China's Scholars (Pastor Hsi): The Culture and Conversion of a Confucianist* and *Pastor Hsi: One of China's Christians*. Alvyn Austin points out that the term "Pastor Hsi" was coined by the CIM and is not commonly mentioned in sources outside the CIM except for a few comments in the *Chinese Recorder*. Austin, *China's Millions*, 172.

2. See Thompson, *Prince with God*, 16; Austin, *China's Millions*, 258.

During the following ten years, their friendship grew. This long-standing relationship had a significant impact upon Hoste, who later became the leader of the CIM – one of the largest foreign missions in China in the early twentieth century. When Hsi passed away in February 1896 at the age of sixty, Hoste grieved the loss of his dear friend.

> A few words as to the general impression made by Pastor Hsi, upon one who was intimately associated with him for nearly ten years, may not be out of place. He has remarkable energy and force of character. His life was an unceasing warfare with the powers of evil. He was habitually burdened in heart about the sins and sorrows of those under his care, and his tears and fasting on their behalf were almost constant. He was a born leader; nothing escaped his keen eye, and he was ever ready to rebuke, instruct, or succour as occasion required. As years went by, his masterful character grew more and more mellowed and softened; until, when he passed away, it is no exaggeration to say that hundreds wept for him as for a father or elder brother.[3]

One can sense Hoste's careful wording as he describes Pastor Hsi's life and work and his fighting spirit, stern style, and imposing character. Over the course of their ten-year association, Hoste observed that Hsi's character changed and grew more approachable. He recognized Hsi's leadership, and this shaped Hoste's view of how the Chinese should lead the Chinese church in the future.

This chapter will highlight the development of the relationship between Hoste and Hsi and how Hsi's influenced and shaped Hoste's leadership capacity. But it is important to first trace the early life of Hoste before he arrived at China, including aspects such as his vision of a China mission, his joining the CIM, and his fellowship with the Cambridge Seven. After that, I will turn to Pastor Hsi's life and his initial contact with Hoste. This will be followed by an analysis of the co-working experience and friendship between Hoste and Hsi. Finally, I will examine how Hoste formulated his preliminary concept of the indigenous Chinese church under the influence of Hsi.

---

3. Taylor, *Pastor Hsi*, xix.

2. Young Life: Military Training and Religious Conversion

Hoste was born in 1861, just four years before the founding of the CIM. Both his father and his grandfather were from a military background – the former was a major general in the Royal Artillery, and the latter was a colonel. So, it is not surprising that Hoste, from his youth, learned the value of "military precision" and following orders. He attended school at Clifton College, one of Britain's elite schools, and the then principal, Dr. John Percival (1834–1918), described Hoste as being "thorough."[4] Hoste paid attention to detail and had an extraordinary ability to concentrate. During his schooldays, he learned by heart many long passages of English poetry, especially Shakespeare, which he could repeat even sixty years later. Hoste was diligent; at nine, he was even reading Greek.[5] However, he himself described his teenage life as being unhappy.[6] Because of his reserved temperament, he had few intimate relationships as he grew up.

Phyllis Thompson records that Hoste entered the Royal Military Academy at Woolwich at the age of seventeen in 1878.[7] Puncher, in his PhD thesis on the Victorian Army and the Cadet Colleges, comments that those who were trained at the Academy were intimately linked with the elite ruling class. With such a background, there was always a question if these young cadets from wealthy backgrounds took the training professionally.[8] Edward Mogg (fl. 1803–1860), a popular writer for newspapers in London in the nineteenth century, described the Academy like this:

> About one hundred and thirty young gentlemen, the sons of military men, and the more respectable classes, who are here instructed in mathematics, land-surveying, with mapping, fortification, engineering, the use of the musket and sword exercise, and fieldpieces; and for whose use twelve brass cannon, three-pounders, are placed in front of the building, practicing with which they acquire a knowledge of their application in

---

4. Thompson, *Prince with God*, 16.
5. Thompson, 17.
6. Thompson, 16–18.
7. Thompson, 17.
8. Puncher, "Victorian Army," 10.

the field of battle. This department is under the direction of a lieutenant-general, an instructor, a professor of mathematics, and a professor of fortification; in addition to which there are French, German, and drawing masters.[9]

It appears that education at the Academy focused mainly on mathematics and the scientific principles of gunnery and fortification, with most of the required readings being in mathematics.[10] Thus, precision was a hallmark of the training Hoste received, which probably influenced his whole life, including his leadership style in the China Inland Mission. In the aftermath of the Boxer Uprising, Hoste insisted that Chinese churches needed to have a careful, accurate assessment of property and lives lost so that no claims by the church would be exaggerated in any way, a point that we will return to in the next chapter.

In 1900, Captain Frederick. G. Guggisberg (1869–1930) published a book about the Royal Military Academy, in which he describes the life of the cadets during the training:

> All luxuries should be removed from the rooms [of the trainees]. Every rug, carpet, tablecloth, armchair etc. was banished. The old system of having tea was banished and we marched to the hall for meals. There were four cadets in each room, the corporal, or head of the room, being in charge. The poor snookers [juniors] usually had a terrible time were severely fagged and unmercifully thrashed with belts and tennis bats . . . We stood to attention at roll-call at 10 pm when the lights were put out, and we turn in as best as we could in the dark. The baths were in the yards, supplied with cold water taps only, in winter those froze, and we had to fill the baths in the mornings with "tosh-cans" from the pumps, a dreadfully cold business when it was freezing or snowing.[11]

---

9. Puncher, 18.

10. "Online Books by Woolwich Royal Military Academy," https://onlinebooks.library.upenn.edu/webbin/book/lookupname?key=Royal%20Military%20Academy%2C%20Woolwich.

11. Guggisberg, *Royal Military Academy*, 92–93.

The tough training at the Military Academy was certainly good preparation for Hoste to endure the rough conditions in the inlands of China in later days. In fact, Hoste – who died in 1945 at the age of eighty-six – outlived all other members of the Cambridge Seven.[12]

According to available records, Hoste commenced his service with the Royal Artillery (RA) on 21 December 1881 and remained there until he joined the CIM in 1885. The military record of 1885 notes that Hoste had received the Crown Honours of CB, the Companion of the Order of the Bath, though the date of conferment cannot be determined.[13]

In 1882, while Hoste was serving with the Royal Artillery, he was converted to the Christian faith through the ministry of the American evangelist D. L. Moody (1837–1899), who visited Brighton where Hoste's parents lived.[14] Hoste, who had initially not wanted to go to the meeting where Moody was the speaker, was later persuaded to attend by his brother William. He was rather relieved that the only seats left were at the back of the hall.[15] When Moody stepped onto the middle of the platform, Hoste seemed unable to take his eyes off him.[16] When Moody prayed, "never before had D. E. Hoste heard such a prayer. Moody talked to God. He talked as though God was there, as though he knew Him, as a man talks to a friend. He talked as though God could be depended upon to do His work in men's hearts, right then and there."[17]

Hoste felt "overwhelmingly conscious of the sin of his ungodly life. He was seized by a conviction that he must be saved now or never."[18] Hoste was converted at that meeting. Hoste recalled that he immediately stopped smoking and, from that moment, never touched tobacco again, which seemed to support the genuineness of his conversion.[19]

---

12. *China's Millions* (1945): 25.
13. Retrieved and available from the British Military Record. The CB would be the medieval equivalent of appointing a knight.
14. Thompson, *Prince with God*, 18–19.
15. Thompson, 19.
16. Thompson, 19.
17. Thompson, 19.
18. Thompson, 20.
19. Thompson, 23.

To Hoste, becoming a Christian and mission service were inseparable. "If this Gospel is true," Hoste thought, "and I know it is, as it has changed my life, I want to make it known where Christ is not known. I want to give my life to this."[20]

It did not take long before Hoste came across Hudson Taylor's little book, *China: Its Spiritual Need and Claims*. Hoste was captured by these words in the book:

> Were all the subjects of the court of Pekin marshalled in single rank and file, allowing one yard between man and man, they would encircle the globe more than ten times at its Equator. Were they to march past the spectator at the rate of thirty miles a day, they would move on and on, day after day, week after week, month after month; and more than twenty-three and a half years would elapse before the last individual had passed by ... Four hundred millions of souls, having no hope, and without God in the world![21]

Like many others who wanted to be involved in mission work in the faraway land in the East, Hoste had never visited China before. Yet the mere number of Chinese who had never had the chance to hear the Christian message caught Hoste's attention. According to Taylor's book, China had 250 million people – ten times the population of England or sixty-seven times that of Scotland.[22] Hoste expressed to his father his desire to go to China. His father, while rejoicing that his son had become a Christian, urged him not to take such an important step rashly, lest he should regret it later. Although initially disappointed, Hoste recognized the wisdom of such a warning. Nearly a year later, in May 1883, his father wrote to him saying that if he still desired to be a missionary, "he could now feel free to resign his commission [from the army]." [23] He would not stand in the way.[24] His father was impressed by Hoste's persistent spirit; and since he himself was from a military background, he understood well the importance of following orders. He believed that

---

20. Thompson, 1.
21. Taylor, *China*, 11.
22. Taylor, 11.
23. Thompson, *Prince with God*, 25.
24. Broomhall, *Shaping of Modern China*, 421.

his son, as one who had given his life to God, was following orders from a higher authority. In 1833, with his father's refusal to allow him to resign his commission from the military overcome, Hoste finally decided to write to the London Office of the CIM and offer himself as a candidate for China.

3. Applying to the China Inland Mission

At the time of his conversion, Hoste became aware of the calls for Christian missions to the East, which had been part of a fervent trend in England and across European countries at that time.

Prior to 1865, almost all Protestant missionary societies had confined their efforts to the coastal areas of China, with just a few exceptions in a handful of cities along the Yangtze River. In 1865, however, Hudson Taylor changed that picture. Founding the China Inland Mission in 1865 with just ten pounds in hand and no support from established societies or churches, Taylor had one goal in mind: the spreading of the gospel in inland China. By 1884, more than eighty workers had joined the workforce, working in fourteen provinces.[25]

Taylor was also conscious of the devastation Shanxi had faced because of the severe famine. Joshua J. Turner (1854–1937) and Francis H. James (1851–1900), both CIM missionaries, arrived in Shanxi in 1876 and were active in the famine relief.[26] Taylor had always had a special place in his heart for Shanxi. Even his second wife, Jennie, went to Shanxi to help with the famine relief between 1878 and 1879 by caring for the orphans and was separated from her husband for more than a year.[27] However, the need continued to be great. Thus, Taylor was excited to find out that this young man, Hoste, just twenty-four years old at that time, was interested in going to China.

On 23 July 1883, Hoste wrote to Taylor, asking to meet with him as he wanted to offer his services to the CIM.[28] Hoste had not met Taylor before, but Taylor's name had become well known both in China and England shortly after the establishment of the CIM in 1865.

---

25. *China's Millions* (1884): 10.

26. Kaiser, *Rushing On*, 5. After three years with the CIM, Joshua Turner joined the Baptist Mission Society (BMS).

27. Broomhall, *Shaping of Modern China*, 335.

28. Broomhall, 421.

The letter to Taylor by Hoste was signed "your obedient servant, D. E. Hoste, Lieutenant, RA [Royal Artillery]."[29] The letter did not reach Taylor right away as he was on a trip away from the CIM headquarters in Newington Green, London. It was only upon his return on 1 August 1883 that Taylor read the letter and immediately arranged for Hoste to meet with him.[30] This date was also significant because Harold Schofield (1851–1883) – an Oxford graduate who had joined the CIM three years earlier and worked in Taiyuan, Shanxi – had died from Typhus while treating a patient. Schofield's death was a great loss to the CIM.[31] For Taylor to have received Hoste's letter at that time must have been a great comfort and encouragement.

Taylor was already a middle-aged man when he met this young lieutenant. Little did the two men know that, in less than twenty years, Hoste himself would be taking the helm of the Mission that Taylor had founded. The future was hidden from them.

They met at the CIM headquarters at Pyrland Road, Newington Green, London, in 1883.[32] Years later, Hoste wrote about that encounter with Taylor. Taylor was careful to set before Hoste the real character of life and work in inland China, telling him quite plainly that it involved isolation, privation, the lack of privacy, exposure to the hostility of the people, hard living conditions, and also many trials of faith, patience, and constancy. Taylor himself also had to endure the contempt with which fellow countrymen regarded this Englishman who identified himself with the Chinese by living among them as one of them.[33] Taylor also did not minimize the suspicion with which foreigners were regarded by the Chinese people. Thus, Taylor advised Hoste to wait, to be prayerful, and to mature as a Christian. Surprisingly, according to Phyllis Thompson's record, Hoste walked away from that interview feeling encouraged: "His enthusiasm had been quickened rather than dampened by what he had heard."[34]

The CIM London Council continued to follow up with Hoste. Two further interviews were conducted by the London Council in 1884, which included

---

29. Broomhall, 421.
30. Broomhall, 421.
31. Broomhall, 421.
32. Broomhall, 421.
33. Thompson, *Prince with God*, 26.
34. Thompson, 27.

a request for testimonials from two or three people who knew Hoste personally in order that "a balanced and impartial view" might be formed of the suitability of Hoste joining the CIM.[35]

One such reference letter was from Hoste's pastor, W. T. Storrs (1883–1919), who had been the vicar of Sandown since 1881. Storrs characterized Hoste as naturally shy, a little impulsive, with just some ability to learn, not able to teach well, not very enterprising, and not fitted for missionary work – with a disclaimer of "but I may be mistaken."[36] Storrs also commented on Hoste's high-pitched voice, which prevented him from being an impressive public speaker. According to this reference, Hoste was not the obvious choice for mission work, let alone for going to China. The London Council probably shared Storrs's view, judging from their requirement for several more interviews without a final decision.

Although Storrs's reference was not particularly promising, the spiritual stature of the "quiet young man" and Hoste's humility and sincerity had not passed unnoticed.[37] The London Council deliberated on the matter carefully, taking into consideration several factors. First, the fact that Hoste came from an elite family and his willingness to renounce what promised to be a distinguished career in the army to "bury himself" in the interior of China was no small matter. Second, the London Council had also received the doctor's report, stating that though Hoste was not physically strong, he was healthy and should be able to endure hardship in China.[38] Third, there was already the momentum created by the intentions of some of the brightest graduates from Cambridge University to join the CIM. Though Hoste was not a Cambridge graduate, the London Council felt that having another young man such as Hoste joining the group to China would be a big boost for the CIM.

According to the minutes of the October 1884 CIM London Council, Hoste was finally accepted to join the CIM as a probationer.[39]

---

35. One interview was conducted in February 1884 and the other in April 1884. For details, see Broomhall, *Shaping of Modern China*, 42.
36. D. E. Hoste's application to the CIM, OMF Archives, OMF Office, UK.
37. Thompson, *Prince with God*, 34.
38. Thompson, 34.
39. Thompson, 35.

4. Becoming a Member of the Cambridge Seven

Initially, many members of the CIM had no formal education or training, although there were a few rare exceptions such as Dr. Harold Schofield, the prominent medical doctor from Oxford who was mentioned earlier in this chapter.

John Pollock, in his book *A Cambridge Movement*, comments that the CIM was catapulted "from comparative obscurity to an almost embarrassing prominence" with the rise of the Cambridge Seven.[40] Initially called the "Cambridge Party," this group of young men were later referred to as the "Cambridge Band." It was only after they had left for China that the term "Cambridge Seven" came into use.[41] Yet not all of the seven were Cambridge graduates – two were military men, namely, Hoste and Cecil Polhill-Turner (1860–1938) – and not all had applied to the CIM simultaneously; but they left for China as a group, catching much attention. A. J. Broomhall comments that when the initial CIM meetings took place in Oxford and Cambridge in November 1884, there was "no Cambridge Seven, not even a Cambridge five."[42] The CIM was just beginning to stir interest in the top universities.

Compared to the rest of the Cambridge Seven, Hoste was perhaps the most unassuming. The most charismatic and colourful personality was Stanley Peregrine Smith (1861–1931), often known as "S. P. S," eldest son of a surgeon and known as a natural public speaker.[43] Smith was most famous for being the captain of his college boats[44] and often captured people's attention at the first contact with his impressive and eloquent speech.[45]

Charles T. Studd (1860–1931), often known as "C. T.," also spoke with great intensity and passion as he gave his personal testimony. "Opposition and criticism were alike disarmed, and professors and students together were in tears."[46] Studd, probably England's best cricketer at that time, was most famous for being the captain of the Cambridge cricket team.[47] However, A

---

40. Pollock, *Cambridge Movement*, 87.
41. Broomhall, *Shaping of Modern China*, 433.
42. Broomhall, 429.
43. Broomhall, 416.
44. Broomhall, 417.
45. Taylor and Taylor, *Growth of a Work of God*, 386–387.
46. Taylor and Taylor, 386–387.
47. Broomhall, *Shaping of Modern China*, 443.

J. Broomhall comments that Studd was often "impulsive, unpredictable, even unbalanced."[48]

William W. Cassels (1858–1925) was twenty-seven, the oldest of the group when he joined the CIM. The only member of the band who was a clergyman, he later became the first Anglican clergyman in the CIM. Cassels later became the first bishop in Western China, while remaining a member of the CIM – an unusual arrangement between the CIM and the Church Missionary Society (CMS), which was an extended arm of the Church of England.

We come then to the Polhill brothers. Arthur Polhill-Turner (1862–1935), at twenty-two, the youngest in the group, joined Cassels in East Sichuan and was ordained by him and remained a close co-worker until Cassels's death in 1925.[49] Cecil Polhill-Turner (1860–1938) was a lieutenant in the Royal Dragoons in Ireland. Later, Cecil found "his niche in the Tibetan marches and embarked on romantic dangerous adventures."[50] The Polhill-Turner brothers had Pentecostal inclinations. Shortly after their arrival in China, they, along with C. T. Studd, had thought language study a laborious substitute for what they considered the biblical way of acquiring a foreign tongue. On the slow journey up the Han River, they had put away their books and "given themselves to prayer" for a Pentecostal gift of speech in Chinese. Within a few months, however, "they saw their mistake, knuckled down to study and in time became fluent."[51]

Finally, Montagu Proctor-Beauchamp (1860–1939) came from a prominent background, being a nephew of Lord Radstock. He renounced a significant family estate that amounted to a quarter of a million pounds to go to China.[52]

John Pollock summarizes the Cambridge Seven in his book *The Cambridge Seven*:

> At first meeting Smith would seem severe, though affectionate and charming on closer acquaintance, but Studd's gentleness almost belied his burning words. Beauchamp with his enormous

---

48. Broomhall, 6:341, 330–332, quoted in Austin, *China's Millions*, 207.
49. Broomhall, 6:208.
50. Broomhall, 6:472, 557–558.
51. Broomhall, 6:444.
52. Broomhall, 6:444.

frame and somewhat florid face and capacity to extract enjoyment from anything, was almost as eloquent as Smith; but Hoste and Cecil Polhill-Turner were shy and found public speaking a trial. Cassels, as quiet as Hoste, as good a speaker as Beauchamp, was in many ways the most mature of them all.[53]

Twice, Pollock refers to Hoste and describes him as a quiet and shy man. From various descriptions and observations, it seems that Hoste was an unassuming person who did not mind staying in the background. Several farewell meetings were held in early 1885, with the final one held at Exeter Hall on 4 February 1885. Comparing the different speeches given by each of the Cambridge Seven, Stanley Smith's speech, as expected, was the longest and the most colourful, containing more than two pages of personal testimony, while Hoste delivered a short and succinct speech about the initial difficulties involved in leaving the army.[54] In comparison with the rest, Hoste's speech was flat and unimpressive.

5. Pastor Hsi's Initial Contact with Hoste

As mentioned earlier, Shanxi had suffered one of the most severe famines between 1876 and 1879. Even by 1885, when the Cambridge Seven arrived in China, the people were barely recovering from the fateful blow dealt by the long period of famine. However, Shanxi had an even bigger problem than famine. It was said that in the province of Shanxi, "eleven out of every ten smoked opium."[55] According to Brian Inglis (1916–1993), in his book *The Opium War*, the East India Company had been producing and selling roughly three thousand chests of opium per annum, each a hundred and forty pounds in weight with a steady revenue of fifteen hundred dollars per chest – giving them a 2000 percent profit.[56] The CIM was not silent about its opposition to the opium trade,[57] and Taylor personally protested strongly against it.

---

53. Pollock, *Cambridge Seven*, 13.
54. *China's Millions* (1885): 34–35.
55. Thompson, *Prince with God*, 43.
56. Broomhall, *Shaping of Modern China*, 55. See also Inglis, *Opium War*, 46–47, 59–61, 202.
57. Christians in England also took on the issue seriously. One example was a meeting held in Exeter Hall on 15 March 1882, organized by James E. Matheson, secretary of the

The CIM addressed the subject strenuously by publishing several articles in *China's Millions* between 1880 and 1885. In one such article – entitled "Who Is Responsible for the Opium Trade?" – Taylor wrote,

> We feel that England is morally responsible for *every ounce of opium* now produced in China, as well as for that imported from abroad . . . The opium trade made England's profession of the Christian faith hollow and insincere. Nothing could have been worse for undermining missionary work in China.[58]

On the one hand, Taylor condemned the opium trade. On the other, he was determined to send some of the young CIM missionaries to Shanxi to face the challenges posed by this problem, particularly the rehabilitation work for opium addicts. Thus, in 1885, the work of the CIM and that of Pastor Hsi began to intersect. This was also the first time that Hoste came into contact with Hsi.

The most extensive coverage on the life of Hsi is found in the writings of Mrs. Howard Taylor, who wrote the two volumes, *One of China's Scholars* and *Pastor Hsi: One of China's Christians*. It is important to note Mrs. Taylor's explanation for writing the two volumes. In her introduction to the books, she explains that the two books were written based on a handwritten manuscript prepared by Hsi himself and with additional information from Hoste, who worked under Hsi for ten years.[59]

The historian Alvyn Austin postulates that it was likely that Hsi had only submitted a few pages of his own manuscript in Chinese and that the rest of the information for Mrs. Taylor's two volumes was supplied by Hoste.[60] If that postulation is true, then the two volumes by Mrs. Howard Taylor are

---

English Presbyterian Mission, with one hundred attendees, mostly missionaries who had served in China. The conclusion of the meeting was recorded: "Having heard the testimony of the missionaries' long residence in China, the meeting condemns the opium trade as unworthy of this country and calls upon the Parliament to give the subject its earliest and earnest consideration." *China's Millions* (1882): 50.

58. *China's Millions* (1882): 39–40, 57. Also, according to the records in the 1875 *China's Millions*, in 1873–1874, exports to China from India were over 11 million pounds sterling, of which 10 million were for opium alone. The land devoted to the cultivation of opium in Central India was 289,062 acres. *China's Millions* (1875): 168.

59. Taylor, *One of China's Scholars*, 16.

60. Austin, *China's Millions*, 172. It was when Mrs. Taylor visited Pastor Hsi in 1894 that she received his handwritten manuscript.

based mainly on Hoste's recollections of the life of Hsi from the ten years he spent with this Chinese leader.

Pastor Hsi, more commonly known as Xi Shengmo (席勝魔), was a Confucian scholar, originally from the Shanxi Province. When he became a Christian, Hsi changed his name to the two-character name "Sheng-mo" (勝魔), meaning devil-overcomer. To Hsi, the devil was a personal foe and a terrible reality, and he wished, henceforth, to be known as "conqueror of the devil." Once an opium addict, in 1879, he converted to the Christian faith through the teaching of David Hill (1840–1896), a missionary from the Wesleyan Mission.[61] Hsi was baptized in 1880 at the age of forty-four and later became an assistant to Hill for a few months, during which time he helped him to write literary tracts. That was the only time Hsi had any "sustained contact with any foreigners in his first six years as a Christian."[62] Hsi later wrote, "Thanks be to God, Mr. Hill led me to the gate, God caused me to enter."[63] However, Hill left Shanxi in 1979 to return to Hankow (漢口, Hankou). Therefore, Hsi's contact with foreigners was limited prior to the arrival of the Cambridge Seven. Though grateful to Hill, Hsi was generally suspicious of foreigners, and more so in regard to work with foreigners.[64]

Hsi soon became a well-known Christian preacher. However, his first call was to help those afflicted by opium addiction. Hsi's work grew rapidly and was large and spreading throughout the province of Shanxi, with meeting places for worship in twenty-seven villages, spread over five counties.[65] Hsi wrote many hymns himself, without the influence of missionaries. In fact, the tunes and the lyrics were of local origin.[66] One significant observation made by Mrs. Taylor relates to the independence and indigenous nature of Hsi's work.

Mrs. Taylor comments that Hsi was "the centre of a large and extended organization, for the support and direction of which he alone was responsible."[67] Hsi's work was independent of the CIM, and he received no salary or

---

61. Broomhall, *Shaping of Modern China*, 32.
62. Austin, *China's Millions*, 172.
63. Broomhall, *Days of Blessing*, 126.
64. Thompson, *Prince with God*, 58.
65. *China's Millions* (September 1884): 113.
66. Taylor, *Pastor Hsi*, 124.
67. Taylor, 45, 137, 351.

remuneration from the CIM or other missions. Entirely independent and run on native lines, the number of opium refuges continued to increase.

By 1884, even before the arrival of the Cambridge Seven, Hsi had already established at least eight opium refuges. From just south of his home in Pingyang to Chao-ch'eng (趙城, Zhaocheng), forty miles to the north, and in villages and hamlets all along the line, little companies of believers were meeting regularly for worship with the help of Hsi and his local co-workers.[68]

The summer of 1885 was an especially exciting time for Hsi. Never before had he been joined by so many new missionaries. The Cambridge Seven, who had departed for China in February 1885, aroused missionary interest on both sides of the Atlantic, especially in the student world. Hudson Taylor assigned four of the Cambridge Seven to Pinyang to join Hsi's work: Stanley P. Smith, the prominent athlete and natural speaker; Rev. W. W. Cassels, who later became the first bishop of Western China; Montague Beauchamp, the wealthy young man; and, finally, Dixon Edward Hoste of the Royal Artillery, the quiet young man.

No records could be traced that indicated how Taylor introduced the Cambridge Seven to Hsi. One can only speculate that some kind of communication must have taken place between Hsi and the CIM prior to the arrival of the Cambridge Seven. The evidence shows that Benjamin Bagnall (1844–1900), the CIM superintendent of Shanxi Province, escorted the four young men to Taiyuan, and they then continued another nine days, finally arriving in Pingyang to see Hsi.[69] Frederick Baller (1852–1922), who had joined the CIM in 1873, was the language supervisor assigned by Taylor to help Cassels, Beauchamp, Smith, and Hoste "find their feet."[70]

When these young British men met Hsi, they found him rather unimpressive at first sight: "He was just a quiet, scholarly man of medium height and slender figure, dressed in simple blue cotton or white muslin grown. The only thing that might have attracted attention was the power of his glance; for his eyes were keen and commanding, in spite of a slight cast that disfigured one of them."[71]

---

68. Taylor, 137–138.

69. Austin, *China's Millions*, 233. Bagnall was killed during the Boxer Rebellion, along with his wife and child.

70. Broomhall, *Shaping of Modern China*, 450.

71. Taylor, *One of China's Scholars*, ix.

However, there was something unique about Hsi. To the missionaries, Hsi could even have seemed a bit intimidating as he was a man of authority. After a later visit, Stevenson, the CIM's China director recorded his impressions of Hsi:

> He [Hsi] was not much to look at. But one could not be in his presence an hour without knowing he was a man with a purpose ... something about his eyes made you feel – here is the clearness of conviction and tremendous intensity. There was nothing dull or slow-going about him. There was no trifling in his presence, no wasting time on side questions. He was a man of one idea, and that the greatest that can absorb the soul. To him God was a reality. In everything and always, he dealt with God. The passion of his life was – saving souls.[72]

Even Hudson Taylor – as recorded in Mrs. Howard Taylor's book *Pastor Hsi: One of China's Scholars* – made a comment that Hsi was a "proud self-centred Confucianist" before his conversion.[73] If there was one thing for which Hsi had always been noted, "it was his antipathy to foreigners and dislike for everything connected with them."[74] Alvyn Austin comments that Hsi "had nothing to do with foreigners [before his conversion]."[75] After Hsi's death, Hoste also wrote that "there were points in his character which rendered his cooperation with foreign missionaries a matter of difficulty. By nature, and by training, his temper was autocratic and independent ... his confidence was not easily won; indeed, a tendency to over-mistrust and suspicion concerning those he did not know well." [76]

Mrs. Taylor comments that as a "cultured Confucianist" with position and influence, a scholar deeply rooted in the Chinese tradition, it was Hsi's "patriotic feeling" that made him dislike foreigners.[77] It is sometimes hard for outsiders to understand the level of aversion and contempt the Chinese educated class felt towards foreigners. However, Mrs. Taylor makes the sharp

---

72. Taylor, vii.
73. Taylor, *Pastor Hsi*, ix.
74. Taylor, 4.
75. Austin, *China's Millions*, 172, 177.
76. Austin, xiii.
77. Taylor, *Pastor Hsi*, 62.

observation that "there is a deeply-rooted conservatism in the heart of the Chinaman that perhaps makes him naturally averse to foreigners. The [great] empire, China, aims at moral greatness not [necessarily] material greatness." Besides, Hsi "knew well who had brought opium to China, who had drained the country millions of money as indemnity for the two unjustifiable [opium] wars, and bound the hands of the nation while driving them to suicide."[78]

Hoste, as a quiet, shy, younger person, must have found Hsi difficult to work with. It seems most unusual for Hsi to have welcomed into his care some of these inexperienced young English aristocrats who could not speak the Chinese language. Hsi had enjoyed a student-teacher relationship with David Hill, but his relationship with other foreigners was not the same. He had been working alone, without foreign help, especially since Hill had left Shanxi in 1879. Perhaps one key factor that induced Hsi to welcome these young missionaries was Taylor himself. Though Hsi only met Taylor a year after the Cambridge Seven's arrival, Taylor's reputation and the work of the CIM work were well known among Chinese Christians. As early as 1876, CIM missionaries, including Turner and James, had arrived in Shanxi with the goal of establishing the first permanent Protestant residence in the province.[79] With the arrival of its missionaries, the CIM had also started famine relief work in 1876. This must have created a positive impression upon Hsi. So, it may not be surprising that he was willing to welcome these foreigners into his midst out of respect for Taylor and the work of the CIM.

Furthermore, Hsi was impressed by the qualities of the CIM missionaries whom he met. For instance, he was amazed by Baller's fluency in Chinese and his scholarly knowledge of the Chinese classics.[80] Baller, who joined the CIM in 1873, had been involved in famine relief work in Shanxi since 1876. He had been assigned by Taylor to help these new CIM missionaries in their Chinese language learning and had accompanied these young missionaries to meet with Hsi for the first time.

For some time, Hsi had been thinking about commencing an opium refuge in the city of Hungtung (洪洞, Hongdong), quite a few miles from Pingyang. In 1886, since the young CIM missionaries were with him, Hsi

---

78. Taylor, 144, 160–161.
79. Kaiser, *Rushing On*, 8.
80. Taylor, *Pastor Hsi*, 149.

took the initiative to invite first Smith and later Hoste to work with him.[81] The missionaries soon found suitable premises for their accommodation on a busy street in Hung-tung, while Hsi took over the front courtyard and transformed it into an opium refuge.[82] Hsi would pay frequent visits to the refuge. One way that Hsi helped the opium addicts was through singing: "Nothing cheered the patients in the Refuges so much or was so speedy a cure for anxious care apart from singing."[83] Hsi had also his own unique way of leading the singing: "He loved to pitch the tunes as high as possible and keep them up to a good swinging pace." There was "nothing dull or drowsy about the Hung-tung meeting."[84]

Hsi also gave advice to Smith and Hoste about how they were to carry out the evangelistic work.[85] They would divide the work into different sections and centres, with Smith and Hoste visiting at least fifteen to twenty centres regularly and local Christians from different villages meeting with them to hear Bible teaching. "Little intervals between these journeys they gave to rest and study."[86] It was strenuous work, but the missionaries accustomed themselves to such conditions by living entirely in Chinese style in the city: "They always ate with chopsticks, slept on heated brick beds like their neighbours, and wore the dress of the ordinary scholar."[87]

Smith, due to his strong personality, sometimes found it hard to work with Hsi. Smith also had some reservations about Hsi, feeling that he had a "weak spot in his character" in his love of power.[88] But, of course, Smith had to submit to Hsi's leadership, which he found challenging. In 1887, Smith felt the urge to start a new work in Luan (潞安), a city seventy miles east of Pingyang.[89] By the summer of that year, he proceeded to the new field. This left Hoste in Hungtung. This was an important period, during which the friendship between Hoste and Hsi began to grow.

---

81. Taylor, 165.
82. Taylor, 166.
83. Taylor, 166.
84. Taylor, 207.
85. Taylor, 204.
86. Taylor, 205.
87. Taylor, 205.
88. Taylor, 214.
89. Thompson, *Prince with God*, 58.

6. Hoste Learning the Chinese Language

Language skills for day-to-day communication and mission activities was a crucial factor for fieldwork in Shanxi. From the outset, Taylor, the founder of the CIM, laid great emphasis on learning the Chinese language and adopting the Chinese way of life. His motto had always been "becoming a Chinese to the Chinese by learning the Chinese language."[90] Even with the first group of CIM missionaries aboard the Lammermuir in 1866, it was reported that language learning continued without relenting "even in rough seas."[91]

By 1871, two CIM language schools had been set up, one in Yangzhou 揚州 in Jiangsu Province, mainly for the women CIM missionaries, the other for the men in Anqing 安慶 in Anhui Province.[92] However, even before the Cambridge Seven arrived in China, there seemed to have been some flexibility in how the CIM missionaries could acquire the language. Dr. Harold Schofield, who joined the CIM in 1880, was allowed to learn the language for a few months in Yantai 烟臺, rather than at the CIM language school, before proceeding to Taiyuan, where he practised medicine in a CIM hospital until he died from diphtheria in 1883, just three years later.[93] Despite this flexibility, learning the Chinese language was always a serious business. When the CIM missionaries found the Chinese language difficult to acquire, they were instructed to spend time with the local people – "the cook, the laundryman and the printers."[94] Taylor argued that the missionaries should "consider six or eight hours a day sacred to the Lord and His work, and let nothing hinder your giving this time to language study and practice till you can preach fluently and intelligibly."[95]

Although there is no detailed record of how Hoste acquired the Chinese language, a few things are clear. First, he like the rest of the Cambridge Seven, did not go to the traditional CIM language school. Instead, Taylor sent along Frederick Baller, the CIM language supervisor, to accompany Hoste, Cassels, and Smith and help them to "find their feet" as they arrived in Shanxi in

---

90. Broomhall, *Shaping of Modern China*, 809.
91. Broomhall, 719.
92. Broomhall, 333–334.
93. Broomhall, 409.
94. Broomhall, 769.
95. Broomhall, 118.

1885.⁹⁶ Baller was the head of the language school in Anqing and had written the language learning manual – the *Mandarin Primer* – for the CIM.⁹⁷ This learning manual outlined in detail six sections of learning the Chinese language. According to the manual, "the first four sections should be passed through in the probationary two years. Should any student fail to pass in at least three sections in that time, his probation will be prolonged."⁹⁸ The language examination for the first four sections included a conversation of not less than fifteen minutes with a Chinese teacher in the presence of the examiner, writing in Chinese character the names of all provinces of China, the recognition and knowledge of one thousand Chinese characters, and a test on the *Book of Hundred Family Names* (百家姓).⁹⁹

From the CIM record, it seems that Baller spent at least a few months with Hoste to help him to gain skills in the Chinese language. Therefore, though Hoste did not go to the CIM language school like the others, he had Baller as a personal tutor at least during the initial period of the first few months in Shanxi.

Apart from Baller's help, it is also clear that Hoste learned the language from the local teachers, probably including Pastor Hsi himself.¹⁰⁰ As we shall see later in this chapter, Pastor Hsi invited Hoste to attend church leadership meetings on a regular basis; therefore, we can infer that Hoste managed to acquire sufficient Chinese language skills – at least in listening and speaking – that would allow him to engage in conversations and discussions on various church affairs with Pastor Hsi and other Chinese Christians during and after the mission work in Shanxi.

---

96. Broomhall, 6:450.

97. Broomhall, 6:471.

98. China Inland Mission, *The Arrangement of the China Inland Mission Comprising – Classified Lists of the Missionaries and Stations, with Their Chinese Names; The Principles and Practice; The Course of Chinese Study in Six Sections and the Instructions for the Private Use of Members of the Mission Only* (Shanghai, China Inland Mission, 1886), 22–26.

99. China Inland Mission., 23–27. The fifth and sixth stages of language learning by CIM missionaries also included a study of the *Analects of Confucius* 論語 and remembering the names of all the Chinese dynasties starting from Xia 夏. See also Baller, *Primer*.

100. Broomhall, *Shaping of Modern China*, 443, 460.

7. Hoste's Support for Pastor Hsi in a Time of Crisis

We may wonder why Hsi was drawn to Hoste, that quiet, unassuming new missionary. Crisis was one key factor that helped to strengthen the bond between Hsi and Hoste. With Hsi's strong character and personality, it is not difficult to imagine that he would have attracted enemies. A rival leader by the name of Fan (范) arose about twenty miles from Hsi's home.[101] He practised a "meditative kind of Christianity that offered release from the transient world."[102] However, Fan became increasingly resentful of Hsi's expanding power and authority.[103]

Fan accused Hsi of gaining favour with the foreigners for his own financial gain. On one occasion, when Smith and Hoste were away visiting other villages, Hsi moved into their house and "took charge of everything," claiming that he was entitled to the "hundred-fold reward" that the Bible proclaimed.[104] To Fan, Hsi was glorying over them "on account of his comfortable quarters rent free, the confidence of the missionaries, and the honour of his position."[105]

Fan set up opposition refuges to compete against Hsi and sold his own prescriptions to help opium addicts. The Hungtung church, with its large number of new believers, was soon divided against itself, with some remaining loyal to Hsi, while others followed Fan.[106] The church that had been progressing so rapidly was weakened by division, while the refuge work seemed in danger of being overthrown. Even some of the missionaries felt that the attack against Hsi might be not without provocation.[107] While deeply appreciative of Hsi's character and work, Hoste was not blind to his faults. Yet he stood by him as few others did even among his own CIM colleagues.[108]

On one occasion, Fan instigated a mob that attempted to physically attack Hsi.[109] After months passed, signs of dissolution became apparent in Fan's

---

101. Alvyn Austin indicates that Fan's full name was never given. See Austin, *China's Millions*, 265.
102. Austin, 266.
103. Thompson, *Prince with God*, 58.
104. Taylor, *Pastor Hsi*, 221.
105. Taylor, 221.
106. Taylor, 221.
107. Taylor, 59.
108. Taylor, 239.
109. Taylor, 222–223.

gang. Once the matter was settled, decisions had to be made about whether Fan, the offender, should be subject to discipline or "drastic action." However, Hsi consulted with Hoste and, "after prayer and consideration," they jointly decided that any attempt to punish Fan would be a mistake as it would only garner sympathy for Fan's followers and justify the position of those who had already accused the leaders of the church of having an contentious spirit. Hsi, with Hoste's encouragement, believed that "God in the end would make it right."[110]

After a few months, things settled down as the revolt lost strength and followers. Mrs. Howard Taylor writes, "Independent as he was by nature, it had been irksome to him to bear with the restraints of even such cooperation . . . [Hsi] discovered the rich treasure of sympathy and friendship [with Hoste] he might otherwise have continued to ignore."[111] Since the crisis in 1887 until he passed away in 1896, Hsi continued to trust Hoste on matters of importance. Hsi's association with Hoste continued for a long time and resulted in a deep friendship such as was rarely known between a Westerner and a Chinese during that time.[112]

This friendship was tested on different occasions. During the time of famine, there were crop failures. This meant that all the opium refuges faced added expenses as well as having fewer patients who could afford to pay for treatment. Hsi, of course, suffered with the rest. It came to Hoste's ears that Hsi and his household were living on limited supplies of coarse bread and millet gruel. Hoste's first impulse, of course, was to help. He had fifteen ounces of silver to spare and decided to take the money to Hsi. During his long walk to Hsi's home, he felt an inner conviction that giving Hsi the money would not be wise as it would only create dependency. When Hoste arrived at Hsi's home, "no complaint was made, and no help was sought or offered. Hoste kept that silver up his sleeve."[113] Though he felt grief at not being able to help his friend because of his conviction, he refrained from giving the money to Hsi.[114] When the famine was over, Hsi himself brought up the subject one

---

110. Taylor, *Pastor Hsi*, 237.
111. Taylor, 238–239.
112. Taylor, 238–239.
113. Taylor, 283.
114. Thompson, *Prince with God*, 67.

day, expressing his appreciation to Hoste that, in that most difficult time, his friend had not given him any money. "It is a special blessing because during the period of privation, a gift from the missionary would be a hindrance to my work."[115] This special experience probably shaped the way Hoste thought about the development of the indigenous Chinese church in the years to come. The Chinese could stand on their own without depending on help from foreign missionaries.

While deeply appreciative of Hsi and his work, Hoste was also keenly aware of Hsi's weaknesses. Hoste indicated that Hsi "was a man who is impatient and is quick to temper."[116] Though Hoste gave Hsi counsel, he always let Hsi bear his own burdens while, at the same time, submitting to Hsi's leadership.[117] Hoste chose to play second fiddle to Hsi.

8. Hsi's Involvement in Hoste's Family

On one occasion, Hsi came to know that Hoste's father was "suffering and out of health."[118] Hsi wrote a long letter to Hoste's father in Chinese and prepared two different kinds of medicine to be forwarded to England for Hoste's father's use. In the letter, Hsi gave some specific instructions about how Hoste's father should take the medicine. The pills were in two large pint-and-a-half bottles with instructions that eight of the red pills should be taken every evening with boiling water and twenty of the black ones every morning before breakfast.[119]

Part of this letter from Hsi was printed in *China's Millions* in the original Chinese. Interestingly, while Hoste's full Chinese name (何斯德) was actually mentioned by Hsi in the letter, Hoste's name was omitted in *China's Millions*. We can only speculate on the reason for this, but it is quite likely that the Hoste himself requested the omission as he did not want to receive any praise or be at the centre of attention. Rather, Hoste wanted people back home in England to know Hsi, the Chinese Christian leader. As expected, Hoste wanted to stay in the background.

---

115. Thompson, 67.
116. Thompson, 59.
117. Taylor, *Pastor Hsi*, 239.
118. Taylor, 329.
119. Thompson, *Prince with God*, 67.

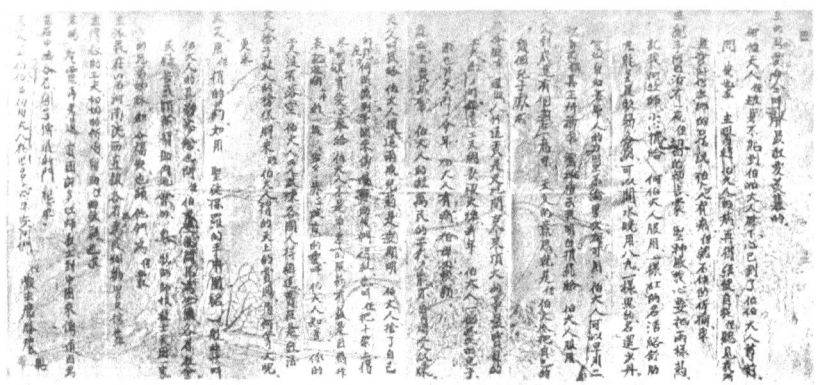

Pastor Hsi's letter to Hoste's father.
Source: Mrs. Howard Taylor, *Pastor Hsi: One of China's Christians* (London: Morgan & Scott, 1903), 332.

The letter also shows Hsi's concern for Hoste's family, particularly for Hoste's father. These carefully chosen words were penned in beautiful handwriting by Hsi:

> By the grace, love, and commandment of our Lord (I may address you as):
>
> Beloved and honoured General Hoste,
> Though in body I cannot come and salute you, yet in spirit I have ere long this been with you inquiring after you. May the Lord relieve you of your sickness, that you may again become strong.
> From the time that I heard my much-loved pastor, Mr. Hoste, say that you were ill, I have not ceased to pray that the Lord would with His own hand heal you. On a certain night, while engaged in fervent prayer, the Holy Spirit put it into my heart to give two kinds of medicine to my pastor, Mr. Hoste, that he might carefully hand them on to you to take. The one kind is red and is called Ho-lo-shu, a supplementary pill, good for curing all kinds of weakness in hands or feet. Take eight pills in the evening with boiling water. The second kind is black and is called Huan-sha-tan; it helps to strengthen aged people, either man or woman may use it. Take twenty pills every morning.

You have taken several of your sons and laid them upon God's altar, for the preaching of the truth in many lands and for the salvation of men. Receive this, then, from your humble servant: it is fervent love out of a pure heart, that you may know that your labour has not been in vain (Abridged translated version).[120]

This letter, which has never been examined in previous research on Hsi and Hoste, is of particular importance as it demonstrates a deep and trusting relationship between the two men.

First, Hsi addresses Hoste's father as General Hoste, which was both accurate and respectful. This shows that Hoste shared his family background with Hsi. Going beyond just the normal honorific language, Hsi, in traditional Chinese style, refers to himself as a "nephew" (侄) and addresses Hoste's father as an "uncle" (伯伯), indicating a more personal relationship. Though Hsi had never met Hoste's father, the language he uses in the letter seems to imply that he was speaking to a senior member of the family. Hsi uses Chinese honorifics not only to show deference and respect to Hoste's father, but, more significantly, the way Hsi addresses Hoste's father indicates that he considered Hoste to be his brother.

Second, Hsi addresses Hoste as "my most-loved pastor" (我所最愛的), which reveals a very intimate friendship between Hsi and Hoste – one that reflects trust and respect. This is particularly significant when we remember that Hsi, all along, had difficulties trusting foreigners. "My much-beloved" is certainly a strong affirmation from Hsi, pointing to his precious friendship with Hoste, which was a rare bonding between a Chinese and a foreigner.

Third, Hsi comments in his letter that Hoste's father was willing to offer up several of his sons for mission work. Hoste came from an elite family with a strong military background. His father was a major-general and his grandfather a colonel. If Hoste had stayed in England, a promising career and a bright future would have awaited him. In the Chinese culture, honouring the family tradition was given utmost priority. However, Hsi saw that Hoste's father had been willing to let go of the family honour by letting Hoste be involved in mission work, and this showed Hsi that Hoste and his father had always put God first.

---

120. Letter to Hoste's father from Pastor Hsi. *China's Millions* (1895): 4.

Fourth, towards the end of the letter, Hsi asks for prayer that more missionaries would be able to come to China. From the letter, it is clear that there was a significant change in Hsi's attitude towards foreigners, and this can probably be attributed to Hsi's relationship with Hoste. In the past, Hsi had virtually nothing to do with foreigners. But Hoste had proven to Hsi that a trusting relationship could be built between a Chinese and a foreigner.

Finally, thrice in his letter, Hsi mentions trials and difficulties that Hoste's father had to endure, including the loss of one of his sons as well as a recent illness. Hsi showed great compassion towards Hoste's parents, even going to the extent of preparing two types of traditional Chinese medicine for them. The first, called "Huoluo shujin wan" (活絡舒筋丸),[121] is described as a supplementary pill for muscle and nerves rejuvenation. The second, called "Huanshao dan" (還少丹), was similar to the traditional Chinese medicine "Lycium barbarum," a potent anti-ageing agent.[122] Both these drugs are well known in Chinese medicine. It is not possible to ascertain the exact ingredients of the pills prepared by Hsi, but they must have been made of Chinese herbal ingredients. Hsi was known to prepare his own pills to help opium addicts and had always claimed that the production of the pills was a "sacred process undertaken by prayer and fasting"[123] However, it was not uncommon to find church members selling "opium curing pills" that contained morphia.[124] Morphia – imported from pharmaceutical companies in the United States – was also used by missionaries at that time and was considered therapeutic in helping opium addicts.[125] Domestic opium production was also common.

---

121. There has been significant recent research on the chemical components of similar types of medicine. See Chen huanzhao 陳煥昭, Chen Shaogang 陳少剛 and Li Changchao 李長潮, etc., "Shujin huoluowan de yaoli yanjiu 舒筋活络丸的药理研究 (The pharmacological study on pills for nerves and muscles rejuvenation), *Shiyong Yixue Zazhi* 實用醫學雜志 3 (1988): 15.

122. Wang Mingfu 王銘富, Dai Weicheng 戴維成, Li Zongxun 李宗勳 and Huang Kefeng 黃克峰, "Huanshaodan yu jianhuan laohua zhi yingyong yanjiu"還少丹於減緩老化之應用研究 (Research on the use of Anti-Aging Pill in slowing ageing), *Journal of Chinese Medicine no Chinese name?* 16, 1(2005): 35–46.

123. Taylor, *Pastor Hsi*, 65.

124. Austin, *China's Millions*, 248, 368.

125. The May 1890 China Council minutes recorded that Hudson Taylor did not agree with the use of morphia for opium addiction treatment. He had given instruction to Dr. Douthwaite, one of the CIM medical missionaries, to prepare a tract to recommend a suitable substitute for the morphia pill.

However, it is not possible to determine what was contained in the pills prepared by Hsi.

9. Hoste Helping Western Readership Appreciate Hsi

As the name "Sheng-mo" indicates, Hsi held a deep conviction that he should work to overcome the power of the devil. After he became a Christian, he felt that the work of opium refuges was part of his calling to fight against the devil. He did not hesitate to perform exorcisms among some of the opium addicts, believing that they were under the bondage of the devil. To Hsi, the devil was ever a personal foe, a watchful and mighty antagonist. This conviction meant that he considered prayer against the evil one a necessity.[126] Mrs. Taylor's book records detailed incidents of Hsi performing exorcisms.[127] "For Hsi had no confidence in medical treatment alone [for opium smokers] to accomplish a permanent cure. A power more terrible than opium lay behind the fascination of the drug, the grip of the devil, chains with which he binds the soul."[128]

It is important to note that Hoste, as a young missionary, had absolutely no experience or training in this respect, and he would have found the whole question of the devil naturally perplexing. Yet Hoste could not help noticing the genuineness of Hsi's convictions, and he saw that the faith underlying Hsi's new name as a Christian was no empty boast.[129] Given Hoste's close working relationship with Hsi, it is quite likely that Hoste would have witnessed how Hsi performed exorcisms among the opium addicts. As Mrs. Taylor had indicated, her book was based not only on Hsi's own manuscript but also on Hoste's testimony, including his ten years of working with Hsi. It would be fair to say that throughout their ten-year association, Hoste adopted a cautious yet open attitude about this matter. Part of the evidence comes from Hoste's own reflection after Hsi's death. Hoste observed that Hsi's casting out of evil spirits in answer to prayer might raise scepticism among Western readers. However, he urged his readers to maintain an open mind as it would be "wiser

---

126. Taylor, *Pastor Hsi*, 10.
127. Taylor, 156–163.
128. Taylor, 71.
129. Taylor, 165.

to abstain from either a sweeping rejection or an unqualified endorsement of the view entertained by our fellow Christians in China." Hoste was trying to help the Western readership appreciate both the context in China and the significant work done by Hsi. His words also demonstrated to Western readers Hoste's respect and appreciation of Hsi as a Chinese church leader involved in work that Westerners were unfamiliar with.

It is well known that, as in many other cultures, Chinese traditionally attributed illnesses to the influence of spirits or gods. Liu Anrong 劉安榮 comments that Chinese people, including those in Shanxi, believed that certain specific gods and spirits control people's health and can bring illnesses if they were offended.[130] Thus, the general public would approach a spirit medium to appease specific gods and obtain cures for their illnesses and restoration of their health.

It was not just opium addicts seeking rehabilitation who came to Hsi. There were also those tormented by uncontrollable seizures, for whose distressing symptoms doctors could find no physical explanation. When such people were brought to Hsi by their family members, he would call the family together and briefly explain that he, like themselves, could do nothing but that the God he worshipped was the living God, who could grant perfect healing and deliverance. They listened with apparent interest while he told them the biblical story of the Saviour's love; and if they were willing to take down their idols, Hsi would pray for them that their trouble might be removed and their sins forgiven.[131] Often, when Hsi laid his hands on the patient's head and prayed, the person would cease struggling, while the onlookers cried out that the evil spirit had left the person. Some were more dramatic, giving a terrible cry and then becoming unconscious as though dead. After some time, however, they would come to their senses and were soon restored to a normal condition. The grateful family members would often begin to attend the chapel run by Hsi.

---

130. These gods include Huatuo 華佗, Yaowang 藥王, Luzuye 呂祖爺, Yaoshifo 藥師佛, Fengzhenniangniang 風疹娘娘, Douzhenniangnang 斗疹娘娘 and so on. See Liu Anrong 劉安榮, "Jindai huaren mushi Xi Shengmo de zhuyao chuanjiao shouduan ji qi zuoyong" 近代華人牧師席勝魔的主要傳教手段及其作用 (The Preaching Method of Paster Hsi Shengmo and it Functions) in *Shenti, linghun, ziran: Zhongguo Jidujiao yu yiliao, shehui shiye yanjiu* 身體、靈魂、自然:中國基督教與醫療、社會事業研究 (Body, Soul, and Nature: Chinese Christianity and medical service), ed. Liu Tianlu 劉天路, (Shanghai: Shanghai Renmin, 2010), 155–157.

131. Taylor, *Pastor Hsi*, 95–96.

Liu, in his research, comments that since the Shanxi people saw the great responsibility of the spirit medium – as the middle person who had to appease their gods to bring healing – they did not have any problem in viewing Hsi in a similar role, as appealing to the God of heaven, according to the Bible.[132] As many local people were amazed by the almost instant healing and deliverance, they began to attend the chapel service organized by Hsi. However, not everyone truly understood and accepted the Christian faith. That is perhaps why Hoste took a more cautious, though open, view on the matter.

10. Building the Indigenous Church Together

Both Hoste and Hsi believed that for the best interest of the Chinese church, they should lay aside all treaty rights, refusing protection by foreign powers and renouncing all tangible benefits. In 1894, Hsi wrote,

> After united prayer and consultation, Mr. Hoste and I decided to bring before the next conference (early in 1891) a resolution that in future all members and inquirers connected with any of the churches in Hungtung district, who might suffer persecution or from disputes, should trust only in the Lord for protection, and not depend upon their treaty rights. This, after full discussion, was unanimously approved by the church, and became a fixed rule.[133]

Hsi's words not only suggest a spirit of independence beyond politics but also testify to his great confidence in Hoste as they collaborated closely in handling church affairs and challenges.

The united nonpolitical stance taken by Hoste and Hsi is important because when disputes occurred between missionaries and the local Chinese, both the Chinese authorities and foreign powers got involved. The Yangzhou riot in 1868 was one such an incident, where CIM missionaries were attacked and their premises burned. Although Taylor, in desperation, went to the Yangzhou governor to seek help to stop the riot, it was never his intention

---

132. See Liu 劉天路, 155–157.
133. Taylor, *Pastor Hsi*, 366.

to seek compensation.[134] However, as Broomhall suggests, Taylor became a "convenient pawn in British power politics."[135] The British consul-general Walter Henry Medhurst (1822–1885) took extreme action by engaging in gunboat diplomacy.[136] Hoste certainly did not want to see history repeat itself yet again.

Hsi and Hoste agreed on the principles of not depending on treaty rights or protection from the authorities but on God alone. The "one mind" of Hoste and Hsi can be seen in an incident in which Hsi was put to the test. A man annexed a portion of Hsi's property – a well-watered piece of land[137] – by secretly altering the boundary markers and taking over the addition as his own. Though Hsi was entitled to "recover his rights and go to law and have the aggressor punished," after praying over the matter, he responded with grace: "It is my Master's land," he said. "I hold it only for His service. If he wants to use it thus, to illustrate the spirit of the Gospel – let it go."[138] However, when the man who had annexed the land unexpectedly became seriously ill, Hsi visited him and provided him with medicine. The man was so impressed that he took the medicine given by Hsi and began to attend chapel services at the opium refuge run by Hsi. Later, the man held back and ceased attending the meetings. Soon after, however, he was suddenly taken ill again and passed away. The villagers watched carefully as Hsi decided not to take any steps to take back the land but left it in the possession of the family, a decision that was strongly supported by Hoste.[139] Hsi laid aside his treaty rights and did not pursue the matter further nor seek help from the authorities.

---

134. Chang, *Christ Alone*, 52.

135. Broomhall, *Shaping of Modern China*,:433.

136. More recent studies have been conducted by Chinese scholars on the Yangzhou Incident. For a more comprehensive review, see Tao Feiya 陶飛亞 and Dai Wanqi 戴婉琦, "Jinnianlai Dalu Zhonghua Neidihui yanjiu zongshu" 近年來大陸中華內地會研究綜述 (Recent Survey of Studies in Mainland China on the China Inland Mission) in *Kuayue Sange Shiji De Chuanjiao Yundong, 1865-2015: Neidihui Laihua Yibaiwushi Nian Xuanjiao Lunwenji* 跨越三個世紀的傳教運動, 1865-2015: 內地會來華一百五十年宣教論文集 edited by Lin, Zhiping 林治平, and Wu Yoxing 吳昶興, (Christian Missions Spanning Three Centuries 1865-2015: Essays on the 150th Anniversary of CIM-OMF Work in China), ed. Lin Zhiping 林治平 and Wu Changxing 吳昶興 (Taiwan: Yuzhouguang, 2016), 68–70.

137. Taylor, *Pastor Hsi*, 367.

138. Taylor, 367.

139. This story was recorded in great detail in Taylor, 278–281.

Hoste was obviously deeply impressed by what this incident revealed about Hsi's character. He commented, "For if anyone had reason for confidence in the flesh, it was dear Hsi. But he was entirely weaned from that spirit. He placed no reliance on his own judgment apart from the guidance of God. Hsi is a man raised up of God to shepherd the flock to this district."[140] Hoste also said, "The Lord has given him authority in the sight of people."[141] It was Hsi who ultimately made the decision not to take back the land. However, Hoste's support for him made a difference. Through this incident, Hoste saw Hsi's spiritual strength in leadership. Hsi's response in not insisting on his rights even when wronged most likely influenced Hoste when he had to deal with the compensation issue after the Boxer Uprising. We will come back to this point in the next chapter.

Apart from laying aside their rights, Hsi and Hoste also shared a common conviction regarding indigenous leadership. Hoste likened indigenous leadership to a living organism: "If you have a living thing, it will grow; and grow after the order of its own life."[142] Hoste insisted that missionaries should not limit Chinese church leaders like Hsi to conditions that were exactly the forms that the Western Christians had inherited.[143] Hoste was convinced that "new wine must be put in new wine bottles[144]." He was determined to minister to Hsi in spiritual matters only, seeking to deepen Hsi's knowledge of God but leave the responsibility of church matters to Hsi himself.[145]

At the same time, Hsi proved to Hoste the value of indigenous leadership. Hsi certainly demonstrated his ability to manage church affairs on his own. He appointed four "subordinate pastors" or "presbyters" in the province of Shanxi.[146] Hsi was to exercise control over wide portions of the work, while some fifteen or twenty other brethren were made responsible for the supervision of local centres with Hsi as the overall leader with "episcopal authority."[147] The churches were indigenous in nature. None of the men received any salary

---

140. Taylor, 383.
141. Taylor, 153–154.
142. Taylor, 350.
143. Taylor, 350.
144. Taylor, 350.
145. Taylor, 351.
146. Taylor, 352.
147. Taylor, 352.

or pecuniary support from the CIM or any foreign source. They were all self-supporting – either having means of their own or, as was the case with most, working for their living. Services were held in the homes of believers; and when the number became too large, a public hall would be secured in the village for meetings. Expenses were met by the local believers themselves.[148]

At Hsi's invitation, Hoste participated in an annual general meeting of the church officers and representative members from the different churches, with Hsi acting as the overall superintendent. The discussions included deliberations on church affairs and the appointment of church officers and decisions about church policies.[149] Hsi also invited Hoste to join occasional meetings with local church leaders in connection with questions on baptisms and church discipline. In all matters, Hsi wanted Hoste to be involved, and they often decided "on matters together."[150] However, Hoste was keenly conscious of his role as a supporter, very much like that of Aquila supporting the capable and learned Apollos as mentioned in Acts 18:26.[151] Hoste wrote, "My relations with Pastor Hsi grew more and more close and helpful to ourselves and to the church. The work steadily increased and the village gatherings growing both in number and in Christian character."[152]

While Hoste was convinced that he should let go of control, Hsi always wanted to include Hoste in important matters concerning the church. While Hoste was ready to let go of controlling hands, he was ready to offer helping hands when asked to do so by Hsi. Hoste was not aloof or detached in implementing the indigenous principles. The spirit of cooperation was always there. In 1894, just two years before he passed away, Hsi wrote, "In all matters connected with the Church or Refuges, Mr. Hoste and I have united in prayer and consultation and are thus enable to arrange things happily. We mutually help one another, without any distinction of native or foreign; because the Lord has made us one."[153]

---

148. Taylor, 352.
149. Taylor, 354.
150. Taylor, 354.
151. Taylor, 355.
152. Taylor, 351.
153. Taylor, 366.

11. Hoste Getting Ready to Lead

In the summer of 1886, Taylor finally visited Hungtung and met Hsi for the first time. Taylor was already well aware of Hsi's opium refuge work and the churches that he had established in the region. What would be more fitting than that Hsi should be openly acknowledged – by missionaries and Chinese alike – as a key Chinese church leader? Therefore, one special thing that Taylor did was to publicly acknowledge Hsi's role as the "Superintendent Pastor" – the "watcher and feeder of the flock" – of the three districts of South Shanxi.[154] Hsi was already a Christian leader, and it did not need a foreigner to ordain him. However, to publicly confirm Hsi's wider leadership role would have given Taylor an even stronger reason to place CIM missionaries under Hsi's leadership. Hsi was, in fact, already the pastor-in-chief and acknowledged by all to be their leader with the necessary authority. But he had been a Christian less than ten years, and his leadership had often been suspect and challenged by other Chinese Christians. It was timely for Taylor to publicly acknowledge Hsi's wider leadership. Hsi accepted the recognition and, along with Taylor, conducted the Sunday service during Taylor's special visit.[155]

The conferring of the official title "Superintendent Pastor" upon Hsi by Taylor brought about a subtle change in the relationship between the CIM missionaries and the young, emerging Chinese churches that had been brought into being. A readjustment in the attitude of the missionaries towards Chinese church leaders was needed. Hsi showed the missionaries that the Chinese could lead the Chinese church themselves. Taylor also wanted to demonstrate that missionaries should be prepared to work under the leadership of Chinese church leaders. Through all this, Hoste became increasingly convinced of the importance of indigenous Chinese churches.

Taylor often practised his indigenous principles even though he did not formulate or articulate these until much later.[156] Hoste, as a young missionary, observed how Taylor publicly honoured Hsi. He witnessed Taylor's desire that CIM missionaries be willing to come under Chinese leadership. Hoste's willing and humble spirit in working with Hsi must have been an

---

154. Austin, *China's Millions*, 285.
155. Taylor, *Pastor Hsi*, 184.
156. Broomhall, *China's Open Century*, 6:79.

encouragement to Taylor, who saw something unique in Hoste and regarded him as a rare find.

While Hsi's work continued to spread over hundreds of miles, covering the three adjacent provinces of Shanxi, Henan, and Hebei,[157] Hoste further built up his experience and capacity under Hsi. This clearly paved the way for the leadership role that he had not expected. Hoste personally witnessed the ability, the energy, and the vision of Hsi, who led the Chinese church without the help of foreign missionaries. Hoste was able to journey alongside Hsi and gain his trust. It is difficult to ascertain how much Hsi influenced Hoste with regard to his appreciation of the importance of the indigenous principle. However, Hoste witnessed a real-life example of a confident and able Chinese indigenous leader. Though not without fault, Hsi proved to Hoste that the practice of indigenous principles could be one important channel by which Chinese Christians and missionaries could develop cordial friendships and shared responsibility.

Within four years of Hsi's death in 1896, Hoste was asked to take the helm of the CIM at a most unexpected time. Hoste's experience of working with Hsi shaped the way he led the CIM. Hoste was convinced that the "native leaders whose very force and independence of character unfitted them for office under the old regime will come to the front; and proving themselves equal to the facing of danger and bearing of responsibilities, growing into leadership."[158] What Taylor observed about the way Hoste and Hsi worked together was probably the deciding factor in his choice of Hoste as the next leader of the CIM.

---

157. Taylor, *Pastor Hsi*, 351.
158. *Chinese Recorder* (1900): 511.

CHAPTER 2

Hoste Taking the Lead in Responding to the Boxer Crisis

1. Introduction

In the previous chapter, we saw how Hoste, an unassuming British aristocrat, was willing to work under Pastor Hsi – the strong, hot-tempered yet charismatic Chinese Christian leader – for ten years. Unlike other CIM missionaries who saw Hsi's faults, Hoste witnessed a living example of an able and confident Chinese indigenous leader. Hsi's indigenous leadership proved to Hoste that the Chinese church could stand on its own and become truly indigenous without the help of foreign missionaries.

Within four years of Hsi's death in 1896, the CIM encountered one of the most severe and devastating crises in its history when fifty-eight missionaries and twenty-one children were murdered by the Boxers.[1] At this time of crisis, with Taylor ill and no longer able to lead, Hoste was asked to take the helm of the CIM.

This chapter will not cover all aspects of the Boxer Uprising but will only focus on how this crisis impacted the CIM under Hoste's new leadership. I will first examine why and how Hoste was appointed the leader of the CIM at this critical time. This will be followed by a detailed account of how Hoste managed to fulfil the responsibilities of his new appointment and demonstrated his leadership in handling issues related to the Boxer crisis, especially

---

1. *China's Millions* (1902): 39.

the CIM's remarkable stance on indemnity. Hoste's close connections with the Chinese church in such a tumultuous situation is another aspect that will be given special attention. Not only did the Boxers attack the missionaries, but thousands of native Christians were also killed, particularly those living in Shanxi with whom Hoste enjoyed close relationships since he had worked there for more than ten years under Pastor Hsi.[2] Finally, we will also look at Hoste's longer long-term vision as he looked beyond the immediate crisis to the future of the Chinese church. Seeing the unhealthy centre of gravity of power and influence that still rested with the missionaries, Hoste was convinced that the Chinese church should become indigenous. He viewed the unprecedented crisis due to the Boxer Uprising as a good opportunity for the Chinese church to come to the forefront and prove themselves equal to the task of facing danger, bearing responsibility, and growing into leadership.[3]

2. Christian Missions in the Turmoil of the Boxer Uprising

The Boxers – or Yi He Quan (義和拳, Righteous and Harmonious Fists) – created what is probably one of the most widely reported incidents in modern Chinese history. The exact reasons for the Boxer Uprising are debated. At present, historians still maintain different views on nearly all important questions concerning the Boxer Uprising.[4] However, there were multiple interrelated factors – including anger at the seizure of territory by the foreign powers, irritation at the acquisition of properties in the interior by missionaries, offences by foreigners including missionaries acting against time-honoured traditions, the failure of an attempted peaceful reform while the Empress Dowager was still fully in power, and reaction to the unprecedented privileges granted to Roman Catholic priests – that contributed to this crisis.[5] Also, the

---

2. Latourette, *History of Christian Missions*, 501–526.
3. *Chinese Recorder* (1900): 510–513.
4. Mingnan, "Appraisal of the Boxer Movement," 24.
5. Joseph Esherick carries out a detailed analysis of the origin of the Boxers in his book *The Origin of the Boxer Uprising*. He claims that "there is no major incident in China's modern history on which the range of professional interpretation is as great," indicating the complexity involved in understanding the Boxer Incident. Esherick, *Origin*, xiv. Another detailed analysis can be found in Latourette, *History of Christina Missions*, 501–526. Previous work by Chinese scholars can be found in Wu Jingheng 吳敬恒 and Cai Yuanpei 蔡元培, ed., *Yihetuan Yundong*

Chinese could not forget losing both Opium Wars (1839--1842, 1856–1860), which resulted in great humiliation due to the signing of the unequal treaties and the forced opening of treaty ports. Although it is beyond the scope of this thesis to conduct a comprehensive review or meta-analysis of all the reasons for the Boxer Uprising, since the CIM suffered one of the heaviest losses among the Protestant mission societies, I will specifically examine the CIM's perspective on the Boxer Uprising.

Marshall Broomhall, the CIM's editorial secretary, offers his observations in the book *Martyred Missionaries of the China Inland Mission* published in 1901.[6] Broomhall comments that the Europeans completely ignored the significance of China's history and its culture. In addition, significant damage was done to the Chinese people due to the opium trade by Britain. Broomhall argues that ordinary Europeans loved change and admired the lightning-fast rapidity of modern inventions and discoveries. The Chinese, however, had a tenacious love for unchanged traditions. "The Europeans almost worshipped the new, while the Chinese respected the old. While an old English county family would take pride in its genealogies and heraldry, this would be magnified a hundredfold in the Chinese clan."[7] Broomhall states that the "national pride of the Chinese is the aggregate of millions of such families."[8]

More significantly, Broomhall attributes European hegemonic ambition as being a major factor underlying the Boxer Uprising, mentioning one specific example: the partitioning of China became the talk of Europe in those days, with maps of China showing the geographical areas under the control of specific European powers. One particular book was entitled *The Break-up of China*?[9] Broomhall comments, "Was it to be expected that the Chinese

---

Shi 義和團運動史 (History of the Boxer Movement), 75–78. However, more recent studies were conducted and presented in 2001 at a conference at the School of Oriental and African Studies, UK, which resulted in the publication of the book *The Boxers, China, and the World*, which gives a more nuanced understanding of the Boxer Uprising.

6. Broomhall, *Martyred Missionaries*, 3–4. Broomhall joined the CIM in 1890 and was assigned to work in Shanxi but had to return home in 1899 just before the Boxer Uprising because his wife, Florence, was suffering from poor health. He became the editorial secretary of the CIM after his return from China and continued in that role for the next twenty-seven years.

7. Broomhall, 3.

8. Marshall Broomhall's view that Europeans were ignorant of the Chinese is well supported by Chinese scholars including Huang Dashou 黃大受 in his book, *Zhongguo Jindai Shi* 中國近代史 (*China Contemporary History*), (Taipei: Dazhongguo tushu, 1954), 202–203.

9. Broomhall, *Martyred Missionaries*, 5.

Government would calmly ignore the book published to the world under the title of *The Break-up of China*?"[10] More recent studies, including the work by Bickers, concur with Broomhall's finding. Bickers comments that we should understand the broader context of the "the Boxer War in the history of world imperialism."[11]

Most would agree that the Boxer Uprising originated in the Shandong area close to the end of the nineteenth century. Many of those involved were poor peasants living in Shandong.[12] The rural people who initiated the movement were originally motivated by the need to protect themselves from bandits. However, with the increasing famine, drought, and other natural disasters, the movement became increasingly anti-foreign and anti-Christian in nature. Sidney M. Brooks (–1899), a British Anglican missionary, is generally recognized as the first martyr killed by the Boxers in a small Shandong village on the last day of 1899.[13] The major attacks occurred in the Shanxi Province, though other places – including Ho-nan (河南, Henan), Chih-li (直隸, Hebei), and Chekaing (浙江, Zhejiang) – were also affected. These are places where the CIM, just prior to the Boxer Uprising, had a significant number of missionaries – more than one hundred in Shanxi, seventy-four in Zhejiang, twenty-nine in Henan, and twelve in Hebei.[14]

Alvin Austin describes Shanxi in the spring of 1900 as a "volcano about to explode."[15] Out of a total of the 188 foreigners killed during the Boxer crisis, including 135 adult missionaries and 53 of their children, 139 were stationed in the province of Shanxi or across the Mongolian border.[16] Thus, missionaries in the province of Shanxi suffered the most. The CIM suffered the heaviest loss, with forty-seven missionaries and four children killed in

---

10. Broomhall, 5.
11. Bickers, "Introduction," xi.
12. Kaiser, *Rushing On*, 63.
13. Rev. S. M. Brooks, a missionary from the Society for the Propagation of the Gospel, was murdered in Shandong by the Boxers on 31 December 1899. Details are recorded in Broomhall, *Martyred Missionaries*, 18. Kaiser also refers to two German Catholic missionaries being killed two years earlier on 1 November 1897 in Shandong Province. See Kaiser, *Rushing On*, 62.
14. *China's Millions* (1989): 165–168.
15. Austin, *China's Millions*, 394.
16. Broomhall, *Jubilee Story*, 246.

Shanxi alone.¹⁷ Compared to other mission societies, the CIM suffered the most with the loss of fifty-eight CIM missionaries and twenty-one children in total.¹⁸ Apart from Protestant missions, Latourette, in his book *A History of Christian Missions in China*, reports that five Roman Catholic bishops, thirty-one other European priests, and nine Catholic sisters were killed and that it was estimated that more than thirty thousand Chinese Catholics were also murdered.¹⁹

One of the tactics that the Boxers had used was mobilizing youths to attack foreign missionaries. According to one record, Boxers recruited children as young as ten years old.²⁰ Cohen notes that many young children were recruited from among the poor, with the assurance of "perpetual safety from all calamity if the family would give their sons to this righteous crusade."²¹ Many young men were easily swayed by the licence to kill, and Cohen records the testimony of one Chinese scholar who described Taiyuan as having "a terrified population inclined to violence and ready to believe almost anything."²² Multiple factors created a perfect storm of an anti-foreign, anti-Christian campaign including the encouragement by Yu-Hsien 毓賢 (Yuxian 1842–1901), the new governor of Shanxi since March 1900, to attack foreigners, the severe and devastating famine without an end in sight, for which the blame was put on the missionaries, and grievances against the Catholics who were granted the special privilege of not paying taxes. With the official issue of a formal declaration of war by Empress Dowager Cixi (1835–1908) on 21 June 1900, including the edict that "the foreigners must be killed, even if they try to escape, they must be killed,"²³ the attack upon the Christians and missionaries, including CIM missionaries, was in full swing by July 1900.

Surprisingly, over the first three decades in its history, the CIM had never encountered death by violence or accident. The first to suffer a violent death was William Small Fleming (1858–1898), who was murdered in November

---

17. Broomhall, 25. See also Chang, *Christ Alone*, 109.
18. Chang, *Christ Alone*, 109. See also *China's Millions* (1901): 100.
19. Latourette, *History of Christian Missions*, 512.
20. Brandt, *Massacre in Shansi*, 155, 187.
21. Cohen, *History in Three Keys*, 97.
22. Cohen, 149.
23. Austin, *China's Millions*, 401–402.

1898 in the province of Guizhou.²⁴ Therefore, the attack upon the missionaries by the Boxers came as a major shock to the CIM.

Before the edict by Cixi was issued, local Christians in Shanxi were already being attacked. Elder Si, Pastor Hsi's successor, was stabbed and severely injured on 14 May 1900. Widow Hsi and her mother were severely beaten and barely escaped death.²⁵ On 23 May, the Boxers plundered the home of the late Pastor Hsi. At that time, William Cooper (1858–1900), another experienced CIM missionary, was able to visit the CIM stations in both central and south Shanxi, particularly Pingyang, in support of the missionaries and the local Christians.²⁶ However, Cooper himself was killed less than two months later, a significant loss to the CIM.

During the Boxer Uprising, both native believers and missionaries underwent severe trials and suffering. The exact number of local Christians who were killed or attacked cannot be ascertained.²⁷ However, a recent study by Kaiser shows that the Chinese Christians who were killed in association with the different mission societies included 79 from the American Board of Commissioners for Foreign Missions (ABCFM), 156 from the CIM, 112 from the British Missionary Society (BMS), and 27 from the Shouyang Mission (SYM).²⁸ Latourette estimates that nearly two thousand native Christians, including three Mongolians, were killed during the Boxer Uprising, with Shanxi being the worst affected.²⁹

Broomhall reports that many local believers risked their lives assisting the missionaries to escape, offering practical help and hiding places at great cost and demonstrating amazing faith.³⁰ Eva French (1869–1961) from the CIM commented that even though the Shanxi native Christians fully realized the dangers and risks involved, they hid the missionaries in their homes, "not fearing to endanger their lives, denying themselves of food that the missionaries might have it, and sitting up late at night to make chicken-broth for

---

24. Broomhall, *Martyred Missionaries*, ix.
25. Broomhall, 103–106.
26. Broomhall, *Martyred Missionaries*, 103.
27. *Chinese Recorder* (1901): 150.
28. Kaiser, *Rushing On*, 111.
29. Latourette, *History of Christian Missions*, 512, 517.
30. For some examples, see Broomhall, *Martyred Missionaries*, 270.

those of our party who were too ill to eat other food."[31] The local Chinese Christians, though young in faith, offered help to the Western missionaries. The young indigenous church began to show its strength as it went through this baptism of fire. Little was reported in *China's Millions* during the first few months of the Boxer Uprising except to note that there was a "critical state of affairs" because "too little was known for certain."[32] The details of how the Chinese church offered a helping hand to CIM missionaries was only discovered much later.

3. The CIM's Work in Shanxi and the Boxers

It is necessary to know about the CIM's early work in Shanxi in order to clearly understand how severely it was affected by the Boxer crisis.

The CIM commenced its missionary work in Shanxi in 1876. One reason for the timing was that Shanxi was experiencing a severe famine.[33] Both England and America provided considerable relief supplies, which helped to break down a great deal of anti-foreign prejudice.[34]

For the next two decades, the CIM actively participated in missionary work in Shanxi, operating four major bases across the province.[35] In Ping-Yang-Fu (平陽府) in the south, the work was managed by the Swedish Mission, an affiliate of the CIM. In the southcentral region, from Kü-wu (曲沃, Qüwo) to Ping-yao (平遙, Pingyao), the work was covered by the CIM. The central area, mainly the Tai-yuan-fu 太原府, which was the provisional capital, was covered by the Baptist Missionary Society, the American Board, and the Shouyang Mission. Finally, in the north, work was covered by a group of mission societies including the CIM, the Christian and Missionary Alliance, and the Holiness Union Mission.[36]

By early 1900, there were already 103 CIM missionaries in the province of Shanxi.[37] Apart from foreign missionaries, prominent native Chinese

---

31. Broomhall, *Martyred Missionaries*, 270–272.
32. Broomhall, *Shaping of Modern China*, 715.
33. Broomhall, 320.
34. *China's Millions* (1878): 121.
35. Broomhall, *Martyred Missionaries*, 17.
36. Broomhall, 17.
37. *China's Millions* (March 1902): 35.

Christian leaders like Pastor Hsi had already been working in south Shanxi for some time with the anti-opium refuges.

Modern historians have examined in detail the reasons Shanxi was so severely affected by the Boxer Uprising, given that it was not in Shanxi, but in Shandong, that it all began.[38] In the two decades prior to the Boxer Uprising, there had not been a major riot against Christian missionaries in Shanxi. One missionary wrote,

> In disposition, the people are milder and more amiable than those of any other portion of the empire. They are patient and uncomplaining to a high degree. The common people are tolerant in their attitude toward Christianity and foreign missionaries. Almost invariably their first judgement of us is "they are just like us; they do good to accumulate merit."[39]

Many missionaries just could not believe that such animosity was directed towards them. This dilemma can only be explained in connection with a set of factors related to that particular historical context.

First, it is quite easy to put the blame on Yuxian, the governor of Shanxi, who was responsible for the brutal murders. Broomhall calls Yuxian the "Father of the Boxers."[40] Yuxian was the prefect in the province of Shandong and had organized a band of men he called "the patriotic harmony fists." In March 1899, he was promoted as governor of Shandong Province. Later, he took with him to Shanxi "bands of Boxers to Shandong, who mounted and armed, travelled throughout the whole province, stirring up the people and instructing them in the Boxer arts."[41] Broomhall places the blame for the Shanxi massacre by the Boxers largely on Yuxian. However, more recent studies – by other historians like Thompson – have taken a more sympathetic position: "The weight of evidence leads to a conclusion that mob violence,

---

38. Qiao Zhiqiang, ed., *Yihetuan zai Shanxi diqu shilao* 義和團在山西地區史料 (Historical materials concerning the Boxer movement in Shanxi), (Taiyuan: Shanxi Renmin chubanshe, 1982), quoted in Austin, *China's Millions*, 404.

39. Brandt, *Massacre in Shansi*, 148-149.

40. Broomhall, *Shaping of Modern China*, 672-673. See also Brandt, *Massacre in Shansi*, 18.

41. Broomhall, 672-673.

not Yuxian, was directly responsible for a massacre or massacres in Taiyuan that took place in July [1900]."[42]

Second, another historical factor of significance was the involvement of the Roman Catholic Church. Franciscan missionaries had entered Shanxi Province as early as the seventeenth century, long before Protestant missionaries first appeared in this region. Austin highlights the fact that "the Sino-French Convention of 1860 not only allowed Catholic missionaries under French protection to travel and purchase land in the interior, it also confirmed the edict that called for the return of missions property which had been seized after 1724."[43] More significant, the Catholic converts were exempted from paying taxes to support temple activities, including opera performances to the gods of the local religions. This amounted to 40 percent of all taxes that others had to pay and had caused huge discontent among the village people. Thompson argues that "their refusal to pay taxes to support temple activities upset the economic and moral order of the villages."[44] This had become one of the most contentious issues between the converts and the village people. Henrietta Harrison mentions that the Catholic villages, with "their complexes of churches, schools and seminaries had become important regional centres," often located high up in the hills, controlling the water supplies for the villages below.[45] The village people began to believe that their basic needs were being threatened by the foreign missionaries.

A third factor was the serious famine in Shanxi, particularly during the hot summer of 1900. This was not the first time that Shanxi had encountered such a famine. In 1877–1879, the Great North China Famine had claimed five million victims in Shanxi alone, which was one-third of its population.[46] People were desperate. This horrendous situation is described in *China's Millions*: "The husband eats his wife, the parents eat their sons and daughters, and in their turn, children eat their parents."[47] Local people blamed the missionaries

---

42. Thompson, "Taiyuan Massacre," 65.
43. Austin, *China's Millions*, 158.
44. Thompson, "Twilight of the Gods," 56.
45. Henrietta Harrison, "Village Politics and National Politics: The Boxer Movement in Central Shanxi," unpublished paper, quoted in Austin, *China's Millions*, 404. See also Clark, *Heaven in Conflict*, 11–39.
46. Austin., 145.
47. *China's Millions* (1878): 115.

for the famine. Rumours began to spread, and there were stories to the effect that the missionaries had the supernatural power to prevent rain. The local people claimed that clouds were continuously being driven away by fierce winds because of the missionaries. They also found out that the missionaries were teaching the people to stop ancestor worship. Thus, they believed that the armies of heaven were making war against the people.[48] Though the missionaries, including those from the CIM, had been involved in the famine relief, they now became the target of blame. However, not all the attacks on the missionaries were due to mob violence. Among those who were ruthless in their murder, some were highly educated people who held strong convictions and beliefs and were willing to sacrifice themselves to get rid of foreign aggression.[49]

4. The CIM in Severe Crisis

Just before the Boxer Uprising, the CIM had a total of 811 missionaries in China.[50] A key question that arises is this: How did the Boxer Uprising affect the CIM?

The records of cables received in London from the CIM office in Shanghai in 1900 reveal the atrocious and monstrous situation caused by the Boxer Uprising. Here are a few examples:[51]

| 24 July | "Information has been received that Miss Whitchurch and Miss Searell [from South Central Shanxi] have been murdered." |
| 26 July | "Tai-Yuan Fu rioted, no details. Mr. and Mrs. Glover travelling through Ho-nan, robbed, are not able to move. Stations rioted, all destroyed, friends safe, escaped to the country, but there is danger." |

---

48. Broomhall, *Martyred Missionaries*, 68. See also Edwards, *Fire and Sword*, 53.

49. Wu Jingheng 吳敬恆, Cai Yuanpei 蔡元培 and Wang Yunwu 王雲五, eds., *Yihetuan Yundong Shi* 義和團運動史 (The Boxer Movement), 78.

50. Broomhall, *Shaping of Modern China*, 638.

51. Broomhall, *Martyred Missionaries*, 293–297.

27 July	"Authentic information has been received that all missionaries have been murdered in Pao-ting-fu 保定府 (Baoding). We apprehend the worst for Mr. and Mrs. Bagnall and Mr. William Cooper."
15 August	"Mr. E. J. Cooper, Mr. and Mrs. E. A Glover, Miss C. Gates, Mr. and Mrs. A. R. Saunders . . . arrived Hankow.漢口 (Hankou) Miss H. J. Rice murdered. Miss Huston, Mrs. E. J. Cooper, three of Mrs. Saunder's children dead, injuries received travelling."
16 August	D. B. Thompson, Mrs. Thompson, and two children, Miss E. S. Sherwood, Miss M. E. Manchester, Miss J. E. Desmond, 21st ultimo. Mr. G. F. Ward, Mrs. Ward, infant, Miss A. Thirgood, 22nd ultimo, Murdered.
17 September	Mr. and Mrs. Duncan Kay held to ransom. Seven children missing, unable to gather information.
26 November	(last cable received) Mr. Ogren has been killed. Mr. Graham McKie, Miss Chapman, Miss Way, Mrs. Orgren and infant are safe in Tai-yuan-fu 太原府.

Altogether, more than forty cables were received by the CIM London office between 20 July and 26 November 1900, announcing the murder and the death of many CIM missionaries.[52] Nearly one-third of all the CIM missionaries working in the Shanxi Province were murdered within a few months. Among the one hundred and twenty-six missionaries killed in Shanxi, the CIM suffered the most significant loss compared to other mission societies, with the forty-seven missionaries killed mainly in Taiyuan Fu.[53] The CIM lost fifty-eight missionaries and twenty-one children in total. Many other mission societies were also severely affected.[54]

There were long delays in confirming some of the deaths. One such person was William Cooper of the CIM, whose death was not confirmed until 29 October though he was actually murdered on 1 July – a gap of nearly four months.[55] William Cooper, "a quiet saintly but physically powerful" man,

---

52. Broomhall, 293–297.
53. For the names of all martyred CIM missionaries, see Cheung, *Christ Alone*, 109, and Broomhall, *Shaping of Modern China*, 90.
54. Brandt. *Massacre in Shansi*, 264–267.
55. Broomhall, *Shaping of Modern China*, 709.

had won Hudson Taylor's profound confidence and was being groomed for leadership at the highest level.[56] Even before the Boxer Uprising, Cooper was perceived to be a promising younger colleague who could succeed Taylor.[57] His death was a tragic and significant loss to the Mission.

The news of the murders of Cooper and other missionaries came as a great shock to Taylor. He was ill and resting in Switzerland when the news broke about the Boxer crisis. Taylor's second wife, Jennie, had the telegrams in her hands but wanted to break the news gradually to Taylor. Broomhall records Jennie's emotions, noting that she felt that the news of the murder of the CIM missionaries might be too much for Taylor to bear. Thus, Jennie held back some of the letters for later.[58]

Taylor realized that he could not provide leadership at this critical time as he was far too weak. With the death of Cooper, the CIM was faced with the challenge of leadership succession. Taylor had to find someone who understood the China situation well and could take the helm of the Mission to face the crisis. *The Principles and Practice of the China Inland Mission* (P&P), which was the constitution of the CIM, did not clearly stipulate how the next general director was to be appointed.[59] The P&P even stipulated that both the China Council and the Home Departments – represented by the London Council, the North America Council, and the Australasian Council – were only "advisers" to the general director. Since the general director had ultimate decision-making power in all matters of importance, the burden of appointing the next general director to succeed him fell on Taylor's shoulders.

---

56. Broomhall, 450, 578.

57. According to Broomhall, Hudson Taylor wrote to the China Council on 8 January 1900, recommending that William Cooper be appointed as "Visiting China Director" to assist in the work of John Stevenson, who was the China Director at that time. Thos title is interesting because when Hudson Taylor initially wanted to make Cooper the "Assistant China Director," Stevenson objected to having "a partner" to share in his leadership role. The London Council was keen to see William Cooper and Dixon Edward Hoste take over leadership from Stevenson. For details, see Broomhall, *Shaping of Modern China*, 638.

58. Broomhall, 711.

59. The original of *The Principles and Practice of the China Inland Mission* is held at the CIM Archives, OMF International, Singapore.

5. Hoste Appointed as the New Leader of the CIM

By 1900, Taylor was already sixty-eight years old. With the Boxer crisis still looming and given his own ill-health, Taylor realized that he needed to find a successor without delay. Instead of sending a letter, which would have taken too long to arrive, on 8 August 1900, Taylor sent a cable to the CIM headquarters in Shanghai to both John Stevenson (1844–1918), the CIM China director at that time, and Hoste, "expressing sympathy" and concern for Stevenson, acknowledging the pressure on him because of the crisis but, at the same time, appointing Hoste to be "Acting General Director" during Taylor's incapacity so that the responsibility might be shared.[60] What Taylor did was, of course, within his jurisdiction as general director. However, Taylor also wrote a private letter to Theodore Howard (fl. 1891–1913), the chair of the CIM London Council, indicating that the announcement of Hoste's appointment should only be made after "it had been accepted by all Councils."[61] Taylor further wrote, "Hoste was [already] in Shanghai, and difficult though it was to bypass John Stevenson, the nettle had to be grasped."[62] While realizing that not appointing Stevenson would be a disappointment to him, Taylor recognized that Hoste was a more suitable candidate. He also realized that the appointment of Hoste to succeed him needed endorsement and ownership by other leaders in the CIM. It is important to note that Taylor, acting within his jurisdiction, went ahead and made the decision to appoint Hoste as the acting general director during this time of crisis and only later consulted with the councils to seek their endorsement and with the announcement to be made made later. It is interesting to note the differences in leadership style between Taylor and Hoste. As a pioneer and founder of the CIM, Taylor's approach was much more top-down, while Hoste, as will be seen in later chapters, made every effort to seek the "intelligent and cordial concurrence of others."[63]

Hoste, having worked in Shanxi for more than ten years, was already in Shanghai at that time, working at the CIM headquarters. Taylor had instructed him to assist Stevenson, the CIM China director, in facing the "darkening

---

60. Broomhall, *Shaping of Modern China*, 710.
61. Broomhall, 710.
62. Broomhall, 710.
63. "China Council Minutes" (1927): 11, 14.

thunder clouds of early 1900."[64] However, the appointment of Hoste to succeed Taylor seems to have been a rather unusual arrangement. Stevenson had been Taylor's deputy for many years. As a seasoned leader, it seemed only natural to many that Stevenson would be the next general director of the CIM. So, it was a surprise when Taylor appointed a much younger person – Hoste would not turn forty until 23 July 1901 – to be the CIM leader at such a time of crisis. This appointment certainly surprised both Stevenson and Hoste.

The question of who could take the helm of the CIM had been on Taylor's mind for some time, but his decision might have been influenced by the views of his acquaintances.[65] A few years earlier, around May 1897, when Taylor was not well, his wife, Jennie, had taken him to Switzerland to rest. While in Davos, he received a letter from William Sharp (fl.1895–1905) – the CIM lawyer, who was also on the CIM London Council – urging him to name his own successor. However, Sharp also urged Taylor to replace Stevenson as the China director as he had been alienating members more and more because of his "unfeeling harshness in administration."[66] It had also become increasingly clear that Stevenson could not work with the younger Cooper, possibly because he felt threatened by his shared leadership role.[67]

In June 1898, Sharp wrote to Taylor again, warning that

> for the future well-being of the work, Mr. Stevenson must on no account be entrusted with the principal oversight in China. I doubt if the Mission could hold together for six months after you were gone.[68]

Sharp also commented,

> Mr. Cooper is a tried man, loved, trusted, and honoured by all his brethren and well qualified for the work. With him should be associated as his second in command a man of somewhat similar gifts, and proved ability, and one perhaps, who has had a fuller educational training – Dixon Hoste.[69]

---

64. "China Council Minutes" (1927): 708.
65. Broomhall, *Shaping of Modern China*, 610.
66. Broomhall, 610.
67. Broomhall, 611.
68. Broomhall, 619.
69. Broomhall, 631.

Sharp further wrote,

> Dixon Hoste has very valuable qualities for leadership. He and Cooper could work well together.[70]

Taylor trusted Sharp's judgement. To Taylor, the best option seemed to be for Cooper to be the next general director, with Hoste assisting him as the deputy leader.

According to Broomhall's record, Stevenson, a senior administrator and managing director of the CIM, was a man who attended to details and kept his finger on a myriad of matters at the same time. Stevenson's major weakness, however, seems to have been his brusqueness, and he also seemed to have lacked "the essential qualities required of a General Director, the international leader and inspiration of the Mission. Also, he was not good working [with others] in partnership as equals."[71]

Despite Sharp's earlier request in 1897, it seems that Taylor had not yet named his successor by the time the Boxer Uprising broke out. However, it appears that Taylor had Cooper in mind and, after him, Hoste. The death of Cooper during the Boxer Uprising left Taylor with only one choice. Stevenson, though a more senior leader in the CIM, was not the right choice because he lacked the essential qualities of an inspiring international leader.[72] At that point, Hoste seemed to be a much better choice. Besides, Taylor's visit to Hsi in 1886 had confirmed in his mind that Hoste worked well under the Chinese leader. If the next general director was required to be one who could not only lead the CIM but also connect with Chinese church leaders, then Hoste was the ideal candidate.

Having sent a cable to Shanghai, Taylor hoped that Hoste would accept the appointment. But Hoste replied almost straightaway, declining the appointment:

> It would have the effect of weakening and, to a certain extent discrediting Mr. Stevenson . . . without inspiring confidence.

---

70. Broomhall, 631.

71. Broomhall, 609–712.

72. Broomhall wrote, "Stevenson was not good at working in partnership as equals. He had to be told candidly of Hoste's promotion and be trusted to weather the blow. If Cooper should return from the dead, as it would seem if somehow, he survived, the way would still be open for reconsideration of who should become General Director." Broomhall, 711.

Stevenson had done well in his direction of affairs in the crisis, members of the China Council would agree. My appointment to act now on your behalf, during your present incapacity, would come as a complete surprise, and is one to which they would not agree, and would be calculated to weaken and even produce disruption in the Mission. PS. I have not touched on the point of my own unfitness, mental and physical.[73]

Stevenson wrote to Taylor separately, sending a short letter, in which he said, "Mr. Hoste's help at the Council meetings was most valuable and I thank God for his prayerful sympathy and advice. I consult him very freely." Stevenson did not clearly indicate whether he agreed with or disagreed with Taylor's decision to appoint Hoste.

Taylor, however, was determined. He wrote a separate forthright letter to Stevenson on 20 September 1900, affirming his intention to appoint Hoste as the substantive – and not merely acting – general director, though not immediately: "I thought my appointment of Mr. Hoste would help in this way, and also that acting with you in Shanghai, he would be gaining in the necessary experience for becoming General Director at my death."[74] There is no record to indicate whether or not Stevenson replied to Taylor's letter.

Soon after Taylor's cable in August, Hoste went down with a life-threatening attack of typhoid and remained ill for the next few months. Gertrude, Hoste's wife, wrote to Taylor on 5 November, mentioning that Hoste was affected by a serious embolus impacting both arms and legs, keeping him "on a knife-edge of danger."[75] After more than a month, Hoste recovered from this danger and, feeling better, wrote two separate letters to Taylor and Stevenson. In his letter of 23 November to Taylor, Hoste indicated that the thrombosis in his forearm had disappeared and that he was convinced of "the strong love of Christ to spend and be spent for others."[76] He informed Taylor that he would tell Stevenson that "it was my duty to accept the appointment." On 15 December, Hoste wrote to Stevenson: "I feel I ought to

---

73. Broomhall, 711.
74. Broomhall, 712.
75. Broomhall, 713.
76. Broomhall, 713.

accept the appointment; if, however, you do not see your way to agreeing, I shall [be] free from responsibility."⁷⁷

Stevenson not only readily agreed but pledged his full support to Hoste: "the Lord had given me not only peace about it but joy in the assurance that it was of God and would be for blessing."⁷⁸

On the last day of 1900, a special prayer gathering was held at the hall of the CIM headquarters in Shanghai. Stevenson, the China director, formally called upon Hoste to address the congregation attended by CIM missionaries.⁷⁹ Two things stand out about this event. First, Stevenson openly welcomed and invited Hoste to address the assembly. It was significant that Stevenson, the China director, officially affirmed Hoste before the CIM missionaries. Though the official appointment of Hoste as the acting general director was not made public until January 1901, this open endorsement indicated to others that Hoste would play a significant leadership role in the future. Second, exactly a year earlier, in the same CIM hall, it was Cooper who had been asked to give the opening address.⁸⁰ It seems likely that Cooper had already been seen as the potential candidate to succeed Taylor. Now that Cooper had been killed, Hoste was to take his place. This special gathering at the Shanghai CIM headquarters on the last day of 1900 marked a watershed moment in Hoste's life.

In January 1901, in an open letter, Taylor confirmed the appointment of Hoste as the acting general director of the CIM. In this letter, Taylor honoured Stevenson and, at the same time, affirmed Hoste:

> Of course this appointment does not in any way supersede Mr. Stevenson in his position or work but will supply him with the help which I would gladly afford him myself did health permit. Matters that might otherwise need to be referred to me can be dealt with without delay in China, by Mr. Hoste, and I shall not have the mental strain of feeling that I am not adequately attending to my part of the work.⁸¹

---

77. Broomhall, 713–714.
78. Broomhall, 714.
79. *China's Millions* (1900): 60.
80. *China's Millions* (1900): 60.
81. Broomhall, *The Shaping of Modern China*, 714.

Thus, on 23 March 1901, Hoste officially became the acting general director of the CIM.[82] The announcement of his appointment came at a critical time because, just a few weeks later, the governor of Shanxi called for help in resolving the reparation problem due to the Boxer Uprising in his province. Hoste was the one best fitted for this task. His ten-year association with Hsi had won the confidence of the Shanxi church and "scores, hundreds of the persecuted martyrs were personally known to him."[83] Hoste also provided stability and leadership for the CIM in the aftermath of the Boxer Uprising. According to Broomhall, within a year and five months, "the work of the Mission had been re-established in most of the Empire."[84]

6. The Decision on the Boxer Indemnity

The first thing that Hoste did as acting general director was to provide care and support for the CIM missionaries and their families who had been affected by the Boxers. At the same time, he had to handle a request from the Qing authorities. On 22 March 1901, the new governor of Shanxi – Ceng Chunxüan (岑春煊, Chen Chun Xüan), who had replaced Yu Xian – called for help in resolving the compensation problem in his province.[85] Hoste was seen by Ceng as the obvious choice to help. Of course, Hoste was concerned not only about the lives lost but also about the financial impact on the CIM because many churches and CIM stations had been destroyed due to the Boxer Uprising. General donations to the CIM from Britain and the United States had also dropped in the previous year. According to Broomhall, talk of indemnities was highly relevant: "Mission income from all sources in 1900 had been 2,780 taels lower than in the previous year, while travelling and rentals in China had cost 3,504 taels more. Return to the interior and rebuilding wrecked premises would inflate expenses."[86] Hoste knew that he could not avoid the issue of finance.

---

82. Broomhall, 723.
83. Broomhall, 723.
84. Broomhall, 724.
85. Broomhall, 723.
86. Broomhall, 724.

On 30 January 1901, Hoste wrote to Taylor seeking his advice on the issue of compensation.[87] Taylor's reply was clear. He was determined that the CIM was to "claim for *nothing, but to accept*, where offered, compensation for destroyed Mission premises and property."[88] As for private property purchased by the CIM missionaries themselves, Taylor felt that the CIM should leave each missionary free to accept or decline compensation. As for injury or loss of life, Taylor insisted that the CIM should not claim any compensation. However, Taylor made two further important comments. First, he stated that the CIM should be responsible for the orphan children of missionaries. Second, he said that the CIM should reach out to local believers to help them and to care for their bereaved relatives.[89]

In a fuller letter written later to Hoste, Taylor pointed out that to claim compensation for loss of life, injury, or loss of property would be in violation of CIM's *Principles and Practice*, particularly Article 15, which stipulated that "any appeal and demands, indemnification of losses are to be avoided."

However, when Taylor was informed of the atrocities committed by the Allied troops in Beijing, he was distressed by the behaviour of these "Christian" nations. He then changed his mind about accepting compensation if offered "as thousands of Chinese as innocent as our missionaries seem to have been ruined and robbed of their all, and large numbers slain, through the action of the allies, for which China will not be compensated."[90] Broomhall quotes Taylor's words:

> Money-conscious nation like the Chinese could be counted on to recognize such a clear-cut distinction between the motives of the secular powers and those of missionaries as witnesses to Christ and the Gospel. It would show the meekness and gentleness of Christ by not accepting any compensation even if offered.[91]

However, relatives of some members of the CIM had applied directly to the Foreign Office, making claims for compensation for lives lost. The CIM

---

87. Broomhall, 724.
88. Broomhall, 724–725. Emphasis added.
89. Kaiser, *Rushing On,* 112.
90. Broomhall, *Shaping of Modern China,* 724.
91. Broomhall, 724.

London Council responded promptly by writing to the British authority that "this Mission should be entirely disassociated from all claims for life, or bodily injury, that may be put forward by (relatives or friends) of members."[92]

At the end of February 1901, the CIM, under Hoste's leadership, formally decided "not only not to enter any claim against the Qing government, but to refrain from accepting compensation *even if offered*."[93] Since Hoste had been in frequent consultation with Taylor during this time, one might conclude that he was still under the former leader's influence. Nevertheless, the final decision would have been agreeable to Hoste as well. Later, Hoste adopted a firm stance when bringing the CIM's conviction to the negotiation table at Taiyuan-Fu in July 1901.

This decision came at a great cost. As mentioned earlier, since the Boxer Uprising in 1900, the CIM's income had dropped significantly; in addition, returning to the interior and repairing damaged properties had inflated expenses. Although the CIM faced many uncertainties, they remained firm in their decision not to accept compensation. In March 1901, *China's Millions* officially announced that Hoste was the acting general director of the CIM; in the same month, in its editorial note, a declaration was made in accordance with Hoste's decision on the issue of compensation. Among the many burning questions regarding the Boxer Uprising, the proposed indemnity to the Allied powers took foremost place. The CIM, under Hoste's leadership, decided that whatever other foreign powers might do in this matter, it would be well for the CIM, taking a more Christlike course, to gladly suffer even the loss of all things that the gospel might not be hindered.[94] Thus, Hoste made it clear that the CIM had decided to make no claim whatsoever, either for life or property, and had assumed responsibility for the orphan children of the martyred missionaries. This stance made the CIM stand out among other mission societies that had also suffered heavy losses because of the Boxer Uprising.

---

92. Broomhall, 724. Emphasis added.
93. Broomhall, 724.
94. *China's Millions*, North American edition (1901): 62.

7. Hoste's Negotiation for the Chinese Church

Reparation for loss of life or property did not come under debate by different Christian denominations in China until near the end of 1900. In a series of articles in the *Chinese Recorder*, Bishop George Moule (1828–1912) recognized the basic right to require full compensation from the Chinese government for both loss of life and property but held that it would be a good policy not to press such claims.[95]

The Roman Catholics had entered China long before the Protestants, having worked in Sichuan as early as 1704.[96] According to the *North China Herald*, in 1901, the Roman Catholics in Shanxi had asked for 2,225,000 taels (£300,000) in compensation and had already received 140,000 taels (£20,000) in compensation for Henan Province, where forty-four Roman Catholic missionaries – thirty-five men and nine women – had been killed during the Boxer Uprising.[97] *China's Millions* comments that the Catholic demands for compensation were "exorbitant," while, in contrast, the CIM had decided to claim nothing.[98] Even Kaiser comments that the Catholic approach was "aggressive."[99]

The Catholics negotiated with Chinese officials regarding compensation mainly through the French government. Their demands were extensive. Kaiser records these demands in detail.[100] One particular demand was that the military officers' school in Taiyuan should be handed over to the Catholic Church and transformed into a cathedral and a monastery.[101] The provincial government of Shanxi could not provide the exorbitant sum demanded, quite apart from the fact that the famine was not yet over in the province. Initially the Catholic Chuch had demanded even more than the final sum agreed of 2.25 million taels with no mention of land.[102]

Although it had decided to make no claims, the CIM's response to the indemnity issue was not passive. In June 1901, led by Hoste, a party of eight

---

95. Broomhall, *Shaping of Modern China*, 721.
96. Broomhall, 119.
97. *China's Millions* (1901): 168; (March 1902): 38, 80.
98. *China's Millions* (1902): 9.
99. Kaiser, *Rushing On*, 112–113.
100. Kaiser, *Rushing On*, 112.
101. Kaiser, 112.
102. Kaiser, *Rushing On*, 112–113.

from different mission groups headed to the province of Shanxi at the invitation of the governor, Ceng Chunxüan. They were Dr. E. H. Edwards (1856–1916) of the Shouyang Mission, Rev. Moir Duncan (1861–1906) and Dr. Creasy Smith (1873–1929) of the British Missionary Society (BMS), Dr. Irenaeus Atwood (1850–1913) of the American Board, and Archibald Orr-Ewing (1857–1930), Carl Henrik Tjader (1866–1929), and Ernest Taylor (1875–1948), along with Hoste, of the China Inland Mission.[103] They started from Pao-ting-fu (保定府, Baoding Fu) on 26 June 1901 and arrived first in Shouyang (壽陽) on 4 July, where they were received by Elder Qü, Elder Xü, and Elder Si – Pastor Hsi's brother-in-law who was still suffering from the sword thrust from which he was later to die.[104] Hoste was warmly received by the Chinese church leaders from Shanxi. The group finally arrived in Tai-yuan-fu, Shanxi, on 9 July – coincidentally, the first anniversary of the dreadful Boxer killing in that very city.[105] Settlement and indemnity were high on the agenda of the governor.

Hoste's visit to Shanxi was "the most painful experience."[106] Though the governor hosted an elaborate reception, Hoste could not ignore the suffering that had taken place. Hoste and his party were met by the provincial treasurer, the provincial judge, the tartar general, the city prefect, and other mandarins who welcomed them with all politeness and cordiality, repeatedly expressing their regrets for the events of 1900.[107] However, Hoste's priority to give time to the local Christians, particularly the leaders who were waiting for him.

Hoste, representing the CIM, had already made it clear to the officials that the CIM would not claim any compensation for lives lost, bodily injury, or the loss of property.[108] Nevertheless, the CIM was committed to making every effort to help local Christians receive compensation for their losses during the Boxer Uprising. However, Hoste believed that the Chinese Christians were "not in the service of foreigners" and should be under the protection of the Chinese government.[109] Since the local believers had suffered, Hoste believed

---

103. Broomhall, *Shaping of Modern China*, 725–826.
104. Broomhall, 725–826.
105. Wong 黃錫培, *In Remembrance*, 143–144.
106. Broomhall, *Shaping of Modern China*, 727.
107. Broomhall, 726.
108. Broomhall, 730.
109. Broomhall, 724.

that the CIM should offer a helping hand to assist fellow Chinese believers to claim rightful compensation. Therefore, the negotiations between Hoste and the officials were mainly about compensation for the local Chinese Christians rather than for the CIM.

The position on indemnity taken by Hoste, representing the CIM, was different from other mission societies in its understanding of the relationship between the local church and the foreign mission societies. The American mission societies made a united presentation of their claims to the Department of State. The American government included in their demands "indemnities for societies, individuals and Chinese who had suffered in person or in property in consequence of their being *in the service of foreigners*."[110] Thus, many American mission societies argued that the Chinese believers were to serve the purpose of the foreign missionaries, implying that the Chinese church "belonged" to the missionaries, at least from a persuasive rationale of claiming compensation. Thus, to compensate the missionaries for lives and property lost also meant compensating the Chinese. This view was not accepted by the CIM, particularly by Hoste as its general director. Hoste, while insisting that the CIM, as a foreign agent, should not claim "blood money,"[111] was eager to help Chinese believers to receive compensation – not because they belonged to the CIM but, rather, because they were fellow believers. Hoste acknowledged the independence of the local churches and, at the same time, was willing to offer help. This marks the difference between Hoste and other mission leaders in handling the Boxer crisis.

Hoste's concern included far more than just compensation for the Chinese church. He was concerned about the affairs of the local believers in the aftermath of the Boxer Uprising. In place after place, hearing the grim details of torture, maiming, terror, and coercion, Hoste called this "the most painful experience of his life."[112] Despite the crisis, Hoste was impressed by the strength of the indigenous Chinese church and the rising of local leaders. Hoste wrote to Taylor with his observations:

> The sufferings of the Christians have been frightful, and it is almost overwhelming to hear them at first hand and to be living

---

110. Broomhall, 722. Empasis added.
111. Kaiser, *Rushing On*, 110.
112. Broomhall, *Shaping of Modern China*, 729.

> in this place where so many were massacred. Never have I felt so utterly unequal to the responsibilities on me ... One great comfort is that some of the Church Elders have developed much since I last saw them, notably Xü Puyüan. His powers as an administrator are remarkable, and all the others, including Pastor Qü, seem gladly to recognise him as the moving spirit. Very capable, and stronger than Si, Xü showed a robustness and capacity for responsibility.[113]

While Hoste saw the potential of the Chinese churches in the midst of this crisis, others outside the CIM did not necessarily share his perspective. In 1902, the *Chinese Recorder* published an article from the *New York Independent* by Charles Denby (1861–1938), the former minister to China, that emphasized "the rights of missionaries" in the context of the aftermath of the Boxer crisis.

> The missionary does nothing but good. He clothes the naked. He feeds the hungry and comforts the heavy laden. If in addition, he teaches Christianity, can he teach any better system of morality? Let there be reason in all these things, but do not by neglect to secure proper terms to deprive the Chinese of the right to have the assistance of these devoted agents of the cross who are surely but slowly spreading civilization.[114]

Thus, in contrast to Hoste's conviction, the notion that the Chinese church needed to continue to depend on foreign missionaries had remained strong in the mindset of many foreigners. Many Western churches and foreign missions held onto the belief that the Chinese church was too weak to stand on its own. They also perceived that apart from the direct work of evangelization, there was a great need in China for education, medicine, and other social services. To many, the Boxer Uprising proved that China must be Christianized with help from the West. One example was the proposal from Timothy Richard (1845–1919), a Welsh Baptist missionary, to indemnify a Western-style school of higher education in Shanxi. Some even claimed that "the rapidity of the spread and development of Christianity in China will be in exact ratio to the

---

113. Broomhall, 727.
114. *Chinese Recorder* (1902): 147.

amount of finances received from foreign Christian lands."[115] They felt that the idea that the Chinese church was becoming self-supporting was far too premature. Yet Hoste held a very different view. His experience of working with Hsi had proved to him that the Chinese were capable and that ongoing control by missionaries would only impede the growth of the church. I will examine this idea further in the next chapter.

8. Insisting on Integrity on the Matter of Indemnity

Governor Ceng had agreed to offer compensation for the losses of local Christians, and the local church leaders were waiting for Hoste's advice on how to proceed in this matter.[116] Hoste had a challenging job to ensure integrity on both sides – that is, that the local Chinese believers would not exaggerate any claims and that the officials would be fair in compensating the amount due to the local Christians. Both sides looked to Hoste for help. Hoste, who had worked for ten years under the Chinese leader Hsi, had won the confidence of both the local Chinese church leaders and the government. Both sides had little trust in each other. The officials believed that the claimants would inflate their figures, while the claimants felt that the officials would avoid their responsibilities and not give them fair treatment.

The governor invited Hoste to organize the collection of the particulars of losses by the Chinese believers.[117] However, the circuit intendant (道臺 Daotai) Shen Denhe, who worked for the governor and the Foreign Office, laid down a condition for Hoste in reaching agreement about the compensation.[118] He wished to first reduce 20 or 30 percent from whatever was claimed as it was a customary practice to always ask for more and expect a reduction later.[119] Hoste refused to comply with such a condition because to accept such a reduction would be virtually admitting that the Christians had been exorbitant in their estimates. Probably following the principle of precision he had

---

115. *Chinese Recorder* (1900): 506.
116. Broomhall, *Shaping of Modern China*, 728.
117. Broomhall, 726–728.
118. According to Broomhall, Shen Denhe was the circuit intendent who had received Hoste and the team when they arrived in Taiyuan. It is very likely that this is the same person who had insisted on subtracting 20 to 30 percent of the claims as was customary.
119. Broomhall, *Shaping of Modern China*, 728.

developed during his earlier military training, Hoste was eager that all claims be honest and accurate. Therefore, he insisted that each claim be investigated carefully before it was submitted to the governor. He also maintained that there should be no "carelessness or overstating" of the claims, which should be subject to "careful and thorough examinations."[120] Hoste also made it very clear that none of the money received should go to the CIM but only to the native Christians.

To ensure that every claim was carefully investigated, Hoste felt strongly that the help of local church leaders was essential. In working with Elders Qü, Xü, and Si – who had worked closely with Pastor Hsi and had been recognized by the Shanxi churches – Hoste selected over forty local leaders representing the different districts in the province and submitted their names to the governor.[121] The governor accepted the names and informed the local officials that these names were formally appointed and accepted to "superintend the native indemnity."[122]

Subsequently, Hoste wrote a letter to be sent out to all the Chinese church leaders in Shanxi emphasising the importance of integrity.[123] First, Hoste informed the local Christians that if they were willing to forgive their enemies and, therefore, did not wish to claim compensation, they would do well. Second, he cautioned that if they would like to claim compensation because of bodily harm or property loss, "there must be no carelessness or overstating, lest God's name be dishonoured before your enemies."[124] Hoste also insisted that the leaders who had been appointed to manage these affairs must first make a careful and thorough examination of the claims.[125]

There was one more matter that Hoste had to handle. Timothy Richard, an influential Welsh Baptist missionary, wanted to negotiate with the Chinese government to establish a university in Shanxi using compensation money. Richard wanted to form an inter-mission team to work on the matter of indemnity. Hoste's response was that while the CIM would not object to

---

120. Broomhall, 728–729.
121. *China's Millions* (1901): 163.
122. *China's Millions* (1901): 163.
123. Only the English translation is available in *China's Millions*. The original letter that was written in Chinese could not be traced.
124. *China's Millions* (1901): 163.
125. *China's Millions* (1901): 163.

the establishment of a university, this could not be in the name of the CIM.[126] Hoste felt that money received to establish the university must not be used to indemnify the CIM as it had claimed no compensation from the beginning.

The whole process of compensation took several months to complete. According to the record, ultimately, the CIM was granted 73,156 taels on behalf of the CIM-related Chinese churches for the loss of Chinese lives and property.[127] The CIM was careful to ensure that all the money went to the native believers. In comparison, the Baptist Missionary Society (BMS) received 35,776 tales for 112 murdered church members, and the American Board of Commissioners for Foreign Mission (ABCFM) was given 25,000 taels for their 79 dead. The Shouyang Mission (SYM) received 5,600 taels for their loss of 27 adherents.[128] The local believers were satisfied with the settlement.

The CIM was not the only group that had not claimed compensation for themselves. Each mission made its own decision about the position it wished to adopt. For example, the American Board submitted no claim for damaged mission property but actively requisitioned land.[129] The Shouyang Mission (SYM), like the CIM, waived all claims to indemnities. Even the London Missionary Society (LMS) later concluded that compensations did more harm than good and renounced all claims.[130] Perhaps what made the CIM stand out among the other mission groups was not so much that it did not claim compensation for loss of lives or property but, rather, the way it viewed the Chinese church. Under Hoste's leadership, the CIM did not help the Chinese churches claim compensation because they belonged to the CIM but, rather, offered a helping hand to Chinese fellow believers whose churches were becoming independent of foreign missionaries.

Hoste's care and concern for the Chinese church did not go unnoticed, particularly by Governor Ceng. Ceng was impressed by Hoste's meticulous approach in working with the Chinese church and ensuring that the local believers submitted accurate and honest claims.

On 11 October 1901 (the twenty-seventh year of the Kwanghsu [光緒] dynasty), Governor Ceng, with Hoste's agreement, issued an official edict.

---

126. Broomhall, *Shaping of Modern China*, 730.
127. Kaiser, *Rushing On*, 111.
128. Kaiser, 111.
129. Broomhall, *Shaping of Modern China*, 721.
130. Broomhall, 721.

Placards were placed wherever the CIM had worked and suffered throughout Shanxi.[131] Ceng praised the CIM for not claiming compensation. The edict stated that the CIM had sought no indemnity and would rebuild the churches using its own funds. Ceng also commended the behaviour of these missionaries by stating that the Christian faith exhorted all men to live virtuously and discouraged all desire for revenge. But, most important, Ceng particularly commended Hoste for being able to carry out these Christian principles to the full and declared that his actions deserved the fullest approval.[132] Ceng also saw for himself the action taken by the CIM in providing famine relief. During the first six months of 1901, in the aftermath of the Boxer Uprising, the CIM forwarded 15,000 taels to China for famine relief, mainly for the worst-hit Shanxi Province.[133] In response, Ceng himself, of his own accord, allocated another 10,000 taels to be distributed for famine relief.[134]

9. Conclusion

The Boxer Uprising in 1900 wrought havoc in both the missionary community and the Chinese church. The CIM suffered one of the heaviest losses, with fifty-eight missionaries and twenty-one children murdered. Hoste took on leadership of the CIM during this difficult time.

From the time that Hoste took on leadership as the acting general director, he was totally absorbed in the affairs of the CIM and the Chinese church. There must surely have been times of struggle and difficult decisions to make, as well criticism to face. However, as Phyllis Thompson points out, "If he kept a private diary, it has never come to light."[135] Though we may not know much about Hoste's inner struggles as he handled the aftermath of the Boxer Uprising, one thing remains clear – Hoste was deeply concerned about the affairs of the Chinese church. He did not view the Chinese church as serving the purpose of the foreign missionaries. Even in the matter of compensation,

---

131. *China's Millions* (March 1902): 33, 36.
132. *China's Millions* (1902): 36. The record of the full letter in Chinese was published in *China's Millions* (1902): 36. See also 朱金甫, *Qingmo jiaoan* 清末教案 (Late Qing Incidents), Volume III (Beijing: Zhonghua Shuju, 1998), 187–208.
133. *China's Millions* (1901): 146.
134. Broomhall, *Shaping of Modern China*, 731. See also *China's Millions* (1902): 9.
135. Thompson, *Prince with God*, 7.

he was convinced that the CIM was not helping the Chinese church to receive compensation because it worked under the CIM but because the Chinese church had suffered, independently, at the hands of the Boxers. Hoste's leadership in handling the Boxer crisis, at barely the age of forty, won the confidence of colleagues in the CIM as well as leaders of the Chinese church. One key issue that Hoste had to handle was the matter of compensation. Both the Chinese government and the Chinese church in Shanxi requested Hoste's help. The government officials wanted to subtract at least 20 or 30 percent from whatever was claimed, but Hoste completely rejected the idea as it would imply that the claims had been exorbitant. At the same time, Hoste insisted that each claim by the Chinese church be investigated carefully to ensure that there had been no carelessness or overstating of the truth. Hoste's integrity was witnessed and respected by both the government officials and the Chinese church leaders. Though appointed by Taylor, Hoste was able to step out of the founder's shadow and lead with confidence.

Though Hoste made every effort to help the Chinese church claim rightful compensation, he did not focus on the suffering of the Chinese church. Hoste had the foresight to see the potential of the Chinese church to rise to the challenge. He believed that the Boxer Uprising would accelerate the independence of the Chinese church. While it would be fair to say that Taylor was too ill at that time to contemplate the future of the Chinese church, Hoste went beyond Taylor's vision of the rapid evangelization of the inlands of China and grasped the importance of the urgent indigenization of the Chinese church.

Hoste's leadership was appreciated not only by the Chinese church and CIM missionaries; Ceng, the governor of Shanxi, also openly expressed his appreciation of Hoste in a public letter. Ceng's highly positive comment about Hoste, something that had rarely happened with regard to his missionary peers, once again proved the credibility of Hoste's leadership among the different parties involved.

Under Hoste's leadership, the CIM grew in number during the post-Boxer period, reaching 828 CIM missionaries by 1905 and 928 by 1909.[136] Along with this rapid expansion of the CIM, we will see in the next chapter how Hoste went one step further to consolidate his efforts in developing the Chinese church in a new era.

---

136. *China's Millions* (1905): 73; (1909): 20.

CHAPTER 3

Hoste's Vision of the Indigenous Chinese Church

1. Introduction

Right after the Boxer Uprising, Hoste worked closely with Chinese church leaders to ensure that the compensation claim process was done with careful investigation. However, his pursuit at that moment was carried out along with a keen concern about the future of the Chinese church. He believed that the Chinese church would one day grow by itself without dependence on missionaries and that the missionaries must, therefore, learn to let go of control.

Hoste's far-sighted vision did not develop overnight. This chapter will show that some of these ideas and practices of an indigenous Chinese church may be traced back to the work of missionary leaders in previous decades, including the efforts of Hudson Taylor. Moreover, the CIM, in its work in a few places, especially Hangzhou, was also involved in supporting Chinese-led churches that proved the feasibility of the indigenous principles. Hoste himself worked with Pastor Hsi in Shanxi for ten years, during which time he witnessed how this Chinese Christian leader managed to carry out independent evangelistic work and also handle a variety of church affairs on a daily basis. In a sense, the Boxer Uprising provided the much-needed momentum for Hoste to further confirm the importance of the indigenous principles and lead a fundamental change in the CIM in terms of leadership, organization, and financial principles.

Given the tense situation in the aftermath of the Boxer Uprising, Hoste's plan understandably met with some disagreement, and the CIM's stance received strong criticism. However, Hoste was determined to push forward to the new goal in the years to come. Not only did he firmly defend the CIM's approach to the compensation issue and indigenous principles, he also took steps to remove obstacles for the self-support and independent work of Chinese Christians. His leading work in this area made a notable impact on the growth of the indigenous Chinese church and also became an unprecedented model for the missionary-Chinese relationship in the new era.

2. Early Ideas on the Indigenous Principles before Hoste

In order to understand Hoste's view of indigenous principles, we must first go back to the work of some of the missionary leaders who had gone before him. In many ways, Hoste's view of indigenous principles was not totally groundbreaking. Broomhall summarizes it succinctly:

> Two missionary generations were to pass before a determined attempt was made on a large scale in China to apply these principles (of establishing indigenous leadership), enunciated by the SPCK in the early eighteenth century; by Charles Gutzlaff (1803–1852) in 1849–50; re-echoed by Henry Venn (1796–1873) with qualifications in 1851; by William Burns (1815–1868); by the English Presbyterian George Smith (1815–1871) before 1878, and by John Livingstone Nevius (1829–1893) in greater detail in 1864, 1880 and 1885–86; as well as by Hudson Taylor from 1870 onward.[1]

Taylor was greatly inspired by the indigenous principles advocated by Gutzlaff, who firmly believed that "China would ultimately be evangelized by the Chinese themselves."[2] Broomhall categorizes Gutzlaff's indigenous

---

1. SPCK stands for Society for Promoting Christian Knowledge, a Christian charitable organization founded in 1698 in Britain. William Burns was a Scottish evangelist who worked with the English Presbyterian Mission and was in China before Hudson Taylor. He accompanied Hudson Taylor in his initial mission outreaches between 1855 and 1856. See Broomhall, *Shaping of Modern China* 332; 465.

2. Broomhall, *Shaping of Modern China* 144–145.

principles under three main headings. First, Chinese evangelists should work under Chinese supervision. Second, believers and churches should contribute to their own needs and not rely on foreign funding. Third, the evangelization of China should depend on Chinese preachers.[3]

While many in Gutzlaff's day sympathized with the indigenous principles, few took the radical step of believing, like Gutzlaff, that the local church should aim for autonomy from the very start of the relationship between the missionaries and the converts. Gutzlaff was at least a generation before Hoste. Thus, his understanding of indigenous principles impacted Taylor much more than Hoste.

Another person who had influenced Taylor regarding indigenous principles was John Nevius, a missionary of about Taylor's age, who served with the American Presbyterian Board of Foreign Missions. John and his wife, Helen, served in Hangzhou around 1858 but later, in 1861, moved to Chefoo (Yantai) in Shandong.[4] John and Helen Nevius arrived in China in 1854, just a few weeks before Taylor. Over time, a deep friendship developed between the Neviuses and the Taylors, and John Nevius met up with Taylor and discussed the indigenous principles that he was developing in Shandong.[5]

Nevius was a strong advocate of indigenous principles. He insisted, "I believe it is generally admitted that the main work of preaching the gospel in China must eventually be performed by the [Chinese]. The foreigner was too handicapped. His chief role should be to train Chinese."[6]

Some of the earliest records of the indigenous church and native workers related to the CIM are found in the *China's Millions* editions of 1875, about ten years after the establishment of the Mission. The 1875 *China's Millions* carries reports not only about CIM missionaries but also about native workers – including pastors, evangelists, colporteurs, women preachers, and schoolmasters.[7] Names of these local workers were published alongside

---

3. Broomhall, 144–145.
4. Broomhall, 517, 573.
5. Broomhall, 346.
6. Broomhall, 3:573.
7. *China's Millions*, 1875–1876, 234 and several unnumbered pages thereafter; see also the supplement to *China's Millions* (1875–1876): 2–3.

the CIM missionaries, even though the word "assistant" was used to refer to the native workers.[8]

These native workers probably received some kind of financial support from the CIM. However, two years later, in 1877, *China's Millions* published another article entitled "The Work of the China Inland Mission." Though the author is unknown, it is quite possible that Taylor himself wrote this article, which clearly states that the CIM's goal was to see the Chinese church becoming "self-supporting as soon as possible." The missionaries were to carry out the work "only for a time – till native churches can be left to the ministration by native labourers."[9] This is probably one of the earliest records of the phrase "self-supporting" being used in *China's Millions*.

In the preface to the 1878 edition of *China's Millions*, Taylor again emphasized the importance of local Chinese evangelists and pastors going into the interior provinces for Christian work. To Taylor, the CIM's key role was to provide training for these native believers, particularly men, so that they could be better qualified for the work.[10] The same issue also of *China's Millions* published a table showing a list of sixty CIM missionaries together with the names of more than twelve native pastors and Chinese evangelists.[11] However, it was clear that the number of CIM missionaries far exceeded the number of native workers in this early stage of the CIM under Taylor's leadership.

So, in summary, the CIM acknowledged these native local workers as early as 1875. However, they were viewed as "assistants" to the missionaries. Although the long-term goal was to see the Chinese churches becoming self-supporting, no specific strategies had been developed to achieve that goal.

3. An Early CIM Example of Developing an Indigenous Church

John McCarthy (1839–1911), one of the early CIM missionaries in Hangzhou, reported in the monthly *Gleaner* of November 1875 about how an indigenous

---

8. In the 1875–1876 editions of *China's Millions*, the work of the native evangelists and pastors in the different CIM stations was mentioned no less than thirty times.

9. *China's Millions* (1877): 43–44.

10. *China's Millions* (1878): vi.

11. *China's Millions* (1878): xviii. Wang Lae Djün, the pastor from Hangzhou, was first on the list. Wang later supervised CIM missionaries.

church had developed by meeting in the homes of local believers. McCarthy indicated that chapels were often perceived as "foreign" and commented that the "spirit of self-support would be strangled from its very birth." He felt that the "spirit of the gospel should certainly lead [local] men to self-support."[12] Thus, the situation began to change. The church in Hangzhou began to be led by a Chinese pastor named Wang Lae-Djün (王來全, Wang Laiquan, 1835–), who had previously been trained by Taylor for three years and had developed a deep friendship with him.[13]

In 1867, Wang was inducted as the pastor of the church in Hangzhou by a small congregation of just eighteen.[14] Although Wang initially received funds from the CIM, by 1871, he declined a salary from any mission, including the CIM, relying instead on local resources alone.[15] Wang opened four country outposts with church services and supervised seven full-time evangelists and colporteurs.[16] The church in Hangzhou, which was closely associated with the CIM from the beginning, had become one of the earliest churches to adopt the indigenous principles of self-supporting and self-governing; later, it also became self-propagating.

As time went on, and with Taylor's encouragement, Wang became the de facto superintendent-pastor of a network of local churches in Hangzhou.[17] *China's Millions* records the story of how the indigenous principles adopted by Wang positively affected the churches of neighbouring towns and cities beyond Hangzhou. Among these, one small church from Yu-hang (余杭, Yuhang) also began to adopt a similar principle of self-support, showing willingness to support pastors in other churches, while "needing no help from without."[18]

---

12. Broomhall, *Shaping of Modern China* 178.

13. Broomhall, 814. When Grace, one of Hudson Taylor's children, died from pneumonia in 1867, Wang Lae-djün was present at the funeral. Hudson Taylor and Wang went out and bought a Chinese coffin of hardwood, and Wang worked all night preparing it for use.

14. Broomhall 746, 799, 826. Before the arrival of CIM missionaries, others – including John Burdon, and John and Helen Nevius, who had been there since 1859 as early pioneers – were already working in Hangzhou.

15. Broomhall, *Shaping of Modern China* 150.

16. Broomhall, 154.

17. Broomhall, 441.

18. *China's Millions* (1877): 134.

One of the outcomes of implementing the indigenous principles in the early period of the CIM was that the CIM missionaries came under the supervision of Wang. The 1875 edition of *China's Millions* records that Wang was assigned the superintendent role of the Northern Circuit in Zhejiang Province for the CIM.[19] Missionaries like James Meadows (1835–1914) – a senior worker of the CIM – and Dr. Arthur Douthwaite (1848–1899) – a young CIM missionary, who had arrived in China not long before – both came under Wang's supervision for the work in Zhejiang.[20] This was groundbreaking for missionary practice in those days. In some ways, the work by Hsi in Shanxi, which came ten years later, is comparable to the work by Wang in Hangzhou. However, one key difference between the two is that Wang's development of an indigenous work in Hangzhou was with the strong encouragement of the CIM, particularly Taylor, while Hsi's development of the indigenous church and opium refuges in Shanxi was totally independent of missionary influence from the beginning. In fact, some members of the Cambridge Seven only joined Hsi's work after it was established. However, in both cases, Taylor put CIM missionaries under the supervision of local Chinese church leaders.

The year 1877 was significant in the growing understanding of the indigenous principles. This was partly due to a missionary conference in Shanghai, which was attended by missionaries from different mission agencies. Several papers were presented at the conference on the topic of the native church. For example, "The Self-Support of the Native Church" by Stephen. L. Baldwin (1835–1902), "Native Pastorate" by H. Corbette (1835–1920), and "The Advantage and Disadvantages of the Employment of Native Assistants" by Tarleton P. Crawford (1821–1902).[21] Taylor, who attended this conference, listed several important indigenous principles. First, each native church member should be taught and encouraged to give according to his or her ability. Second, missionaries should make it clear to native churches that aid by missionaries was only a temporary measure. Third, local preachers should not be paid salaries higher than the native churches could be expected to pay. Finally, native believers should avoid building "costly churches in foreign style."[22]

---

19. *China's Millions* (1877): 70.
20. *China's Millions* (1875–1876): 70–71.
21. *China's Millions* (1877): 110–111.
22. *China's Millions* (1877): 111–116.

Despite the endorsement of the indigenous principles, the CIM's 1886 *Principles and Practice* (P&P) was silent on the subject. All that was mentioned in the P&P about native workers was that the missionaries could employ these workers at their own expense if approved by the missionary in charge and the superintendent of the respective region.[23] It turned out that Taylor, by working closely with the Chinese pastor Wang, practised the indigenous principles far more than he articulated or formulated them. Nevertheless, a "thoroughly Chinese Church was always Taylor's declared aim."[24] Thus, it would be true to say that by 1880, though CIM missionaries were familiar with the indigenous principles, not many were actively practising them. It took another leader – Taylor's successor, Hoste – to fully articulate the indigenous principles and implement these throughout the different regions where the CIM had been working during the post-Boxer period.

4. Hoste's Claim for Implementing the Indigenous Principles

Hoste's vision of the establishment of the indigenous Chinese church is best explained in an article entitled "Possible Changes and Developments in the Native Churches Arising out of the Present Crisis" published in the October 1900 *Chinese Recorder*.[25] Hoste's document was comprehensive and far-reaching, with several important observations and challenges.[26]

First, Hoste highlighted that change was necessary. Hoste saw that "the future was pregnant with change. The abrupt removal and prolonged absence of the missionary must necessarily lead to great *changes* in its form and character."[27] Of course, at that time, Hoste had no idea whether missionaries would be able to return to China after the Boxer Uprising. He had assumed that perhaps missionaries could not return in the long term. Hoste was concerned that similar crises could occur in the near future and missionaries

---

23. CIM, *The Principles and Practice of the China Inland Mission* (Shanghai: China Inland Mission, 1886).
24. Broomhall, *Shaping of Modern China*, Appendix XXIX.
25. Hoste, "Possible Changes," 509–512. See also Broomhall, *Martyred Missionaries*, 279–281.
26. Broomhall, *Martyred Missionaries*, 279–281.
27. Broomhall, 279.

might no longer be allowed to work in China. Hoste, who wrote this article in October 1900 – just four months after the CIM had suffered its worst loss since its establishment in 1865 – looked beyond the immediate impact.

Second, Hoste pointed out that the current system employed by missionaries did not encourage self-government in the native churches. He commented that, under the current system, the work centred around the missionaries, who carried executive authority and financial control in their hands. Thus, the local believers were dependent on funds administered by missionaries. "Such a relationship was not, to say the least, in the direction of developing in them the independence of thought and initiative in action."[28] Though Hudson Taylor himself was a firm believer in developing the indigenous Chinese church, Hoste observed that CIM missionaries fell far short of that standard.

Third, Hoste insisted that the authority of the missionaries should be spiritual in nature and that they should only act as guides and exemplars, avoiding dependency. However, Hoste observed that the current system did not tend to produce such a relationship between the missionary and the native believers. Therefore, he commented that the current system had "practically postponed the independence and self-government in the native churches indefinitely" though that was the original goal.[29] Hoste felt that this unhealthy relationship would hinder Chinese minds, leading them to "withstand the missionary action and combat their views."[30] Failure to let go of control would only indefinitely postpone the independence and self-government of the native churches.

Fourth, Hoste believed that the present crisis, the Boxer Uprising, might, in the end, provide an opportunity for the native church to take on leadership in the absence of missionaries. Greater changes would certainly take place with the absence of missionaries "in whom the centre of gravity of power, influence, and initiative had rested."[31] This would lead to a period of greater rearrangement in the mutual relationship with the native leaders. Hoste observed that those local Chinese leaders who were used to remaining in the background "under the old regime would come to the front; and proving

---

28. Broomhall, 279.
29. Broomhall, 280.
30. Broomhall, 280.
31. Broomhall, 280.

themselves equal to the facing of danger and bearing of responsibility, grow into leadership."[32] Hoste was not assuming that the mere fact of the Boxer Uprising would automatically produce strong, mature, and influential native leaders of the Chinese church. In fact, he realized that, practically speaking, the independence of the Chinese church "would be hedged round with risk and difficulty."[33] He also realized that not all would rise to the challenge. However, he insisted that there must be a new rearrangement in the relationship between the missionaries and the native leaders by increasing trust.

Fifth, Hoste urged that all CIM missionaries who were prepared to return after the Boxer Uprising recognize a change of role compared to the past. Hoste urged the missionaries to be prepared to have a change of attitude as they might find that their plans and opinions would not always be received with that "docile acquiescence to which they were formerly accustomed."[34] Local believers would no longer be dependent upon foreign sources for pecuniary support. They would be free and, at times, prepared to voice their own opinions and views that were not the same as that of the missionaries. Hoste recognized that there were factions or unruly men who in a time of change might usurp authority in the name of liberty However, "direct responsibility for action must rest with the native rather than, as of old, with missionaries."[35]

Finally, Hoste urged all CIM missionaries to show sympathy and exercise much humility. Hoste recognized that while local believers were not free from faults, peculiar to their temperament and position, missionaries would need to "exercise much humility and patience in dealing with their self-will and self-complacency, calling for much tact, power of sympathy and quiet firmness in the foreigner."[36] Hoste recognized that this was a considerable challenge to the CIM missionary community. However, he felt that the pain of a mindset change would be nothing compared to "the fundamental injuries to character, mental and spiritual caused by the bondage of an artificial relationship which much the individuals concerned may honestly wish it otherwise, produce uniformity of will and thought at the expense of manhood."[37]

---

32. Broomhall, 281.
33. Broomhall, 281.
34. Broomhall, 281.
35. Broomhall, 281–282.
36. Broomhall, 281–282.
37. Broomhall, 281–282.

Hoste's article provided much food for thought not only for the CIM missionaries but also for the wider missionary community of his day. Hoste advocated his strong conviction of Chinese independence and the growth of the indigenous Chinese church. Hoste believed that the native Christians should be given the space to be self-governing, self-supporting, and self-propagating.[38]

The initial uncertainty about the future of missionary activity because of the Boxer Uprising did not last long. The official signing of the Peace Protocol took place in September 1901 under the leadership of China's statesman Li Hung-Chang (李鴻章, 1823–1901).[39] By the end of 1901, a year after the outbreak of the troubles, most missionaries, including those of the CIM, were able to resume their work in most parts of China. By the end of 1902, all foreign governments also gave permission for women missionaries to return to Shanxi, thus removing the last restriction imposed upon missionary labour since the outbreak of persecution.[40] By 1905, throughout the eighteen provinces where the CIM had worked, there was "peace and general tranquillity."[41]

5. Defence of the CIM's Stance on the Boxer Indemnity

The missionary community did not welcome Hoste's message because some mission groups still believed that the Chinese church was too weak to stand on its own. In the same issue of the *Chinese Recorder* where Hoste's article was published, five more articles were written by members of different mission groups, claiming the right to apply for indemnity for loss of lives and property due to the Boxer Uprising.[42] In his paper "Christian Missions in China Should Be Protected by Western Nations," D. Z. Sheffield (1841–1913), a missionary from the American Board of Commissioners for Foreign Missions

---

38. Although Hoste did not use the full phrase "self-governing, self-supporting and self-propagating" directly in the article published in October 1900, he advocated these concepts using the phrase "self-government in the native churches" in this article. The full phrase "self-governing, self-supporting and self-propagating Chinese churches" started to appear much more frequently in *China's Millions* by 1928.

39. Broomhall, *Jubilee Story*, 258.

40. Broomhall, 260

41. Broomhall, *Land of Sinim*, 12.

42. *Chinese Recorder* (1900): 537, 540, 543, 548, 617.

(ABCFM), explicitly took an assertive stance in this respect.[43] He believed that Western nations that professed the Christian faith should protect the Christians and Christian mission societies in China. In his eyes, the Boxers were the product of pure ignorance and superstition, compounded by evil. Sheffield insisted that Christian nations must act promptly and compel China to fulfil its treaty obligation to give protection to Christians so that they could enjoy their religious rights. In his article, he referred to the treaty's signing at the end of the Opium War and emphasized that China should carry out its obligations. Sheffield felt that Western nations had been too sluggish, feeble, and inadequate in making demands upon the Chinese government to protect native converts in their right to profess Christianity.

Sheffield claimed that "missionaries are not the representatives of a narrow propagandism" but, rather, the "apostles of human rights." He further insisted that "China needed to be saved from herself through the wise interference of Western nations helping the spirit of progress."[44] One cannot help but sense the tone of Western superiority in Sheffield's words. Sheffield claimed that the Boxer Uprising reflected "an old China with its attachment to traditional institutions and fear of innovation."[45] But he completely ignored the multiple factors that had caused the Boxer Uprising, including political distrust, commercial and trade antagonism, and religious intolerance.[46]

Sheffield's article is important, not so much because it declared the right to claim indemnity but, rather, because of what it represents and promotes. According to Sheffield, what China needed at that time was "Christianizing China" in order to the save the nation. He also advocated that the role of all Western missionaries was to be "apostles of human rights" and urged Christian nations to discharge their obligations to China by their interference. China was viewed as a weak, backward, superstitious nation that was in desperate need of salvation. Human rights, as understood from the Western perspective, was the major underlying theme. Thus, to many from the West, China needed "to be saved by Western interference," in order to help "the spirit of progress." Missionaries had been given this noble task, and all the

---

43. *Chinese Recorder* (1900): 544.
44. *Chinese Recorder* (1900): 547.
45. *Chinese Recorder* (1900): 544.
46. A more balanced view was expressed in an article by Geo A. Stuart, "The Demand for Indemnity," *Chinese Recorder* (1900): 543.

rights of the missionaries needed to be protected. Logically, the churches that these missionaries had established needed to be protected as well.

However, Hoste's focus was never political nor centred on "Christianizing China." Rather, he felt that what China needed was the Christian message, the gospel, but not necessarily in a European form. For example, though he was not against establishing a Christian university in Shanxi, he was completely against establishing it in the name of the CIM.[47] Hoste's view was vastly different from that of Timothy Richard [48] and other mission leaders of the time. Hoste's emphasis was to evangelize and build up the Chinese church. He also asserted – in his article published in the *Chinese Recorder* in 1900 – that the Chinese church should mature and become self-governing. Though Hoste realized that the native Christians were not free from faults, he insisted that the missionaries should exercise much humility in refraining from being "the centre of gravity of power and influence."[49] Though the Boxer Uprising brought much pain to both the Chinese church and missionaries, Hoste believed that suffering and enduring hardship was part of the calling of all Christians, whether from the West or from China.[50]

The CIM's position of not claiming indemnity resulted in some serious debates with other mission groups who felt that the CIM had put itself above others by being critical of those who had claimed compensation. This feeling continued for ten years and was rekindled in 1910 at the World Missionary Conference in Edinburgh, which was a major historical event for all world missionary activities. Walter. B. Sloan (1858–1943), a representative leader of the CIM, made an appeal to the delegates not to claim indemnities in the course of mission service.[51] Sloan gave an example of a riot in Changsha in which two CIM missionaries had died, after which the CIM refused indemnities. However, this appeal was met with strong objections by some leaders at the World Missionary Conference. Gilbert G. Warren (1861–1927), a

---

47. Broomhall, *Shaping of Modern China* , 730.

48. Broomhall, 734. Timothy Richard was a well-known Baptist missionary who, after the Boxer Uprising, managed to establish a university in Shanxi – a state institution that remained under foreign control.

49. Broomhall, *Martyred Missionaries*, 280–281.

50. *China's Millions* (1906): 6.

51. Walter B. Sloan joined the CIM in 1891 and later became the general secretary for the China Inland Mission in Britain after Benjamin Broomhall. For details, see *Chinese Recorder* (1910): 736–737.

missionary leader from the Methodist Mission, working in Henan, challenged Sloan's view.

Warren argued from the position of the British legal system. According to British law, murder cases are always considered *Rex versus*, meaning that the demands made did not depend on the "views of the relatives, the mission, or the firm" with which the deceased had been connected, though their views would be given due consideration by the court. In applying this principle to the Boxer Uprising, Warren argued that the decision to claim compensation, too, was that of the British government. Thus, though the CIM had the right not to claim compensation or even to refuse it if offered, it was not right for the CIM to bind other missions to follow its policy "for the CIM did not have such rights."[52]

Sloan gave a robust response, arguing that he had never attempted to assert that his proposal was binding on anyone. He insisted that each group was entitled to pursue their own course of action in the event of such a case occurring in the future. However, he felt that the CIM had the right to make such an appeal and that a world missionary conference was a fit place to make it.[53] Sloan's view certainly corresponds to that of Hoste since Sloan was representing the CIM at the conference. The CIM's voice was significant as it had more missionaries than any other mission society at that time and there were also other societies with similar objectives associated with the CIM.[54] Perhaps some may have felt that the CIM's position might jeopardize their own claim for compensation.

The CIM's stance of not claiming compensation has broader implications since it recognized that China needed time to recover not only from the Boxer calamity but also from other natural disasters – including the severe famine in Shanxi. Furthermore, many local people were still afraid of another possible outburst of violence, not just something similar to the Boxer Uprising but also a repetition of foreign aggression as demonstrated by the "Eight Nation Alliance" in 1900. The deaths of many church leaders during the Boxer Uprising also posed a significant threat and challenge to the future of the church in the affected provinces. A severe indemnity would most likely

---

52. *Chinese Recorder* (1910): 736–737.
53. *Chinese Recorder* (1911): 111–112.
54. Latourette, *History of Christian Missions*, 581.

mean heavier tax for the ordinary people. Thus, the CIM's position was that "it would be wiser not to accept compensation in view of the effect which such acceptance would have upon the native Christians. The settlement of this extremely difficult and complex matter should be carried out in the spirit and the mind of Christ."[55]

6. The Start of Change in Organization and Cooperation

The initial fear that all mission activities would be curtailed after the Boxer Uprising was soon dispelled. Massive changes had taken place since 1900, both to the nation's infrastructure as well as to the Chinese church.[56] Kaiser called the post-Boxer period the "Golden Age of Mission."[57] Not only were missionaries allowed to return, they were also welcomed back to China. Changes were taking place in the broader context, too. The great Siberian railway, linking the eastern and western hemispheres, was opened in 1901. Other new railroads were opened within the country. China was on the way to modernization. In September 1905, the old education system was finally abolished by edict and replaced by the emergence of colleges and universities for Western learning.[58] Even more exciting, the native Chinese church faced one of the great revivals of its time with the rapid growth of many independent churches.[59] Nationwide, China reported having over three hundred and fifty thousand Protestant believers and nearly two million Chinese Catholics in 1920.[60]

Even within the CIM, there was encouraging growth. With the reorganization of the work in Shanxi after the Boxer Uprising, the CIM's surviving missionaries began to return by the end of 1901, with new missionaries joining as well.

---

55. *China's Millions*, North American edition (1901): 62. See also Kaiser, *Rushing On*, 105–106.

56. Broomhall, *Jubilee Story*, 263–265.

57. Kaiser, *Rushing On*, 118–177.

58. According to Marshall Broomhall, the old Examination Hall in Peking was transformed into a Naval College, and Chinese students flocked to Japan, where nearly 9,000 such students were in residence during 1905. Broomhall, *Jubilee Story*, 264

59. Kaiser, *Rushing On*, 141.

60. Kaiser, 136.

According to the CIM statistics, there were 79 CIM missionaries working in the province of Shansi by August 1903, compared to 103 in early 1900, just before the Boxer Uprising. But by 1904, the total number of CIM missionaries in the Shanxi Province had grown to 137.[61] The overall total number of CIM missionaries also continued to grow. There were 735 CIM missionaries by the end of 1901,[62] still less than the 811 who were in place before the Boxer Uprising.[63] But by 1905, this number had increased to 825 and, by 1909, to a total of 928 missionaries.[64] By 1915, the CIM had 1050 missionaries.[65]

What was most significant to Hoste, however, was not so much the growth in the number of CIM missionaries but, rather, the increasing number of native Chinese workers associated with the CIM. *The Land of Sinim: An Illustrated Report of the China Inland Mission 1905* gives a surprising report of 332 "unpaid self-supporting native helpers." Along with these self-supporting native workers, the report also mentions other Chinese pastors, assistant pastors, colporteurs, and schoolteachers, who were all paid by the CIM.[66] According to Marshall Broomhall, the self-supporting local workers in 1905 accounted for nearly 20 percent of the total workforce in the CIM,[67] demonstrating that the CIM was changing under Hoste's leadership. A new trend had emerged in that many local workers who joined the CIM were either self-supporting or were supported by local churches without relying on the CIM.

However, it is important to note that the term "helper" was still maintained in referring to these Chinese workers despite the fact that many of them were already working as pastors or Bible teachers with the CIM. These self-supporting Chinese workers were not yet seen as equals with the CIM missionaries. It would take some time for CIM missionaries to adopt this new mindset. It was in 1915, at the CIM Jubilee, that the term "Chinese workers"

---

61. *China's Millions* (1903): 111–116. See also Broomhall, *Jubilee Story*, Appendix III, which shows statistics of the CIM both before and after the Boxer Uprising.

62. *China's Millions* (June 1902): 73, 88.

63. Broomhall, *Shaping of Modern China*, 638.

64. *China's Millions* (1909): 20.

65. Broomhall, *Jubilee Story*, 265.

66. Broomhall, *Land of Sinim*, 178.

67. Broomhall, 178.

was used for the first time by Marshall Broomhall.[68] Broomhall comments that Hoste, who had worked closely with Pastor Hsi, set the example of working with indigenous leaders. By 1935, the phrase "Chinese helper" was finally dropped from *China's Millions* and replaced with "Chinese workers including men and women" serving alongside CIM missionaries.[69] This change had taken twenty years. Although we cannot ascertain if Hoste personally initiated this change, his efforts in promoting and adopting the indigenous principles had clearly begun to take effect.

Thus, the "Golden Period" for the CIM (1900–1920) was not just that the missionaries could return to the interior areas of China after the Boxer Uprising. Rather, it was the growth of the Chinese church, with an increasing number of self-supporting workers joining the CIM work.

There was quite a bit of excitement and many enthusiastic initiatives instigated by local believers. The missionaries were encouraged to see land and buildings freely offered by the local people in many stations.[70] Shopowners offered their shops as chapels, and crowds gathered daily to hear the Christian message preached.[71] Massive Christian movements were observed, particularly in the province of Sichuan.[72] Many CIM missionaries in different provinces observed similar responses from local people. The phrase "as never before" became common in many of the CIM reports: "men crowd into our preaching halls as never before;" "eagerness for education as never before;" "friendliness towards the missionary as never before."[73] In many of the meetings, it was the local evangelists who did the preaching, with the CIM missionaries playing a supporting role.[74]

Bishop Cassels – one of the Cambridge Seven, who was working in Sichuan – reported at least a threefold increase in the number of CIM stations in 1905.[75] However, he raised the important concern that CIM missionaries might still be "doing too much" which was hindering the growth of

---

68. Broomhall, *Jubilee Story*, 266.
69. *China's Millions* (January 1935): cover page.
70. Broomhall, *Jubilee Story*, 268.
71. Broomhall, 268.
72. Broomhall, 267.
73. Broomhall, 268.
74. Broomhall, 270–271.
75. Broomhall, 267–268.

the Chinese church. Cassels reported that CIM missionaries were surprised by what the local people could do when left alone to organize their own resources. "It is terribly true that in some senses we are doing far too little. But it is also true that we are in *danger of doing far too much*."[76] Cassels warned that the CIM might be in danger of not allowing the believers "sufficient scope for natural development, pressing them into too narrow channels, of moulding them in Western moulds." He wrote, "Christianity was founded in Asiatic soil, and it will yet reach its fullest development in an Eastern atmosphere. Thus, sufficient room must be given to local believers to develop in their way."[77]

The Chinese church was experiencing rapid growth. According to one CIM report, there were 700 baptisms in 1895; ten years later, the number had reached 2,500; in 1914 and 1915, the annual baptisms were 4,500 and 5,000.[78] With the rapid growth of the Chinese church, Hoste had already seen the need for the CIM to adopt a different posture, particularly in the way CIM missionaries worked with local believers.

It is heartening to see that there was increasing cooperation between CIM missionaries and local Chinese workers, with encouraging results. One such example was the work in Shanxi near Hungtung, where Hoste had previously spent a significant amount of time with Pastor Hsi. In 1908, Albert Lutley (1865–1934), a CIM missionary, observed how Wang Chi-tai, a young, local Chinese evangelist in Hungtung, took a prominent role in preaching.[79] This resulted in a large number of conversions. One evidence of the fruit of this work was that some who had previously stolen returned the money to their masters and stolen properties were also returned.[80] The result was that the CIM missionaries began to take on a more supportive role in encouraging the local leaders to take on evangelistic responsibilities

According to Marshall Broomhall, the number of unpaid, self-supporting Chinese workers jumped significantly from 108 in the third decade of the CIM (1885–1895) to 332 in the fourth decade (1895–1905) and 1,071 in the

---

76. *China's Millions* (August 1904): 104. Empasis added.

77. *China's Millions* (August 1904): 104.

78. Broomhall, *Jubilee Story*, 269. Broomhall divides the first fifty years of the CIM into five decades: First Decade – 1865–1875; Second Decade – 1875–1885; Third Decade – 1885–1895; Fourth Decade – 1895–-1905; Fifth Decade – 1905–1915.

79. Broomhall, 270.

80. Broomhall, 271–272.

fifth decade (1905–1915) – an almost tenfold increase within twenty years. In addition, by 1915, the total number of self-supporting local workers exceeded the number of CIM missionaries, which stood at 1,063.[81] Though still in the early emergent stage, the indigenous Chinese church was beginning to show forth its strength. It was not until 1940, however, that *China's Millions* began to publish some detailed records of local Chinese workers, some of whom had become prominent indigenous leaders, a point we will return to in the next chapter.

Kaiser, in his book *The Rushing On of the Purposes of God*, gives an even wider picture of the overall church situation in China between 1900 and 1920. In 1918, there were 7,000 Protestant schools with 213,000 students and over 300 missionary hospitals across the country. *China Mission Yearbook* in 1916 reported that the CIM had 1,250 Chinese workers serving across China.[82] In 1917, there were sixty-four theological and Bible schools across China.[83] During this golden period in the aftermath of the Boxer Uprising, the church in China was growing rapidly. Wong Sikpui – in his book *In Remembrance of Martyrs a Century Ago* – records that there were altogether 6,250 Protestant missionaries in China by 1907, an increase of nearly 1,000 compared to just before 1900.[84] With the increase in the number of self-supporting local workers, there was greater cooperation between the CIM and the Chinese church.

7. Hoste's Warning against Denominationalism

After 1900, the missionary community held several important conferences – including the China Centenary Missionary Conference in 1907 – with a focus on the future of the Chinese church. A "self-supporting and self-governing Chinese church" became one of the key topics for discussion, with missionaries divided about the idea of a "self-supporting Chinese Church." However, Hoste had one major concern. He felt that the main problem they were facing did not have to do with the Chinese but with the missionaries – and more so with the mission societies. Hoste was convinced that for the Chinese church

---

81. Broomhall, , 373.
82. *China Mission Yearbook* (1916): 145–146.
83. Kaiser, *Rushing On*, 136.
84. Wong, *In Remembrance*, 732.

to be totally "self-supporting, self-governing and self-propagating," the missionary community must get their act together and get rid of territorialism.

In his article published in 1907 – "Should the Denomination Distinctions of Christian Lands Be Perpetuated in Mission Fields?" – addressing the problems posed by a new situation, Hoste presented some more developed ideas than the ones he had proposed seven years earlier.[85] The title of the paper gives the impression that the issue was denominations. However, a careful study of the paper reveals that the discussion went far beyond denominational issues.[86]

Hoste's main emphasis was the future of the Chinese church. According to Hoste, holding onto denominational distinctions would only be a hindrance to the development of self-supporting, self-governing, and self-propagating Chinese churches. Hoste used some strong words in his article to express how disturbed he was that missionaries were more concerned about preserving their traditions than about developing the Chinese church.

First, Hoste insisted that missionaries must be delivered from "stupid parochialism," which tended to obliterate the individuality and initiative of local believers by introducing practices and arrangements merely because of old habits or traditions.[87] Hoste noted that the time was rapidly approaching when "provincialism which imagines missionaries had all the knowledge and wisdom would meet with well-merited rebuke."[88]

Second, Hoste was also deeply troubled by the way Westerners viewed the Chinese as uncivilized and uneducated. He referred to China's long history, rich in achievements "in the domain of government probably unsurpassed in the history of mankind" and said that "it is much to be desired that China's past political and social history should be more widely and intelligently studied in Western lands than has hitherto been the case." He continued, "until this is done, reproaches of the Chinese on the score of their ignorance and self-conceit seem out of place. We cannot afford to despise a race."[89]

---

85. First published in the *American Journal of Theology*, April 1907, and later republished in the *Chinese Recorder* (1907): 427–430.
86. Hoste referred to denominations as "church orders."
87. *Chinese Recorder* (1907): 429.
88. *Chinese Recorder* (1907): 429.
89. *Chinese Recorder* (1907): 430.

Third, Hoste predicted that, as time went on, "China will give to the Christian believers fitted for leadership and endowed with organizing power on a large scale." Hoste acknowledged that the Chinese people possessed an "independent spirit" and any attempt to force upon them the denominationalism system from the Western homelands would certainly end in disaster. Therefore, Hoste urged all missionaries to exercise the utmost self-restraint and discrimination between *essentials* and *incidentals*, as "one should not put new wine into old bottles."[90] Hoste warned against the danger of "governing too much."[91]

Hoste used strong words throughout the article, condemning the danger of parochialism and provincialism by missionaries. He also criticized the missionaries' attitude of superiority and their unwillingness to let go of control. This insistence that foreign missionaries should let go of power and control in order that the Chinese church could be what it should be – that is, self-governing and self-supporting – represents one of the clearest expressions of Hoste's position on the future of the Chinese church.

Almost ten years later, Hoste published another paper entitled "The Effect of the War on Missions in China" in the *Chinese Recorder*. The paper was written in the midst of the First World War, while conflict was still raging in Europe. Hoste urged missionaries not to be involved in the political propaganda of either side but to give more attention to the development of the "self-help" and "self-supporting" Chinese church.[92] Compared to what he had written ten years before, Hoste had hardly wavered in his position on the importance of the indigenous church. In many ways, he viewed the war in Europe as a reminder to missionaries that elaborate organization, large expenditures, and control of the Chinese churches should be avoided as foreign funds had been either cut off or restricted on account of the war. Hoste concluded that

> where [Chinese] Christians have from the beginning been left to support themselves and also to be largely responsible for carrying on their own services, they will, with a due measure of oversight and teaching, prove equal to the task. It is absurd to

---

90. *Chinese Recorder* (1907): 430–431.
91. *Chinese Recorder* (1907): 428.
92. *Chinese Recorder* (1916): 21–23.

say that the Chinese as a people are lacking in capacity; their whole history disproves it.[93]

By 1915, after fifteen years of leadership as the general director of the CIM, Hoste had certainly grown in confidence in articulating his vision and convictions about the indigenous Chinese church.

8. Creating an Indigenous Model in Shanxi

Hoste realized that implementing the indigenous principles across the whole CIM community in different provinces would take time. He felt that initiating a pilot project on a smaller scale would encourage CIM missionaries to take ownership, and it seemed natural to start with the province of Shanxi, where Hoste had served under Hsi for ten years.

Thus, in 1919, with Hoste's encouragement, the Shanxi churches enthusiastically initiated the formation of a Home Missionary Movement for the province.[94] According to this initiative, the Chinese church was to take responsibility for the evangelization of several "hsien" (縣, *xian*, county) districts that had hitherto been largely unreached.

The formation of a Home Missionary Movement in 1919 was preceded, in 1918, by a CIM Shanxi Church Conference, where some far-reaching decisions were made. At this conference, an executive body was formed, comprised mainly of Chinese pastors from the province. This executive body was to act on behalf of all the churches in Shanxi to deal with all questions affecting the work of the church as a whole. One CIM missionary from each mission station in Shanxi was also to be elected to the executive body. By this arrangement, Hoste ensured that the Chinese delegates outnumbered the missionaries by about two to one. Hoste recommended that this ratio should continue to increase gradually from year to year along with the increase in the number of churches. In this way, the responsibility for the government of the church would gradually be devolved to the Chinese pastors and church delegates.[95]

---

93. *Chinese Recorder* (1916): 22.
94. *China's Millions* (1919): 70.
95. *China's Millions* (1919): 101–102.

At this conference in 1918, a special topic entitled "A Special Mission Field for the Shansi Province" was introduced by the chairman of the conference – a local pastor from Shanxi named Liu Kao Cheng – and a young evangelist named Wang Tsong-tao.[96] Wang gave a forceful appeal that "thrilled his audience." He divided his talk into "special field," "special contribution," and "special workers." Apart from their regular contributions, he appealed to the Chinese believers to donate "one cash" (a small unit of money) per day for the urgent evangelization of the unreached "hsien" in Shanxi.[97] This proposal was received enthusiastically.

> He [Wang] had no sooner sat down, than one of the most liberal men in the church, a member of the Hotsin Church, who was believed to be giving to his utmost ability, got up and promised to give one cash per day for himself, his wife, mother, and several children. Others followed with similar promises. Others followed in quick succession, and it was manifest that many hearts were moved. Present was a poor cobbler from one of the more distant stations, a visitor, who asked if he might say a few words, and upon this being granted, said, "My heart is so full as I think of God's great love to me that I cannot keep silent any longer. I have a little money here that I intended for my journey home, but I want to give it that others may have the Gospel." With these few words he placed about a dollar on the table and resumed his seat. Many were visibly touched, and almost immediately there were requests from different parts of the hall that a collection should be taken up at once. Slips of paper were passed around, and in a short time, about $150 had been either given or promised.[98]

Within a few months of the conference, two Chinese evangelists were sent out by the local churches under the Shanxi Forward Missionary Movement initiatives to three cities in Shanxi: Chinhsien (沁縣, Qin County), Chin-yuan (沁源, Qinyuan County), and Hsiang-ning (襄陵, Xiangning 鄉寧), under

---

96. *China's Millions* (1919): 101–102.
97. *China's Millions* (1919): 101–102.
98. *China's Millions* (October 1918): 103.

the direction of local pastors. The Pingyang fu church, which had a close connection with Hoste, made a commitment to provide half the evangelists' salaries.[99] It was expected that other churches would follow their example.[100] This would certainly have been a great encouragement to Hoste, who had such a deep connection with the Shanxi churches.

In early 1920, Hoste wrote a letter to all the church leaders in Shanxi, with an appeal that "the local native church should even take a larger share in the support and management of their workers."[101] Hoste's view was supported by the secretary of the China Continuation Committee (CCC), Cheng Ching-Yi (誠靜怡, Cheng Jingyi, 1881–1939).[102] The CCC had been formed in 1912 as a result of the 1910 Edinburgh World Missionary Conference. Cheng's speech was published in the 1920 edition of *China's Millions*. Cheng noted that "foreign missions in China were the scaffolding and the Church the permanent building itself. All [mission] policy and work should be church-centric rather than mission-centric. It is not a day too soon to begin to lay more emphasis on the strengthening of the church."[103] These words, particularly the image of the "scaffolding," closely echoed the views of Hoste and also Taylor, the founder of the CIM.[104]

Hoste then worked further on the details of how the funds for local workers should be managed. Subsequently, he proposed that a joint committee be formed to centrally manage all the funds available for the support of these local evangelists, whether contributed by the CIM or by the local churches in Shanxi.[105] This joint committee comprised members from among both missionaries and local church pastors. It was also decided that "the proportion of Mission money to Chinese contribution is to be gradually decreased" and that all special funds for the support of individual workers would be pooled.[106] In this way, the Chinese churches would be encouraged to feel that the work was theirs, be given greater opportunities to exercise their gifts of

---

99. *China's Millions* (October 1918): 103.
100. *China's Millions* (October 1918): 103.
101. *China's Millions* (1920): 9.
102. Ng, "Cheng Jing-yi," 14–16.
103. *China's Millions* (1920): 53.
104. Broomhall, *Shaping of Modern China*, 192.
105. *China's Millions* (1920): 53.
106. *China's Millions* (1920): 53.

administration, and be gradually led to full independence. This important decision was communicated to the CIM missionaries at the 1920 Shanxi provincial conference.[107]

9. Hoste's Resolution of Financial Problems

While Hoste pushed forward with the Chinese church becoming self-supporting and self-governing, a very significant unparalleled pull factor made the indigenizing process even more urgent. By 1920, the unfavourable exchange rate had caused many mission societies to face an unprecedented financial challenge.[108] The exchange rate problem had been going on for several years but had become much worse by 1920, partly due to the war.[109]

John N. Hayward (1858–1919), who worked in the treasury department of the CIM's headquarters in Shanghai, had warned Hoste of the problem as early as 1917. Silver – also known as tael – was the Chinese currency at that time. Since 1915, the exchange rate between British sterling and Chinese silver had been somewhat volatile. In 1915, the CIM could purchase one ounce of Chinese silver for every 2s. 4d.[110] By 1916, this had increased to more than 2s. 11d and, by 1917, it was 3s. 7d. The CIM estimated that it had lost a sum of £17,408 just based on the exchange rate difference between 1915 and 1916, in addition to it being a year of war.[111] Considering that the total income received in Britain for the CIM was only £37,608, this loss was significant.[112] The exchange rate continued to worsen against the stronger China tael and, by January 1918, stood at 4s 10½d.[113] The CIM was somewhat relieved by income received from North America and Australasia, which compensated for the exchange loss.[114] But the exchange rate crisis was not yet over. In the 1918 issue of *China's Millions*, the CIM emphasized the "dire situation,"

---

107. *China's Millions* (1920): 53.

108. *China's Millions* (1920): 8.

109. *Federal Reserve Bulletin* (January 1920): 49–51, 111–112; see also Clements and Frenkel, "Exchange Rates," 249–262.

110. British currency at that time was made up of pounds (£), shillings (s, of which there were 20 in a pound), and pence (d, of which there were 12 in a shilling).

111. *China's Millions* (1917): 77, 119.

112. *China's Millions* (1917): 119; (1918): 23.

113. *China's Millions* (1918): 23

114. *China's Millions* (1918): 65.

explaining that the demand for silver had exceeded the supply and that it was anticipated that by 1919, the demand for silver would again exceed the world's production owing to the requirements of Indian and European coinage.[115]

This unfavourable exchange rate led to a significant debate at the CIM's China Council meeting in 1918. Money previously provided to support the daily needs of Chinese workers, which had formerly been adequate, was now proven inadequate because of the adverse exchange rate. It had always been the policy of the CIM, when funds were low, to give priority to the claims of Chinese workers.[116] The missionaries had adopted such principles for the support of the Chinese workers since the early days of the CIM. However, the exchange rate in 1918 made adequate support for the Chinese workers an increasingly acute issue, which in turn affected the support for the CIM missionaries.

Thus, it was felt that the time had come for more definite steps to be taken to transfer the responsibility of support for Chinese workers from the CIM to the Chinese church, with the goal of seeing self-supporting and self-governing Chinese churches established. In December 1918, the China Council discussed this subject under Hoste's leadership and came to the following conclusions regarding support for Chinese workers.[117]

First, the CIM affirmed that the Mission's support for Chinese workers until the churches had sufficient strength to undertake this burden was a matter of Christian love. However, the CIM also noted that, in many instances, the Chinese Christians had come to regard it as the business and responsibility of the CIM to support their Chinese helpers. Therefore, it was of great importance that steps should be taken to rectify "the above mistake" as the support of local workers was a duty "devolving upon the churches."[118]

Second, CIM leadership also affirmed that the support and supervision of these local workers should be gradually transferred from the Mission to the local churches. They specified that this should include responsibilities beyond the merely financial . They also stated that arrangements should be made in the selection, control, and, when necessary, discipline of workers,

---

115. *China's Millions* (1918): 36.
116. *China's Millions* (1919): 42.
117. "China Council Minutes" (December 1918): 6–7.
118. "China Council Minutes" (December 1918): 6.

and that some central body of Chinees church leaders should be instituted to deal with these matters in cooperation with the missionaries.

Third, it was recognized that since some of the Chinese workers serving with the CIM were deemed unsuitable for various reasons, it was unlikely that the Chinese church would support them. While it was considered desirable that such workers should be retired, it was also felt that due care should be taken to avoid any injustice or hardship.

Fourth, in view of the wide extent and the varying contexts in which CIM missionaries were working, the adoption of a strictly uniform procedure regarding the matter was impracticable. It was agreed that, in this interim period, the special funds for the support of existing Chinese workers be pooled.

Fifth, it was agreed that letters on the subject should be sent by Hoste to both fellow CIM workers and the Chinese churches, emphasizing the vision of developing self-supporting Chinese churches. The CIM China Council also agreed that steps should be taken "for the development of Church government in their districts in order to organize the collection and administration of funds for Church buildings, and also for other matters connected with the life of the church."[119]

Hoste had to tackle the adverse exchange rate crisis. With the significant financial loss due to the high tael value, the needs of both missionaries and local workers were barely being met. Hoste grasped the nettle and introduced a structural change to resolve how local workers should be funded. While Taylor was keen to see indigenous churches established and local believers rise to leadership, Hoste gave attention to the details of ensuring that the indigenous process be implemented and accelerated. Hoste tried to rectify the long-held view of the Chinese church that it was the CIM's duty to support the churches. Though the general direction of encouraging indigenous churches had been decided on, Hoste realized that time would be needed for the process of implementing the principles gradually across different provinces as the context in each province was different.

However, the Anti-Christian Movement in the 1920s showed to Hoste that implementing this indigenous process needed to take precedence and should not be delayed. In the next chapter, we will consider how Hoste introduced

---

119. "China Council Minutes" (December 1918): 6–7.

structural change within the CIM to expedite the indigenous process for the Chinese church.

10. Hoste and Women's Leadership in the CIM

While Hoste devoted much of his attention to developing the indigenous Chinese church with self-supporting local workers, he did not ignore some of the emerging needs from within the CIM, particularly the representation of women on the China Council.

The role of women had been an important issue since the founding of the CIM. According to Valarie Griffiths, "None [of Hudson Taylor's] policies was more radical than his decision to send single women as well as men to go to China as equal members of the mission. In accepting women as missionaries on an equal basis with men in 1865, Hudson Taylor led the way in mobilizing men and women to work together in evangelism and church-planting."[120]

By 1885, the CIM had more women missionaries than men.[121] By 1900, fifteen years later, there were about two CIM women missionaries for every male missionary.[122] These women found opportunities to use their gifts in the work of teaching and evangelism in China in ways that would have been impossible in their churches at home.

Despite Taylor's innovative spirit in mobilizing both single women and married women with their husbands for the work in China, leadership of the CIM remained primarily with the men. Griffiths observes that though Taylor affirmed the role of women – whether married or single – in mission work, "he still accepted the common interpretation of the Bible at that time, that the final authority and leadership must be restricted to men."[123] CIM women were "already more directly involved in church work and evangelism than women in most other missions, but at the same time they were left walking a knife-edge between being what they were and conforming to what people thought they should be."[124]

---

120. Griffiths, *Not Less Than Everything*, 74.
121. Austin, *China's Millions*, 196.
122. Griffiths, *Not Less Than Everything*, 10, 324.
123. Grifiths, 320–321.
124. Grifiths, 320–321.

It was under Hoste that the CIM showed some signs of structural change regarding women in leadership. Just before Hoste took on the role of acting general director of the CIM in 1900, the China Council members were all men.[125] According to the China Council minutes, the first time that the issue of women in leadership was raised at the China Council during the time Hoste was the general director was in 1921 when a CIM missionary named Jessie Gregg (1871–1942) wrote a letter to the China Council requesting strengthening of pastoral support for women CIM missionaries on the field. Gregg suggested the formation of an "Auxiliary Ladies Council to whom the sisters can turn."[126] This proposal was debated at the China Council but turned down, acknowledging that while this model might be helpful to help young missionary women candidates at home, it would not apply to the China situation. For the Auxiliary Ladies Council to be involved in "giving advice to the ordinary affairs of missionary work was not called for and might indeed sometimes tend to embarrass rather than help the administration of the Mission."[127]

The following year, however, Hoste took up this subject again at the China Council, acknowledging that "the point of view and work of the sisters [women] should be more adequately brought to the China administration."[128] The Council was of the view that it would be beneficial to invite two or three female missionaries to be on the Council rather than forming a separate body composed entirely of women.[129] For practical reasons, the Council felt that single women would be better suited for this task. The Council felt that since the proposal endorsed by Hoste involved a distinctly new departure in the practice of the Mission and had a significant bearing upon the Home Councils, "the benefit and the judgement of the Home Directors and the Home Councils should be obtained before any final decision was reached."[130]

---

125. According to the 1897–1899 China Council minutes, the members were John W. Stevenson, William Cooper, Charles. T. Fishe, James G. Broumton, Archibald Orr-Ewing, and John N. Hayward.

126. "China Council Minutes" (November 1921): 11.

127. "China Council Minutes" (November 1921): 12.

128. "China Council Minutes" (April 1922): 9.

129. "China Council Minutes" (April 1922): 9.

130. "China Council Minutes" (April 1922): 9.

The China Council minutes of June 1923 reveal that while the London Council accepted the proposal to have women on the China Council, the North America Council was against it and the Australasia Council, while prepared to accept the proposal, cautioned that this practice should not set a precedent that the Australasia Council would be compelled to follow.[131] The minutes also show that a "considerable number of CIM women workers on the field expressed their disapproval of the proposal."[132] Thus, the China Council decided that "it would be neither wise or right to proceed further with the matter at the present time."[133]

Moreover, it appeared that many CIM female missionaries at that time adopted the more conservative view that leadership in the Mission should be carried out by men.[134] Thus, when Hoste stepped down from leadership in 1935, the China Council still consisted only of men.[135] As Valerie Griffiths writes, "It took another sixty years for the first woman leader to be appointed by the Mission."[136]

With the doctrinal debate with the National Christian Council (NCC) in the early 1920s – which ultimately led to the withdrawal of the CIM from the NCC – Hoste was probably too busy to pursue the matter of including women missionaries in the China Council. Though Hoste gave much weight to the role of women in mission work, he did not did not push for structural change to include woman in the leadership in the CIM.

---

131. "China Council Minutes" (June 1923): 10.

132. "China Council Minutes" (June 1923): 10; see also "China Council Minutes" (December 1925): 12.

133. "China Council Minutes" (December 1925): 12.

134. "China Council Minutes" (December 1925): 12; (November 1927): 24.

135. Members of the China Council in 1935 included Dixon Hoste, George Gibb, William Warren, Frederick Charles Henry Dreyer, William Embery, Charles Fairclough, Henry Ford, William Hanna, Arthur Lewis, Alexander Macpherson, Andrew Moore, Gladstone Porteous, Augustus Trudinger, Ernest Weller and James Stark. See "China Council Minutes" (1935).

136. Rosemary Aldis (1940–) was the first woman leader appointed as OMF's International Director of Personnel in 1987. See Griffiths, *Not Less Than Everything*, 325, and OMF International Headquarters Directors' Meeting Minutes, June 1987, 274, (OMF International Headquarters Archive Department).

11. Conclusion

The post-Boxer period was indeed a golden period for all missionary activities, including those of the CIM. The CIM, which had begun like a mustard seed in 1865, had grown under Hoste's leadership so that, by 1915, there were 1,050 missionaries serving in China.[137] However, what was most significant to Hoste was not so much the growth in the number of CIM missionaries but, rather, the increasing number of self-supporting native Chinese workers associated with to the CIM. Hoste had enabled a different kind of growth – not so much of the CIM but, rather, of the Chinese church. While different mission leaders had previously advocated indigenous principles, Hoste had applied these concepts to the post-Boxer context.

The paper by Hoste, published in the October 1900 *Chinese Recorder*, was a defining document for the CIM. Hoste insisted that the authority of the missionaries should be of a spiritual nature and that they should only serve as guides and exemplars, with the goal of avoiding dependency. If the missionaries failed to let go of control, the independence and self-government of the native churches would be postponed indefinitely.[138]

Hoste knew that it would challenging to achieve a widespread indigenous process within a short time. However, his pilot project, the Shanxi Forward Movement met with success, as an indigenous church network led by local leaders was formed.

While Taylor provided visionary leadership so that the Chinese church could be indigenous, Hoste provided executive leadership in implementing the details of these indigenous principles. He bravely corrected a long-accepted notion of dependency on missionaries. Hoste held that not only should the Chinese church be self-supporting, it should also be self-governing. However, both the CIM community and the Chinese church had not anticipated another major crisis, which was yet to come, that further accelerated the indigenization process. As the next chapter will show, the nationalistic Anti-Christian Movement proved to be a major catalyst for the next major crisis affecting many missionaries.

---

137. Broomhall, *Jubilee Story*, 265.
138. *Chinese Recorder* (October 1900): 509–512.

CHAPTER 4

Hoste Launching the Statement of Policy and the Forward Movement

1. Introduction: CIM and the Anti-Christian Movement

Following the Boxer Uprising, the golden period of the rapid growth of the Chinese church and the expansion of Christian mission in China lasted for about twenty years. There was increased cooperation among different mission societies for the work in China, including the formation of the China Christian Federation at the 1907 Centenary China Missionary Conference.[1] There was great enthusiasm when the China Continuation Committee (CCC) was formed in 1913 – following the vision of John R. Mott (1865–1955) as laid out at the Edinburgh World Missionary Conference in 1910 – to promote Christian cooperation and unity. The formation of the China Continuation Committee also symbolizes the increasing role that Chinese church leadership played in moving from a paradigm of "union" to "cooperation" with various mission societies for the growth and development of the church in China.[2] The CCC was composed of both foreign missionaries and Chinese Christians, with at least one-third of the committee members being Chinese.[3]

---

1. See details in Zhao Tian En, *Zhongguo Jiaohui shi lunwenji*, 90.
2. Zhao, 91.
3. Yao, *Fundamentalist Movement*, 186.

However, China was changing. The 1911 Revolution did not provide adequate answers to the nation's search for its national and cultural identity. According to Richard T. Phillips, the revolution of 1911 remained "superficial." The immediate fundamental changes usually associated with a revolution – such as changes in the social structure or in the distribution of wealth and economic activities – did not take place.[4] At the same time, China continued to be exploited by foreign powers. Nationalism, particularly in the urban centres, began to dominate and, influenced by Marxist and Leninist ideology, became increasingly confrontational.[5] Patriotism was often coupled with an increasing anti-imperialist sentiment. As Jessie G. Lutz points out, with increasing social and political turmoil, nationalism became the cement that held China together.[6] Lam Wing Hung (林榮洪) comments that the Chinese were looking for an opportunity "to release their long-suppressed nationalistic feeling."[7] Lam gives a detailed analysis on how the Christian church was condemned as the instrument of Western imperialists to enslave the Chinese people mentally and spiritually.[8]

The May Fourth Movement of 1917 to 1921 not only gave rise to an overhaul of traditional Chinese culture and an appreciation of democracy and science, it also allowed "a free market for thought and turning from their common hostility to the traditional order and were confronted with a diversity of social philosophies and models."[9] Many young Chinese intellectuals and urban elites were questioning if China needed Christianity at all.[10] There was a growing belief that Christianity was retarding modern progress and that the Chinese should save China from Western domination.[11] Interestingly, the weapons used against religious groups were taken from Western philosophers and thinkers such as Descartes, Darwin, and Marx. The major argument against religion was that all religious faith is dogmatic and, hence, unscientific

---

4. Phillips, *China since 1911*, 32.

5. Phillips, 28–29.

6. Lutz, *Chinese Politics*, 285.

7. Lam Wing Hung 林榮洪, *Fengchaozhong fenqi de Zhongguo jiaohui* 風潮中奮起的中國教會 (Chinese Theology in Construction), 138–145.

8. Lam Wing Hung, Chinese Theology in Construction, 138–145.

9. Chow, *May Fourth Movement*, 215–216.

10. *Chinese Recorder* (1921): 804.

11. *Chinese Recorder* (1921): 804.

and emotional instead of rational.[12] According to this argument, all religions originated from the ignorance and fear of primitive people.

The Anti-Christian Movement was formalized with the formation of the Anti-Christian Student Federation by a group of nationalistic students in March 1922. Many of China's intellectuals felt that China must be forged into a strong progressive nation without the influence and control of the imperial West. National campaigns demanded the elimination of mission schools and religious teaching by foreigners.[13] Thus, at the World Student Christian Federation Conference held in Beijing in April 1922, a group of radical students from Shanghai openly denounced Christianity as the "running dog" of the capitalist class from the West.[14] The Anti-Christian Movement was perceived as a war against Western cultural aggression as part of anti-imperialism.[15]

Tension was already high, with increasing hostility towards Christians and missionaries in some major cities, and there were anti-Christian demonstrations, particularly following the May Thirtieth Incident in 1925, where Chinese students were killed. The National Students' Union of China had determined to launch a major demonstration against Christians in different cities on Christmas Day 1925.[16] A new periodical entitled "Anti-Christianity" made its appearance in 1926 to advocate for the Anti-Christian Movement.[17] As an example of the agitation, Chinese staff went on strike at the CIM Kaifeng Hospital in Henan.[18] The CIM considered Henan one of the provinces most affected by anti-Christian propaganda. "The schoolboys in the province were taught to sing a hymn of hate, the refrain of which was 'hate Britain, hate Japan, down with Imperialism.'"[19]

By 1927, the situation had deteriorated further. Many of the churches established by the CIM faced demonstrations and, sometimes, severe attacks

---

12. Chow, *May Fourth Movement*, 324–325.
13. Latourette, *History of Christian Missions*, 697.
14. Lutz, *Chinese Politics*, 55.
15. Tao Feiya 陶飛亞 has a detailed analysis on this subject in his book *Christianity and Contemporary China Politics*, 19–43.
16. *China's Millions* (February 1926): 31.
17. *China's Millions* (March 1926): 46.
18. *China's Millions* (March 1926): 40.
19. *China's Millions* (July 1926): 106.

by mobs. Threats and slogans such as "Destroy Christianity," "Down with the church," and "Do away with Christians" were issued everywhere.[20] In August 1927, James Stark (1867–1958), secretary of the China Council of the CIM, reported that almost all the British and American missionaries of the CIM and all except forty from Scandinavia had to withdraw to the coastal cities as the consuls of the different countries had called upon all their nationals to withdraw to the coast.[21] The tide of xenophobia was on the rise. By the end of 1927, there was a massive exodus of more than 5,000 of the 8,300 Protestant missionaries in China.[22] This was one of the most severe crises that the Christian missionary community had encountered since the Boxer Uprising.

It is against this historical backdrop that this chapter attempts to explore how Hoste, as the leader of the CIM, responded to the crisis.

First, we will look at the relationship between the Chinese church and the CIM in this context. As mentioned earlier, the Edinburgh World Missionary Conference in 1910 facilitated the formation of the China Continuation Committee (CCC) in 1913 with the visit of John R. Mott to China. The CCC was only meant to be a temporary body, composed of both missionaries and Chinese Christians. However, the most significant development arising as a result of the CCC was the formation of the National Christian Council (NCC) in 1922. The CIM, one of the largest mission organizations at that time, was deeply involved in the discussions during the formation of the NCC. Hoste was totally committed to the NCC's goal of helping the Chinese church to be self-supporting, self-governing, and self-propagating. The NCC also aimed to promote evangelization in China and facilitate communication between missionaries and Chinese Christians.[23] However, Hoste was extremely uncomfortable with the increasingly liberal position taken by the NCC and, ultimately, this led to the decision to sever the relationship between the CIM and the NCC.

---

20. *China's Millions* (July 1927): 105.

21. *China's Millions* (August 1927): 118. Some of the Scandinavian missionaries had to return to their stations because bandits attacked them along the way and also because the railway track had been destroyed. For details, see *China's Millions* (August 1927): 118.

22. Latourette, *History of Christian Missions*, 820; see also Boynton and Boynton, *Handbook*, 447–515.

23. Yao, *Fundamentalist Movement*, 187.

Second, we will examine the "Statement of Policy" introduced by Hoste in establishing self-governing, self-supporting, and self-propagating churches. In comparison with *The Principles and Practice* (P&P) – which was basically the constitution of the CIM, formulated by its founder, Taylor – the Statement of Policy introduced by Hoste was a fresh interpretation of the P&P, particularly with regard to the CIM's relationship with the Chinese church. The Statement of Policy fundamentally changed the way the CIM operated, clearly placing the missionaries in a supporting role to the Chinese churches rather than in a leading role. The missionaries were to model the way by spiritual influence but avoid direct control over church matters.

Third, we will look at the response to the Statement of Policy by the CIM missionaries and the Chinese churches. The Statement of Policy was intended to be applicable to all CIM workers in the different provinces. However, it was noted that not all the churches had reached the same stage of mature development with regard to either organization or Christian experience. Thus, Hoste realized that the implementation of the Statement of Policy had to be done in stages. A critical survey carried out in 1931 revealed that in many districts many churches were still not prepared to take on the challenge of leadership as they were too accustomed to depending on CIM missionaries. Hoste's "Statement of Policy" clearly outlined what CIM missionaries should do to hasten the indigenization process.[24]

Finally, we will examine Hoste's two-pronged strategy in leading the CIM with the Forward Movement in 1929. Hoste was committed both to establishing the indigenous Chinese church and also to moving forward by sending more CIM missionaries to the inlands of China where churches had not yet been established. During the period 1929–1931, the CIM successfully received over two hundred new missionaries. However, the road towards establishing indigenous churches was not so straightforward. I will critically review the Forward Movement to reveal some of its achievements and failures and the reasons behind these.

---

24. *China's Millions* (July 1931): 120.

2. Dilemma concerning the National Christian Council

Hoste had always advocated the establishment of a strong, self-supporting, self-governing Chinese church, but the Anti-Christian Movement had made this need even more urgent. However, it was not always easy to clearly determine who represented the Chinese church and to whom the CIM should officially relate.

In May 1922, the National Christian Council (NCC) was established at the Chinese National Christian Conference held in Shanghai. The main function of the NCC was "to serve as a central body whereby all Christian forces in China might express themselves unitedly upon great moral questions, and to take action in matters of common interest."[25] Four CIM missionaries, including Hoste, and four Chinese church leaders associated with the CIM were elected to be on the National Christian Council.[26]

The NCC spoke strongly about the "Sinification of Christianity," urging missionaries to blend into the Chinese Christian community by not forcing development into any Western form but contributing to the spirit of Christianity, leaving that spirit to express itself in purely Chinese fashion.[27] This view was supported by the CIM. However, the CIM was increasingly concerned about the growing influence of liberal theology and how this might affect the NCC. The CIM had always maintained a conservative theological and doctrinal position, centred on biblical authority, the deity of Christ, and commitment to the proclamation of the gospel.[28] The CIM was extremely concerned that the NCC was beginning to drift away from the traditional beliefs in the ultimate authority of the Bible and a supernatural Christology. Instead, like other liberal groups, the NCC was overemphasizing the social and ethical implications of Christology rather than the salvation of Christ.[29] The NCC had taken the position that "China needs a Christ who is simple and not hopelessly entangled in creeds and dogmas."[30] Hence, the relevance of the virgin birth, the miracles performed by Jesus, and bodily resurrection

---

25. *China's Millions* (May 1926): 7
26. *China's Millions* (May 1926): 7.
27. *Chinese Recorder* (1922): 169–170.
28. "China Council Minutes" (September 1928): 8.
29. Yao, *Fundamentalist Movement*, 52.
30. *Chinese Recorder* (March 1931): 175.

were all downplayed. Instead, Jesus Christ was portrayed as a perfect human moral example, and his sacrifice on the cross was viewed purely as a call for mutual love among humans.[31]

Even before the official formation of the NCC in May 1922, the CIM China Council held a separate meeting in April to deliberate on this issue. At that meeting, Hoste had expressed caution about the NCC's theological position and his dilemma regarding the CIM's relationship with the NCC. On the one hand, the CIM China Council valued the strategic role of the NCC in assisting the development of indigenous churches. On the other, they felt the need to remain "vigilant" to ensure that the doctrinal position of the CIM was upheld.[32]

Initially, Hoste pushed the NCC to adopt a doctrinal resolution consistent with the CIM's core beliefs.[33] The proposed doctrinal resolution focused on the authority of the Bible, the deity of Christ, and salvation through his atonement.[34] This doctrinal position was based on Article 7 of the CIM's *Principles and Practice* (P&P) that had been formulated by its founder, Hudson Taylor. However, Hoste's proposal was rejected by some leaders at the Chinese National Christian Conference in 1922. This was not because of the doctrines themselves but because they felt that the NCC – which was the official central body representing Christians in China – should be just an advisory body, helping churches to work together, but having no authority on doctrinal or ecclesiastical matters. In the end, a compromise was reached and a decision made to pass a doctrinal resolution at the Business Committee of the National Christian Conference instead of formally inserting a statement into the National Christian Council (NCC) constitution. Hoste seemed to have felt that this decision was a reasonable compromise.

Unlike in the case of the previous three conferences, over half of the 1,200 delegates at the Chinese National Christian Conference in 1922 were Chinese, with all Protestant denominations represented.[35] Hoste was keen to maintain unity and not cause division among missionary organizations. In the end, the

---

31. *Chinese Recorder* (March 1931): 175.
32. "China Council Minutes" (April 1922): 1.
33. Yao, *Fundamentalist Movement*, 198.
34. "China Council Minutes" (1922): 1.
35. Kepler, "Movements for Christian Unity," 83.

CIM, under Hoste's leadership, agreed to join the NCC because they felt that it was important for the CIM to stand in solidarity with the Chinese church.[36]

Some CIM missionaries misunderstood Hoste's intention and were concerned that the Mission might have compromised its own theological stance by joining the NCC. One such missionary, John Fall (1872–1961), wrote to Hoste, objecting to the CIM joining the NCC and expressing the view that it was inconsistent to have fellowship with the NCC, which did not hold the doctrinal tenets of the CIM. Fall felt that the NCC might give in to the pressure and assist in "strengthening the Anti-Christian Movement."[37] Thus, he, together with his wife, felt obliged to tender their resignation. In response to this sign of mistrust, Hoste replied graciously, indicating that the CIM's principle should be one of cooperation without compromising essential truth.[38] Based on what Hoste wrote, Fall and his wife withdrew their resignation. However, Hoste's decision that the CIM should join the NCC caused quite a stir among CIM missionaries and supporters. In fact, the London Council of the CIM wrote requesting that Hoste send out a letter to all the Home Councils, reassuring them that the CIM had not compromised its doctrinal position.[39] Unfortunately, the concerns expressed regarding the NCC by some CIM missionaries and the Home Councils came true only too soon.

The NCC's lack of a conservative doctrinal statement at its inauguration in 1922 allowed the organization to move towards a much more liberal position in days to come. Between 1920 and 1930, the NCC leadership began to steer the organization further and further towards the liberal side under the theme of "applied Christianity" with an emphasis on "social and industrial issues," "international relations," etc, with the proclamation of a clearly social gospel agenda.[40]

In 1925, less than three years after the NCC was founded, the China Council of the CIM, under Hoste's leadership, had to deliberate on whether the difficult decision to consider withdrawing from the NCC was necessary. One main reason was that the NCC had increasingly taken on a liberal

---

36. "Report of the CIM Mission Conference Shanghai, 1 May 1922," CIM Papers, 3–40, CIM Philadelphia Archives, Billy Graham Center Archives, Wheaton College, 124.
37. "China Council Minutes" (January 1923): 11.
38. "China Council Minutes" (January 1923): 12.
39. "China Council Minutes" (April 1923): 11.
40. Hodgkin, "National Christian Council," 67; see also Yao, *Fundamentalist Movement*, 192.

Modernist view, questioning the deity of Christ.[41] Hoste, representing the CIM, defended the evangelical Mission's tradition of upholding biblical authority and the deity of Christ.[42] The1926 CIM China Council minutes also noted that the NCC had adopted a stance that supported violent protests against foreigners. Hoste, along with other CIM leaders, felt that the NCC had "constituted unwarranted interference in political affairs lying outside its proper sphere."[43] Hoste considered withdrawing from the NCC "extremely undesirable" as such a decision could be perceived by others as indicating that the CIM lacked "a sympathy with Chinese Christians"; nevertheless, he recognized that such withdrawal was necessary.[44] Before making this drastic decision, the China Council felt that it would be appropriate for Hoste to first seek advice from some key Chinese Christian leaders.

Towards this end, Hoste made a special trip to Hangchow (Hangzhou) to visit Pastor Ren Chengyuan (任櫸園, 1852–1929), just three years before Ren passed away.[45] Ren was the CIM's senior Chinese delegate on the NCC, and Hoste consulted him on this challenging matter. Pastor Ren, "whilst on some grounds regretting the possible severance of CIM's connection with the National Christian Council, felt that in the circumstances given, this was called for."[46] Thus, the CIM officially left the NCC on 15 March 1926 when Hoste wrote a letter to the secretary of the NCC indicating the Mission's withdrawal.[47] The CIM was not the only mission that severed its association with the NCC. The Christian and Missionary Alliance also withdrew from the NCC in 1926.[48]

---

41. "China Council Minutes" (March 1926): 8.

42. Yao, *Fundamentalist Movement*, 285.

43. "China Council Minutes" (December 1925):14; see also Hamrin and Bieler, *More Lives of Faith*, 50–51.

44. "China Council Minutes" (December 1925): 15.

45. Pastor Ren established one of the first self-supporting churches of the CIM in Hangzhou around 1877. For details, see Tiedemann, *Handbook of Christianity*, 269.

46. "China Council Minutes" (March 1926): 1.

47. *China's Millions* (May 1926): 79.

48. Yao, *Fundamentalist Movement*, 205.

The CIM's decision to withdraw from the NCC was inevitable as the gap between the evangelicals and the liberals was too large to bridge.[49] However, it must have been a painful decision for Hoste because he deeply honoured the CIM fundamental value of unity and oneness within the Christian community in China, and particularly with the Chinese church. Hoste believed that the CIM should make every effort to contribute to this cause without compromising essential truth. Even Taylor, the founder of the CIM, was able to be involved in committees consisting of people with theological positions different from those of the CIM.[50] But the NCC had strayed too far from the CIM's doctrinal and theological position.

Now that the decision to withdraw had been made this allowed Hoste to devote his undivided energy to something much more important than to being entangled in church politics brought on by doctrinal differences. In order to see the establishment of a truly self-supporting and self-governing Chinese church, Hoste recognized that changes within the CIM had to be a priority. To this end, he addressed the CIM's approach to missionary work and its mode of operation by issuing the "Statement of Policy" in the late 1920s.

3. Hoste and the Groundbreaking "Statement of Policy"

After the May Thirtieth Incident in Shanghai in 1925 – which highlighted a rising anti-foreigner sentiment – many mission organizations were forced to rethink their relationship with the Chinese church. A preliminary discussion was carried out at the CIM's China Council in July 1927 in the context of the Anti-Christian Movement during the period that many missionaries were not yet able to return to the fields after the massive exodus from the inlands. Despite this difficult situation, the China Council concluded that there would still be "openings for preaching the Gospel and teaching the Scriptures by foreign missionaries in the future."[51] Hoste made his personal view clear by stressing that, although it would be unwise to issue a pronouncement right

---

49. Hoste left the NCC but became a member of the Bible Union of China, a conservative group established in 1920 that counteracted the liberal position of the NCC. See Lam, Wing Hung, *A Half Century of Chinese Theology*, 300–301.

50. "China Council Minutes" (January 1923): 1–39.

51. "China Council Minutes" (July 1927): 7.

away, the role of CIM missionaries should only be that of "advisers" and "helpers" to the Chinese leaders in Chinese church affairs.[52] The Council agreed that further consideration should be given Hoste's recommendation.[53]

The words "advisers" and "helpers" were carefully chosen by Hoste. Being "advisers and helpers" represented a significant philosophical change for the CIM's mode of operation. Since the time of Taylor, the CIM founder, although local Christian workers had worked together with CIM missionaries in many CIM stations in the different provinces, they had only been considered "helpers" to the CIM missionaries. Now, Hoste was proposing a complete reversal in the role of CIM missionaries – they were to become helpers to the Chinese church and church leaders, rather than the other way round.

Hoste felt that in order to gain support for this significant change, he should consult with his own troops. Three special consultation gatherings were arranged in Chefoo (芝罘, that is, Yantai, 烟臺), Tientsin (天津, Tianjin), and Shanghai during the period July–October 1927 to consider the opinions of CIM missionaries about the future of their work and its relationship to the Chinese church. Hoste was keen to "secure the intelligent and cordial concurrence of all those concerned."[54] The goal was to come up with a "Statement of Policy" for the guidance of the missionaries in future work.

After the three consultations, careful steps were taken. Two sub-councils were formed, with one group – chaired by George W. Gibb (1869–1940), a China Council member and also deputy director of the CIM – to draft a "Statement of Policy" and the other group, chaired by Hoste, to "outline a method of procedures whereby the stated policy could be best brought to the notice of and commended to the Chinese leaders as well as the most effective means by which the conclusions ultimately reached could be put into practice."[55]

It was noted that a total of 417 missionaries of the CIM from fourteen provinces were present at these three consultations. Great care was also taken to consult with leaders from the Home Councils, including those in Great Britain, North America, and Australasia, as well as with missionaries from

---

52. "China Council Minutes" (July 1927): 6–7.
53. "China Council Minutes" (July 1927): 6–7.
54. "China Council Minutes" (November 1927): 3.
55. "China Council Minutes" (November 1927): 4.

the interior. Accordingly, an important conference was held in London on 7 February 1928, attended by most of the CIM missionaries on furlough and by representatives of the Home Council, members of the Home Staff, retired missionaries, and trainees.[56] Rarely had a consultation on such a large scale been carried out across the whole enterprise of the CIM. Acknowledging Hoste's critical leadership and his long-term relationship with the Chinese, the China Council believed that Hoste should be the person to communicate the final decision to the Chinese church leaders.

While consultations with various Home Councils were still continuing on the matter of the Statement of Policy, an editorial with the interesting title – "A New Policy?" – was published in the March 1928 edition of *China's Millions*.[57] This article was published in response to some who questioned if the new policy that Hoste had proposed was really new. The editorial comments in *China's Millions* clearly state that it would be a "serious misconception" to construe that the CIM was embarking on a new policy. Since the CIM was adhering to its goal of establishing self-supporting, self-governing, and self-propagating churches in China, the proposals now under consideration were in no sense new. The CIM was not "adopting an opportunist policy, dictated by the exigencies of an ever-changing situation." Rather, Hoste's proposal was, in fact, an outgrowth and development of the first principles of the CIM because of "the current conditions which imperatively demanded the change and at the same time provided an unprecedented opportunity for the application of those principles, which are themselves based on Apostolic method and practice."[58]

In order to help CIM supporters understand the intention behind Hoste's proposal, *China's Millions* clearly indicated that the "Statement of Policy" was not a diversion from the original direction and purpose of Taylor, Hoste's predecessor. Many supporters of the CIM were still faithful admirers of Taylor, subscribing to strong values of faith and prayer. Any hint that Hoste's proposal was opportunistic or merely a tactical response to a rising need, particularly financial needs, would have been seen as deviating from the CIM's fundamental principle of trusting in God alone. Thus, Hoste was careful to

---

56. *China's Millions* (March 1928): 47.
57. *China's Millions* (March 1928): 24.
58. *China's Millions* (March 1928): 24.

demonstrate that the proposed change had to do with the maturity and the growth of the Chinese church, which was in line with Taylor's original vision of the indigenous church.

A man with a careful mind, Hoste assigned Gibb to visit all the Home Councils in Britain, Australia, and the United States to seek their views on the proposed Statement of Policy – a process that took nine months.[59] Finally, at the September 1928 China Council meeting, Hoste, with the whole China Council, hammered out the details of the Statement of Policy based on feedback received from CIM missionaries and the Home Councils. The Statement of Policy consisted of six main topics that cover three major concerns: church organization, Chinese workers, institutional work, finance, the future ministry of missionaries, and mission property.[60]

The Statement of Policy basically examined three main areas: church organization and leadership, actual operation, and financial matters.

First, with regard to church organization and leadership, Hoste and the China Council proposed that all churches established by the CIM should proceed without delay with "the nomination, election and appointment of Chinese Church officers in order to carry out the Mission policy of establishing self-supporting, self-governing, self-propagating churches."[61] In addition, they proposed that the oversight of church matters – including the appointment of church officers and workers – be handed over to the local leadership and that CIM missionaries assigned to a particular station should not be entitled to any office in the Chinese church. It was recognized that for a missionary to assume such an office would retard the process of the Chinese church in becoming self-supporting and self-governing.

The key emphasis of this policy, which particularly addressed the Chinese church leadership and their relationship with the missionaries, was "without delay." Delay could be due to many factors, including the reluctance of the missionaries to let go of authority, the unwillingness of Chinese church leaders to take on leadership, or just plain procrastination. Hoste was keen to see changes happening on the ground as soon as possible.

---

59. "China Council Minutes" (November 1917): 1, 14.
60. "China Council Minutes" (September 1928): 6.
61. "China Council Minutes" (September 1928): 6.

Second, on the actual operations, all Chinese workers should be jointly selected by and under the supervision of a district or provincial committee of the Chinese church leaders together with the CIM missionaries assigned to that region. The Chinese church was also expected to assume responsibility "on a gradual increasing scale," including financial support of these Chinese workers. Chinese workers for whose support the Chinese church did not assume any responsibility should be retired. The intention was to encourage the Chinese church to take on increasing responsibility for their own workers associated with the CIM.

However, when it came to institutional work, particularly in relation to Bible institutions and CIM-run hospitals, it was recommended that CIM missionaries continue to take on leadership responsibilities, while committees composed of both "Chinese Christians and foreign missionaries" would oversee the appointment, management, and discipline of Chinese members of the staff of such institutions. The difference in the recommendation between institutions and churches was probably because the Chinese church was not yet ready to supply the more trained personnel required for hospitals and Bible schools.

Third, regarding financial matters, it was recommended that any foreign contribution for the support of local Chinese workers within the jurisdiction of the church be paid to the church committee and that any such foreign assistance should be progressively reduced with a view to final termination. Yearly statements of accounts, showing the proportion from Chinese and foreign sources, should be regarded as a condition for continuing such grants. The aim of this policy was to see the local churches take on full financial responsibility for supporting local Chinese workers, with a view to terminating foreign support in the long term.

Finally, the Statement of Policy gave rise to the challenging task of repositioning the role of the CIM long-term missionaries to be "advisers" of the Chinese church with no official authority but only spiritual influence. The policy specified that administrative oversight be given to Chinese church leaders and that great efforts be taken to "develop younger churches along self-supporting and self-governing lines."

Hoste, with the China Council, recommended that property for missionary residences should, if possible, be rented rather than purchased.[62] This

---

62. "China Council Minutes" (September 1928): 10.

would make it possible for the missionaries to "pass onto other spheres as soon as the church has been gathered." They also specified that the Provincial Council of the CIM should give definite consideration "to the question of the entire or partial withdrawal of missionaries from some of the stations where there were already strong churches"[63] and that the CIM should give "sympathetic consideration" to the request of Chinese church leaders and allow CIM property to come under church control. If the church was already self-supporting and self-governing, the CIM should consider transferring the property to a central board of trustees under the Chinese church. A committee of Chinese church leaders and missionaries should be appointed to determine what sum, if any, the church should pay for the property.[64]

A few points regarding the Statement of Policy are worthy of particular attention.

First, the editorial comments in the March 1928 *China's Millions* declaring that the proposal of the Statement of Policy was not new are important. Since the days of Hudson Taylor, the establishment of self-supporting, self-governing, and self-propagating churches in China had always been the aim of the CIM. In fact, Taylor used the analogy of a "scaffolding" to refer to the CIM, stating that he looked "on foreign missionaries as the scaffolding around a rising building, the sooner it can be dispensed with, the better – or rather, the sooner it can be transferred to other places to serve the same temporary purpose."[65] Therefore, what Hoste was proposing was a detailed implementation of Taylor's concept.

Second, there was a strong emphasis on the transfer of church leadership to the Chinese. Following from this, CIM missionaries could not unilaterally recruit any Chinese workers without the endorsement of the local church. At times, CIM missionaries had taken on Chinese workers whom the local Chinese churches were not willing to support financially because they had deemed them unsuitable or unqualified. The implication of this policy was that the CIM should not work alone but always serve in cooperation with the Chinese church. It is also important to note that Hoste proposed that missionary residences should not be purchased but rented to enable

---

63. "China Council Minutes" (September 1928): 10–12.
64. "China Council Minutes" (September 1928): 10–11.
65. Taylor and Taylor, *Growth of a Work of God*, 232.

missionaries to remain mobile and free to move on to other places once the church was established.

Third, there seems to be a difference between churches and institutions – such as Bible schools and hospitals – when it came to the way the transfer of leadership was handled. While the transfer of leadership in the Chinese church context was intended to be definite and immediate, the transfer of leadership in institutions seemed to have only been partial. This might have been because institutions such as hospitals would have required leadership with professional skills and Bible schools might have required staff who had gone through at least some level of theological training. For example, almost all CIM-run hospitals were led by qualified medical missionaries such as Dr. Harold Schofield, who was responsible for medical work in Taiyuan.[66] The Chinese church had not yet reached the stage where it could provide such trained human resources.

Fourth, Hoste took great care to achieve a consensus in confirming the Statement of Policy. Prior to Hoste, under Taylor's leadership, decision-making within the CIM had been much more centralized and directive. To gain support for the Statement of Policy, Hoste scheduled three special consultations in Shanghai, Tientsin (Tianjin), and Chefoo, attended by more than four hundred CIM missionaries. In addition, a special envoy led by George. W. Gibb was sent to the Home Council, particularly in England and the US, to seek the support and endorsement of Council members there. Hoste was keen to "secure the intelligent and cordial concurrence of all those involved."[67] In addition, an abridged version of the Statement of Policy in Chinese that included a cover note from Hoste was provided for Chinese church leaders.[68]

Finally, there was an initial discussion and debate within the CIM China Council about whether the Statement of Policy was to be promulgated as instructions or as recommendations to the Mission.[69] In the process of dis-

---

66. Broomhall, *Shaping of Modern China*, 338; see also Broomhall, 119. In fact, Taylor was concerned that all CIM missionaries involved in medical mission work should be fully qualified professionally. In 1870, he wrote to the Home Council in Britain saying that "in future candidates should complete their medical training or do none at all."

67. "China Council Minutes" (November 1927): 3.

68. "China Council Minutes" (November 1927): 11. Although this was also recorded in "China Council Minutes" (28 September 1928): 14–15, this copy of the Chinese translation cannot be traced.

69. "China Council Minutes" (November 1927): 18.

cussion, even the constitutional rights of CIM missionaries were considered.[70] In the end, the China Council decided that neither the term "Instructions" nor "Recommendations" should be employed and that it would be better to issue the Statement of Policy as coming from the China Council based upon the recommendations of the three consultative conferences held in Shanghai, Tientsin, and Chefoo. The Council, under Hoste's leadership, also stated that due consideration would be given to the circumstances of particular stations, recognizing that the implementation of the Policy would need to be done in stages in some cases.[71]

After much discussion and debate, with many rounds of revisions to the draft, the Statement of Policy, including a doctrinal section, was finally completed and confirmed at the China Council meeting in September 1928,[72] and Hoste wrote to all the CIM missionaries on 3 November 1928, informing them about the Statement.[73] A review of the records of the China Council minutes, particularly between 1927 and 1929, the period during which the Statement of Policy was introduced and discussed, does not reveal a single record of resignation by CIM missionaries due to the Statement of Policy. It would be fair to conclude that the Statement of Policy was generally accepted by CIM missionaries. However, when the Statement of Policy was initially launched, the CIM missionaries discovered that many Chinese churches were not quite ready for the change.[74] We will explore this further in our next section.

4. Concerns of the Chinese Church

In April 1929, James Stark, the secretary of the CIM based at the Shanghai mission headquarters, reported that Hoste had sent a letter explaining the Statement of Policy to the Chinese church leaders in the various provinces. However, it was noted that "not a few unforeseen problems had arisen as the churches had not all reached the same stage of development either as regards to organization or spiritual experience. Many were still small and weak."[75]

---

70. "China Council Minutes" (November 1927): 19.
71. "China Council Minutes" (November 1927): 19.
72. "China Council Minutes" (September 1928): 8.
73. *China's Millions* (May 1929): 67.
74. *China's Millions* (April 1929): 56.
75. *China's Millions* (April 1929): 56.

Moreover, in some of the provinces, famine conditions had seriously affected the financial resources of the church members, reducing their ability to give. Thus, some churches requested that the implementation of the Statement of Policy be delayed.[76]

G. W. Bailey (1898–1951), a CIM missionary who worked in Kinhwa (金華, Jinhua) in Zhejiang, published an insightful article entitled "Transference of Oversight to the Chinese Church" in *China's Millions* in May 1929. Bailey highlighted three problems that the Chinese church had encountered when the CIM attempted to implement the Statement of Policy – namely, "Method, Money and Men."[77] First, the Chinese church leaders realized that in their attempt to be self-governing, they could not just use the methods previously adopted by the missionaries because they desired to come up with their own methods. Second, regarding money or self-support, they felt that it was important to streamline the resources, thus reducing the number of CIM stations. Third, regarding workers, they felt that some of the local workers recruited by the CIM missionaries were unsuitable and did not meet the requirement of the church council. Thus, CIM missionaries were asked by the churches involved to retire these local workers. It became obvious that once the Statement of Policy was truly implemented, the CIM missionaries would need to learn to let go of control.

It became clear that the Chinese church and the missionaries operated in very different ways. It is also important to see that when the Chinese leaders were able to express their own views and perspectives – which often differed from those of the CIM missionaries – a breakthrough was achieved, leading to the maturity of the Chinese church. At times, these Chinese church leaders even challenged the way the CIM missionaries operated. Nearly thirty years after his paper was first published in 1900 in the *Chinese Recorder*, Hoste's prediction that the Chinese native leaders "will prove themselves equal to the facing of danger and bearing of responsibilities, grow into leadership and would come to the front" had indeed come true.[78]

In some provinces, there were encouraging reports of considerable progress with the implementation of the Statement of Policy. One such report

---

76. *China's Millions* (April 1929): 56.
77. *China's Millions* (May 1929): 76.
78. Hoste, "Possible Changes," 509–512.

came from Wenchow (溫州, Wenzhou), where the general oversight of the churches had fallen upon the local pastors. All the regular quarterly and annual meetings were presided over, in every detail, by Chinese leaders. It was reported that "the missionary was no longer the deciding factor."[79] The churches were all moving towards self-support and self-government. Another report came from Hopei (河北, Hebei), indicating that the Chinese version of the Statement of Policy had been distributed to the church members and that the Chinese Christians "appreciated the goodwill which permeated the whole."[80] The churches in Hebei, similar to those in Wenzhou, were moving towards self-support and self-government. Yet another report came from Tali (大理, Dali), Yunnan, indicating that one church in particular was "enthusiastic" about the Statement of Policy. It had thus begun to formulate its church constitution, and the the church now had a free hand in the choice of officers and evangelists, while previous evangelists paid by the CIM had stepped down.[81] From these three examples, we can see that there was a trend towards CIM-related churches moving towards indigenization, marked by self-support and self-government.

Despite the positive response from the CIM-related Chinese churches, the initial implementation of the Statement of Policy introduced by Hoste was rather slow and patchy among the different CIM stations. By 1929, though missionaries were allowed to move back into the interior of China, many were still recovering from the aftermath of the Anti-Christian Movement. Both the Chinese churches and CIM missionaries were trying to understand and work out how they should relate to each other. Hoste reminded the missionaries that for the Statement of Policy to be realized, there needed to be cooperation between the CIM and the Chinese church. He reiterated that without the active involvement of the Chinese church, the work would be fruitless. As Hoste saw it, the availability of Chinese church leadership was a key factor. So, in his research, pointed out that "the training of capable Chinese leaders" thus became a priority that was of utmost importance to the CIM.[82] So's research on Leslie Lyall, a CIM missionary who worked among Chinese intellectuals

---

79. *China's Millions* (May 1929): 76.
80. *China's Millions* (April 1929): 59–60.
81. *China's Millions* (1929): 71.
82. So, "Passion for a Greater Vision," 120–121. Leslie Lyall coined the term "Forward Movement" for his work among students and intellectuals in preparation for the future of the

with the vision of preparing the future of the Chinese church, illustrates the CIM's desire to develop future Chinese church leaders.[83]

5. Hoste and the Forward Movement

While the situation in 1927 was challenging, with most CIM missionaries forced out of the inland because of the anti-Christian sentiment, by the end of 1928, things had become much more stable. However, the return of CIM missionaries to the inland took place in a different setting and under a different paradigm after the introduction of the Statement of Policy. More CIM missionaries were freer to move into the interior, focusing on pioneering work by reassigning the administration of existing churches to the Chinese Christians.

By the end of 1928, as the Anti-Christian Movement came to an end, more than 840 CIM missionaries had already returned to the field.[84] Many who had been evacuated from the interior since 1927 because of the Anti-Christian Movement were eager to go back into inland China. With the doors to inland China being reopened, the 1928 edition of *China's Millions* revealed that even more workers were needed.

The 1928 *China's Millions* presented a convincing case as to why more missionaries were needed in the interior. First, surveys were being conducted to assess all "walled-cities and strategic points" to know the extent of the need.[85] According to the CIM, there were still 333 counties – with 166,500 towns and villages and a population of 38,508,305 – without a single evangelistic centre or a single Christian in inland China.[86] The CIM had so far assumed mission responsibility in only seventy out of the three hundred counties in the inland, with the majority still largely unreached.[87] Second, consideration was given to work beyond China. Mildred Cable (1878–1952), one of the CIM missionaries, prepared the "Survey of Central Asia," challenging the CIM to accept the responsibility for evangelism in Central Asia beyond China's

---

Chinese church. He became a significant leader of the third generation of the CIM, particularly in the transition from the old CIM to the Overseas Missionary Fellowship (OMF) after 1951.

83. So, 120–121.
84. *China's Millions* (June 1929): 86.
85. *China's Millions* (April 1928): 57.
86. *China's Millions* (March 1928): 47.
87. *China's Millions* (November 1929): 168.

borders.[88] The statistics undoubtedly showed a compelling reason for the launching of such a Forward Movement.

Faced with this new challenge, Hoste advocated and launched a significant campaign called the Forward Movement (initially called the Forward Evangelistic Movement).[89] The term was used for the first time in 1928 by Frank Houghton (1894–1972) – a CIM missionary in West China and the editorial secretary of *China's Millions* – who claimed, "God is calling us to a forward movement of widespread evangelism."[90] Hoste recognized that the Chinese churches, on whose cooperation the CIM largely depended, had hardly emerged from a period of intense struggle from the Anti-Christian Movement. The financial losses caused by the destruction of Mission property might make any serious advance impracticable.[91] But he was convinced that the time had come for the CIM to advance in the name of a Forward Movement to take "not the defensive but the offensive" posture in the preaching of the Christian faith to the millions in the inlands of China.[92]

In preparation for the launch of this Forward Movement, CIM missionary Thomas Cook (1882–1959) explained Hoste's vision at a CIM meeting in London in February 1928.[93] First, instead of taking charge of all aspects of the evangelistic work, as done in the past, the CIM missionaries should now serve as "an impetus" to inspire and "consolidate" the indigenous church. Second, the missionaries should free themselves so as to engage with the Forward Evangelization by going into the inland frontiers to begin work in the many counties where there was no church.[94] For this to happen, a "full transfer of oversight of the churches from the missionaries to the Chinese leaders should happen."[95] Thus, the Forward Movement was to consist of the two parallel aspects of an "advance": the Chinese church advancing to be fully

---

88. *China's Millions* (November 1929): 168.

89. The term "Forward Evangelistic Movement" was used in *China's Millions* (March 1928): 47, but was later discontinued. In *China's Millions* (December 1928): 190, the term "Forward Movement" was officially adopted though this term had already been used before by Hudson Taylor in 1880 in another context.

90. *China's Millions* (April 1928): 52.

91. *China's Millions* (April 1928): 52.

92. *China's Millions* (April 1928): 52; see also *China's Millions* (June 1929): 84.

93. *China's Millions* (May 1928): 72.

94. *China's Millions* (May 1928): 72.

95. Hoste, "Great Advance," 22.

independent and the CIM missionaries advancing to the work in other places in interior China where people had not been touched by the word of God.

Bearing in mind this vision, Hoste made an appeal for two hundred more workers. Although no records were published to show how Hoste came up with the number two hundred, the China Council defended this number by stating that the figure came from a careful survey of provinces where the CIM had been working to estimate the number of workers needed. The total sum came to 199 – hence the appeal for 200.[96]

On 15 March 1929, Hoste wrote an open letter to all friends and supporters of the CIM. The vision and the challenge of the Forward Movement were rolled out, as signalled by the words on the front page of the 1929 edition of *China's Millions*: "Two hundred workers needed within two years – an appeal from China to you."[97] In the letter, Hoste referred to Taylor, the founder of the Mission, who had made a similar appeal in 1882 for seventy new workers and, in 1887, for one hundred new workers.[98] Quoting Taylor, Hoste wrote, "Mere romantic feeling will soon die out in the toilsome labour and constant discomforts and trials of inland work and will not be worth much when severe illness arises and perhaps all the money is gone."[99] Hoste was well aware of the cost involved. He wrote further, "It should be added that all engaging in this forward movement must have good health and sound nerves, this being especially important in the case of those working in the more remote and isolated regions, as, in most instances, they will be without medical or nursing help."[100]

In Hoste's appeal to the churches back home to send two hundred new workers to China, one stipulation stood out. There was a strong preference for single men, who were required to be prepared to remain single for five years as they would be working in the toughest environment in the most remote and isolated areas in China.[101] In fact, when Hoste asked for two hundred work-

---

96. *China's Millions* (May 1929): 79.
97. *China's Millions* (May 1929): front page, 67.
98. *China's Millions* (June 1929): 84.
99. *China's Millions* (May 1929): 67. When Hudson Taylor made the appeal for one hundred workers in 1887, six hundred candidates applied to the China Inland Mission. The proportion of those finally accepted was only one in six. For details, see *China's Millions* (July 1929): 110.
100. *China's Millions* (May 1929): 67.
101. *China's Millions* (May 1929): 68.

ers, he asked that at least one hundred of these should be single men. Hoste was aware of the risks involved in going into the inland areas. As recently as 1928, eight CIM missionaries had died while serving on the field, and of these, five were women – including one woman who was murdered by bandits.[102]

There was active mobilization by the CIM Home Councils, particularly in Great Britain and North America. The term "Taking the Offensive" was used in *China's Millions* in 1929: "We have adopted an aggressive policy – we are taking the offensive and preparing for a great advance."[103] "Advance" leaflets were produced for recruitment.[104] Of course, this was never meant to have any political connotations but pertained only to religious beliefs. When the CIM coined the term "taking the offensive" in response to the "enemy's offensive" of persecution, it was referring to a counteroffensive in aggressive evangelization in cooperation with the Chinese church and not to offensive action by political means.[105] The CIM, under Hoste's leadership, made an impassioned appeal to the Christian public, particularly in Great Britain and North America, in view of the spiritual need of China in the aftermath of the Anti-Christian Movement.[106] As a result of this mobilization campaign, by the initial phase in October 1929, fifty-eight men and fifty-one women had applied to the CIM, with sixteen being accepted for training.[107]

By March 1930, it became apparent that "the number of men candidates accepted has been considerably less than that of the women."[108] Hoste was fully aware of the challenges ahead and spoke of a "deepened sense of tremendous opposition and dangers, both material and spiritual" that CIM missionaries had to encounter and of the uncertainty of the outlook in China.[109] Subsequently, he wrote another letter, published in the April 1930 edition of *China's Millions*, indicating that he was much "exercised in mind and heart" as he believed that "danger and death was one of the normal conditions which indeed may justly be called fundamental" for all those who might respond

---

102. *China's Millions* (June 1929): 86.
103. *China's Millions* (June 1929): 85.
104. *China's Millions* (July 1929): 110.
105. *China's Millions* (June 1929): 86.
106. *China's Millions* (June 1929): 85.
107. *China's Millions* (November 1929): 175.
108. *China's Millions* (March 1930): 46.
109. *China's Millions* (March 1930): 46. .

to the appeal for the Two Hundred.¹¹⁰ Despite Hoste's warning, more new workers continued to join the CIM.

With Hoste's strong appeal, these words appeared in the editorial of *China's Millions* in 1932: "The Completion of the Two Hundred – by December 31, 1931, the Two Hundred [had] sailed for China."¹¹¹ Hoste's appeal for two hundred new workers was a success. With the arrival of more workers, eighteen new CIM stations were opened by the end of 1929 as part of the Forward Movement; and by October 1930, more than twenty new stations were opened.¹¹² These new stations were scattered in the nineteen provinces where the CIM was already working. Most of the efforts were directed at sending workers to the inlands, which was the CIM's focus was.¹¹³

By June 1932, the CIM had received 203 new workers to work in eleven provinces out of the nineteen where the CIM was serving.¹¹⁴ Between 1928 and 1932, seventy new stations were established.¹¹⁵ The the number of CIM missionaries grew significantly under Hoste's leadership. There were 735 missionaries at the end of 1901, 900 CIM missionaries on the active list in 1907, 1,000 missionaries in 1911, 1,200 by the end of 1926, a slight decrease with 1,162 missionaries in 1929, but – with the increase of new workers due to the appeal for the two hundred between 1929 and 1932 – a total of 1,327 CIM missionaries by December 1932.¹¹⁶

With the growth in the number of CIM missionaries in response to the Forward Movement campaign, Hoste was under no illusion about the cost of this advance. The call to recruit two hundred workers came with a price. Quite a few young missionaries died within a few years of their arrival in China. One such person was Dr. Emil Fischbacher (1903–1933), who succumbed to typhoid fever after caring for wounded soldiers.¹¹⁷ He was thirty years

---

110. *China's Millions* (April 1930): 63.
111. *China's Millions* (January 1932): 3.
112. *China's Millions* (July 1930): 84, 94, 103, 121, 147, 152, 168, 193.
113. *China's Millions* (June 1931): 108.
114. *China's Millions* (June 1932): 122. See also *China's Millions* (1932), viii–x. New Forward Movement stations were established in the provinces of Anhwei (Anhui), Chekiang (Zhejiang), Kansu (Gansu), Kiangsi (Jiangxi), Kiangsu (Jiangsu), Kweichow (Guizhou), Shansi (Shanxi), Shensi (Shaanxi), Shantung (Shandong), Sinkiang (Xinjiang), and Szechuan (Sichuan).
115. *China's Millions* (December 1933): 236.
116. *China's Millions* (March 1933): 58.
117. *China's Millions* (December 1933): 135, 237.

old when he died, having barely joined the Two Hundred for the Forward Movement. In addition, many of the young missionaries who joined the Forward Movement were often isolated, being at least five or six days away from any other missionary.[118]

From the start, the Forward Movement always had a two-pronged approach, namely, the recruitment of two hundred new missionaries from the West as well as the indigenization of the Chinese church with transfer of leadership to locals. It was the latter that was proving particularly difficult to implement. As So points out, the Forward Movement was always seen by Hoste as a "joint project" between the CIM and the Chinese church.[119] However, it appeared that the Chinese church was not quite ready to play its part.

Albert Lutley (1865-1934), the CIM superintendent of Shanxi, gave some of the reasons for this unreadiness to play its part. Chinese church leaders, having grown accustomed to depending upon the missionaries for guidance, had in many cases been unwilling, or found it difficult, to take up actual leadership responsibility. There was also a lack of teaching about the importance of local Christians assuming responsibility for the support of their own churches. At the same time, a great deal of the CIM missionaries' time and strength had been taken up in attending to the details of church matters, as result of which the systematic evangelization of the surrounding towns and villages had been neglected.[120]

Lutley also pointed out that, in many places, church and mission property had been occupied by the military or brigand bands and that, in some cases, local church leaders had been killed, while others had been robbed. With civil strife, brigandage, and lawlessness, along with the loss of crops due to drought or natural disasters, many local Christians found it hard to even support their own families. Thus, the indigenization process continued to meet with difficulties in many CIM stations.[121]

---

118. *China's Millions* (March,1931): 40. See also *China's Millions* (March 1933): 58. One of these new CIM missionaries, Dr. Emil Fischbacher, who was assigned to the Xinjiang area, was at least 1,800 miles away from the nearest CIM missionary.

119. So, "Passion for a Greater Vision," 120.

120. *China's Millions* (1931): 120.

121. *China's Millions* (1931): 120.

6. Emphasis on "Brotherly" Cooperation with the Chinese Church

By 1931, Hoste was seventy years old and had been in leadership as the general director for thirty years. Since the days of the aftermath of the Boxer Uprising, he had always advocated that the Chinese church should become indigenous, self-supporting, self-governing, and self-propagating. The launching of the Forward Movement (1929–1931), with its two-pronged approach, was Hoste's final attempt to encourage both CIM missionaries and Chinese church leaders to cooperate and take the indigenization process of the Chinese church seriously before he stepped down as the general director.

One of the best summaries of how Hoste viewed the Forward Movement can be seen in his statement entitled "An Urgent Call to Action," published in *China's Millions* in March 1931. He wrote, "It is essential to the best success of the Forward Movement that the missionaries in it should have the co-operation and fellowship of Chinese colleagues. We are persuaded that the brotherly cooperation of Chinese and Westerners is, as a rule, essential for the work of widespread evangelism."[122] We can see that the primary role of the Chinese church was very much on Hoste's mind. He recognized that while there was still a long way to go for the Chinese church to rise to the challenge of self-government, it was on its way to doing so. According to Hoste, the role of the missionaries was to focus on the training and mobilization of the Chinese church.[123]

Lutley gave an insightful review of the Forward Movement, commenting that, while there was great rejoicing over the growth in the number of CIM missionaries to 1,200 with the recent addition of the two hundred, he was still concerned that there was a great deficiency in two areas. First, the lack of training of a "large number" of Chinese leaders, including evangelists and pastors who would work in the different stations, districts, and provinces. Second, the lack of a widespread "rapid transfer to Chinese leadership of the pastoral care and oversight of the Chinese Churches connected with the CIM."[124] From what Lutley wrote, it is clear that the large-scale indigenous

---

122. *China's Millions* (March 1931): 39–40.

123. One example was the work by Howard S. Cliff (1891–1963), one of the CIM missionaries in Shanxi, who promoted the mobilization of five hundred Chinese workers for the work of the Forward Movement. For details, see *China's Millions* (March 1932): 54.

124. *China's Millions* (1931): 120.

development of the Chinese churches associated with the CIM that Hoste had hoped for still had a long way to go.

In retrospect, it would be fair to say that the recruitment of the two hundred new missionary workers enabled the opening of at least seventy new CIM stations in the inlands of China by 1932.[125] However, despite some encouraging examples on a smaller scale, there was still much to be desired to see the indigenous process go forward.[126]

From a broader historical perspective, the picture was still encouraging. So comments that by the 1930s, there were already three main groups of indigenous churches, many of which were beyond the influence of the CIM.[127] The first group was represented by church leaders such as Cheng Jingyi (誠靜怡, 1881–1939), who was associated with the NCC. The second group was represented by leaders of the more Pentecostal True Jesus Church. The third group was basically evangelical in faith, represented by leaders such as Wang Mingdao (王明道, 1900–1991), John Sung (宋尚節, 1901–1944), Andrew Gih (計志文, 1901–1985), David Yang (楊紹唐, 1898–1969), and Watchman Nee (倪柝聲, 1903–1972). The CIM maintained a close cooperative relationship with these groups, particularly with the third group with whom they shared a similar evangelical doctrinal and theological position. Since the CIM was interdenominational, it did not have difficulties relating to the different evangelical church leaders.

7. Conclusion

The two crises, the Boxer Uprising and the Anti-Christian Movement, accelerated the process of indigenization in the Chinese church. However, it took another major political change almost twenty years later, that demanded the complete exodus of all missionaries, to see Hoste's vision come true.

Looking at the wider historical context, the Chinese church had continued to grow both in numbers and in strength since the Boxer Uprising. According to Latourette, church communicant membership increased fivefold between

---

125. *China's Millions* December (1933): 236.

126. *China's Millions* (May 1934): 93. One such example was reported by a CIM missionary named Adelaide I. Hill (1891–1968) from Tsishan (稷山, Jishan) in Shanxi, where the local church had become self-supporting and was able to support three full-time local preachers.

127. So, "Passion for a Greater Vision," 172.

1889 and 1905, and contributions by the Chinese church increased ninefold.[128] Organizations like the Young Men's Christian Association (YMCA) also placed Chinese believers in positions of leadership and insisted on self-support. In the year 1915, C. T. Wang (fl. 1915–1926), a local Chinese leader, succeeded Fletcher Brockman (1867–1944) as the national general secretary of the YMCA, followed by David Yui (fl.1926–1949).[129] The number of local ordained ministers rose from 764 in 1915 to 846 in 1917.[130]

Despite signs of encouraging growth and the increase in indigenous leadership, the Chinese church was confronted with two key issues.

First, Latourette makes the sharp observation that the Chinese church in general was still under foreign control. "With all this devolution, the Church remained primarily a foreign institution in both leadership and support. The task of attaining self-support was rendered difficult by the [continual] flow of funds from what seemed to the Chinese the exhaustless spring of foreign benevolence. The [Chinese] Church would obviously remain the creature of the Westerner, dependent upon artificial respiration."[131]

Second, contextualization had not been adequately addressed. In addition to Latourette, Lam presents a related but different emphasis on the needs of the Chinese church. With the impact of the May Fourth Movement (1917–1921), followed by the Anti-Christian Movement in the 1920s that produced an increasing nationalistic and patriotic sentiment, the Chinese church was condemned as the instrument of Western imperialism and cultural aggression. Lam points out that the Chinese church was struggling to find its own cultural and national identity.[132] What the Chinese church needed was not just indigenization but also contextualization, embracing a gospel that is for the Chinese. The Chinese church not only needed the missionaries to let go

---

128. Latourette, *History of Christian Missions*, 675.
129. Latourette, 763.
130. Latourette, 762.
131. Latourette, 763, 805.

132. Lam Wing Hung 林榮洪, *Fengchaozhong fenqi de Zhongguo jiaohui* 風潮中奮起的中國教會 (Chinese Theology in Construction), 138–145. Also see Zhao Tianen 趙天恩 *Zhongguo jiaohuishi lunwenji* 中國教會史論文集 (Essays on Chinese Church History), 225; Lam Wing Hung 林榮洪, "Zhanzheng yu kunan" 戰爭與苦難 in *Zhonghua shenxue wushinian* 中華神學五十年 (A Half Century of Chinese Theology), 300–301; Leung Ka-lun 梁家麟 *Fulin Zhonghua- Zhongguo jindai jiaohuishi shijiang* 福臨中華—中國近代教會史十講 (Blessing Upon China: Ten Talks on the Contemporary Church History of China), 166.

of control, what was even more important was for the missionaries to understand and appreciate Chinese culture and how the gospel could be relevant to Chinese society and the Chinese context.[133]

So points out that the Chinese church had not taken theology seriously and contextually and had not thought about how to apply the Christian faith to the Chinese culture. He attributes this to the "simple" approach adopted by the CIM.[134] So gives the example of the use of the "Wordless Book" by the CIM missionaries. According to So, the "Wordless Book" tended to oversimplify the Christian faith. Apart from creating an "anti-intellectual" impression, the "Wordless Book" also seemed to have resulted in misinterpretation as it ignored the cultural aspects of colour symbols.[135] Another scholar, Tao, also comments on the importance of missionaries understanding Chinese culture, which contributed to the critical spreading of the Christian faith and the development of education among the Chinese.[136]

Coming back to the CIM, the Statement of Policy launched by Hoste did not appear to have had an immediate significant impact on the broader Chinese church. A more recent study by Wu Yaqun (吳亞群), who focuses solely on Hoste's work, does not comment on the Statement of Policy and only touches briefly on the Forward Movement.[137]

It was always Hoste's vision to see a fully developed self-supporting, self-governing, and self-propagating Chinese church. Yet the Forward Movement, with the Statement of Policy advocated by Hoste, brought to the surface a problem that was probably known to the CIM in the past but had not been adequately addressed. Many of the churches established by the CIM were

---

133. Lam, 138–145.

134. So, "Passion for a Greater Vision," 83–86.

135. The "Wordless Book" was a tool used by CIM missionaries to explain the Christian faith simply, in a visual form, using colours to illustrate God's plan of salvation. Black stands for sin, red for Jesus's sacrifice on the cross, white for sanctification, and gold for heaven. However, while Christians associate the colour red with death, red is the symbol of good fortune in Chinese culture.

136. Tao Fei Ya 陶飛亞 "Wanqing chuanjiaoshi dui Zhongguo wenhua de yanjiu" 晚清傳教士對中國文化的研究 (The study of late-Qing missionaries and Chinese Culture) in *Bianyuan de lishi- Jidujiao yu jindai Zhongguo* 邊緣的歷史- 基督教與近代中國(Marginal History: Christianity and Contemporary China), 127–140.

137. Wu Yaqun 吳亞群. "Zhongguo Neidihui dierdai zongzhuren He-side yanjiu" 中國內地會第二代總主任何斯德研究 (A study on Dixon Edward Hoste, the second General Director of the CIM), 6–7.

not ready to rise to the challenge of taking up leadership even when the missionaries were no longer in place. For a long time, church leaders had been accustomed to depending upon the missionaries for guidance and had, in many cases, been unwilling, or found it difficult, to undertake actual leadership responsibility. One reason for this seems to have been the lack of teaching about the importance of local Christians assuming responsibility for the support of their own churches. Besides, the external adverse environment with lawlessness in many places and frequent attacks by bandits had caused much fear and unwillingness among local believers to take on responsibilities for the church.

The Statement of Policy, along with the Forward Movement in 1928–1929, was a good test case for an all-out indigenization process, revealing that both the Chinese church and the CIM were not quite ready. Yet Hoste's vision of the indigenous movement had inspired both the CIM and the Chinese church, and momentum was not lost even when Hoste had to step down from leadership. At the same time, by the 1930s, indigenous movements of the Chinese church outside CIM influence were already taking place.

It took nearly twenty years more for the Chinese church to become truly indigenous, self-supporting, self-governing, and self-propagating. This did not happen because someone adopted any strategies or methods to accomplish this but because of the reluctant exodus of all missionaries from China. As I will show in the next chapter, what Hoste did – particularly with the implementation of the Statement of Policy – laid a solid foundation and paved the way for the Chinese church to become truly indigenous when the time was ripe, which was when the Communists came into this power.[138]

---

138. Lea, "Mission and Church," 47.

CHAPTER 5

Hoste's Legacy to the CIM and the Chinese Church

1. Introduction

The spirit of "to live to be forgotten" was a key value that Hoste had held onto throughout his sixty years of missionary life in China.[1] By 1935, he was seventy-four years old and had been in China for nearly fifty years. With the China Council's regretful agreement, Hoste chaired the China Council as its general director for the last time in June 1935. It is important to note that his predecessor, Hudson Taylor, had led the CIM for thirty-five years (1865–1900). Similarly, Hoste led the CIM for the next thirty-five years (1930–1935). George W. Gibb (1869–1940) became the third general director of the CIM in 1935. However, because of ill-health, Gibb had to step down from leadership after just five years. Bishop Frank Houghton (1894–1972) became the fourth general director of the CIM in 1940.

This chapter will examine Hoste's legacy and the impact of his vision for the CIM and the Chinese church.

First, we will explore how Hoste's vision for the indigenous church continued to be realized after he stepped down as the general director of the CIM. The CIM had entered a period of turmoil during the Second Sino-Japanese War (1937–1945). Despite this, the Mission continued to grow, not only in terms of the number of missionaries but also showing significant growth in

---

1. Fung, *Live to Be Forgotten*, cover page.

the number of self-supporting Chinese workers associated with the CIM. In 1940, some 1,363 missionaries worked in 125 centres in fifteen provinces of China, joined by more than 2,800 self-supporting Chinese workers.[2]

Second, we will examine the "New Emphasis" proposed by Bishop Frank Houghton, the general director of the CIM from 1940 to 1951. Houghton continued in the same vein as Hoste but stressed that indigenization was not just letting go of "controlling hands" but also offering "helping hands." What the Chinese church desired was mutual cooperation, not abandonment.

Third, we will also examine the changing relationship between the CIM and the indigenous churches in view of the changing political context. This includes a focus on the reluctant exodus of all the CIM missionaries in 1951. The last two CIM missionaries – Rupert Clarke (1912–1991) and Arthur Mathews (1912–1978) – left China on 20 July 1953, marking the end of the CIM's work in China. In the years that followed, the CIM became the Overseas Missionary Fellowship (OMF), and though it moved its work to East Asia outside China, the OMF continued to embrace the indigenous principles.

After the Boxer Uprising in 1900, Hoste revealed his vision of the Chinese church "coming to the front, bearing responsibilities, and growing into leadership." With the exodus of all missionaries from China, this vision finally became a reality.

2. Hoste Handing Over the Directorship

The June 1931 China Council minutes record the first suggestion that Hoste might step down from serving as general director. On 13 June, during one of the regular China Council meetings, without prior notice, Hoste vacated as the chair and handed over the role to George W. Gibb. He asked Gibb to read to the Council members a letter that he had prepared, which stated that he and his wife "place themselves at the disposal of the Directors and Councils of the Mission, in China and in the three Home countries, with a view to retirement."[3] Though this decision should not have been a big surprise, given Hoste's age and long service in the CIM, the Council was clearly unprepared for this pronouncement. Considering it "with a solemn sense of

---

2. *China's Millions* (1940): index page.
3. "China Council Minutes" (June 1931): 12.

the seriousness of the matter," the Council felt that "it would be against the best interests of the Mission for Hoste to retire at the present time" as age should not be a deciding factor for retirement. Thus, it was their unambiguous desire that Hoste retain his office until "further light in regard to his successor was received."[4]

The *Principles and Practice* (P&P) of the CIM had no clear stipulation regarding the appointment of a new general director. Reviewing the records of the P&P, which had been revised in 1914 during Hoste's leadership, there were only minor changes compared to the original version drafted by Taylor. Again, there was no indication of how a general director should be appointed. When Taylor was ill in 1900, he had basically hand-picked Hoste to be his successor after having consulted the chair of the London Council, Theodore Howard (1837–1914).[5] There was no legal stipulation regarding the process of finding a successor for the general director of the CIM.

Though the China Council expressed the view that more time was needed for "further light" to be received regarding Hoste's successor, in the end, they agreed to Hoste's proposals. As a temporary measure, Hoste appointed Gibb as the China director.[6] Up to that point, Hoste had also been fulfilling the role of China director by virtue of his office as general director, and Gibb had been a member of the China Council for some time.

Some of the reasons Gibb was chosen by Hoste are made clear in a report printed in *China's Millions*.[7] First, Gibb had served with the CIM as a frontline worker for many years since 1884, particularly in the province of Anhui. Therefore, he had first-hand experience as a field missionary. In 1914, he was appointed the CIM superintendent of Anhui Province. Second, Gibb was proficient in the Chinese language and had developed strong relationships with Chinese church leaders. Third, he was a strong administrator, who had been working at the CIM headquarters in Shanghai since 1918, and he also served on the China Council. It was said that Gibb helped Hoste

---

4. "China Council Minutes" (June 1931): 13.
5. *China's Millions* (1903): 87.
6. "China Council Minutes" (June 1931): 12.
7. *China's Millions* (1941): 22.

significantly and made "useful contributions to the deliberations and business of the China Council."[8]

The June 1931 China Council meeting included a significant discussion on what was "legally binding" with regard to the appointment of a general director. Hoste pointed out that there was "no legal document of binding authority on the subject."[9] Even his own appointment as general director had not been "legally binding."[10] At the conclusion of that China Council meeting, Hoste initially proposed that a legal document should be framed to guide the Council in the selection of the next general director, with an emphasis on seeking the concurrence of the various councils and senior members of the CIM.[11] However, when the China Council asked Hoste for his personal view on subject of the search for the next general director, he felt strongly that it would be appropriate for the China Council to nominate the person since they would be "in the position to judge on many points as to who would be most suitable and acceptable."[12] Hoste's perspective was different to the way Taylor had selected his successor as Taylor had basically hand-picked Hoste to succeed him.

After several rounds of discussions, the China Council finally concluded that "there were distinct advantages in the Mission not being bound by any strictly legal document" in the appointment of the general director.[13] The reason given for this decision, which was recorded in the China Council minutes, was a spiritual one. The Council recalled the words of their founder, Taylor: "If the Directors and Members of the Mission are godly and wise, walking in the spirit of unity and love, they will not lack divine guidance in important matters and at critical times."[14] From the time of its establishment in 1865, the CIM, although it was registered as a legal body in England, had always been a faith-based Mission. The ethos of corporate spiritual discernment was probably considered even more important than legal governance from our contemporary perspective. In the end, Hoste did not insist on his

---

8. *China's Millions* (1941): 22.
9. *China's Millions* (1941): 12–13.
10. "China Council Minutes" (June 1931): 12.
11. "China Council Minutes" (June 1931): 13–14.
12. "China Council Minutes" (June 1931): 13–14.
13. "China Council Minutes" (September 1931): 8–9.
14. "China Council Minutes" (September 1931): 9.

view that the Council should first formulate a legal framework for selecting the next general director. Thus, no change was made to the P&P by Hoste and the China Council with regard to the appointment and selection process of the general director.

While the China Council was hoping to find a successor earlier, it actually took another four years for them to confirm the next general director. Initially, the China Council nominated William H. Aldis (1871–1948), the British CIM home director, as a possible candidate to succeed Hoste.[15] Aldis was well known among CIM colleagues, had been interviewed and accepted by the London Council back in 1897, and had sailed to China in October of the same year. He had been ordained to the ministry of the Church of England in 1900 by W. W. Cassels, the first bishop of the East Sichuan Diocese, who was also with the CIM. Aldis later became the assistant superintendent of the CIM East Sichuan district and, thus, assisted Cassels. In 1916, Aldis had to return home to England for his second furlough but could not return to China because of the First World War. He then joined the home staff of the CIM and was appointed the home director.[16]

The China Council had unanimously agreed that the next general director should be someone residing in China. This made Aldis an unlikely candidate since he had left China in 1916 and had not had any first-hand knowledge and understanding of the work in China for nearly twenty years. Though Aldis was well-versed in the Chinese language and understood Chinese culture, the China Council felt strongly that the next leader needed to be someone who was based in China and who understood its current context.

Gibb, then the China director, was considered a likely candidate by Hoste. Even so, the December 1934 China Council minutes show that only sixteen out of twenty-four official members of the China Council initially agreed to the nomination of Gibb to serve as general director. Their objection was his age. Gibb would be sixty-six years old in 1935, and so the appointment of Gibb would result in a short-term directorship. The subsequent Council minutes in March 1935 record agreement on the nomination by all except one member, who indicated that he would not oppose the nomination although

---

15. "China Council Minutes" (December 1931): 18.
16. *China's Millions* (1948): 42.

he did not agree with it.[17] In the end, Gibb's nomination was unanimously approved by the home directors and the other councils in 1935.[18]

Hoste chaired the China Council meeting for the last time on 12 June 1935. At eleven o'clock the next day, an inauguration meeting was held at the Shanghai headquarters of the CIM. Hoste officially stepped down as the general director after having led the CIM for thirty-five years. He was obviously deeply appreciated by his colleagues since the China Council unanimously extended a cordial invitation to both Hoste and his wife to occupy the room at the CIM headquarters in Shanghai for "as long a period as they may desire to do so."[19]

According to the minutes, the last time Hoste attended the CIM China Council was in June 1935. It was noted that when he stepped down as general director, he also resigned as a member of the China Council. From 1946 onwards, Hoste was described in *China's Millions* as "General Director 1900–1935 (Retired)." It is important to note that in every issue of *China's Millions* that described Hoste as "General Director (Retired)," the following words were also included on the same page: "It is the purpose of the Mission to found self-governing, self-supporting, and self-propagating churches throughout the whole of inland China." It is clear that the vision of the indigenous church that was advocated by Hoste continued to reverberate.

On 14 June 1935, *China Press* 中國報 – the local Shanghai newspaper – announced Hoste's retirement from his leadership role as general director.[20] The news report mentioned three specific things about Hoste. First, he had been in China for sixty years and was the only surviving member of the Cambridge Seven. Second, he had worked in Shanxi for his first seven years in China and was later transferred to Henan. Third, he had led the CIM for nearly thirty-five years. The report was short and concise, but the emphasis was on Hoste's long duration of service in China, including his work in Shanxi. The mention of Shanxi has at least two significant implications. First, it was

---

17. "China Council Minutes" (March 1935): 2.

18. "China Council Minutes" (June 1935): 2. The councils mentioned include the London Council, the North America Council, and the Australasia Council.

19. "China Council Minutes" (June 1935): 3.

20. "Hoste Retires as Head of China Inland Mission," *China Press*, 14 June 1935, 3, accessed 28 June 2022, https://www-cnbksy-com.eproxy.lib.hku.hk/literature/literature/0fee7816309ed14a4f30d9004220a8a6.

one of the most severely affected provinces during the great famine (1876–1879), and the damaging effects could still be felt throughout the 1880s and the 1890s.[21] It was in 1885 that Hoste commenced work in Shanxi, serving under the leadership of Pastor Hsi. Shanxi was also the most severely affected province during the Boxer Uprising in 1900, with hundreds of missionaries killed, including those serving in the CIM. Hoste's long-term commitment to China and its people, even during difficult times, was highlighted in the news report.

Though the era under Hoste's leadership came to an end, his vision for the establishment of an indigenous Chinese church continued to have an effect on the CIM and the Chinese church, and we will come to this point in the following section.

3. Continual Growth of the Indigenous Churches after Hoste

The years following Hoste's stepping down from CIM leadership was a period of turmoil for China. Although the Second Sino-Japanese War only started in 1937, the CIM headquarters, like other parts of Shanghai, had faced Japanese bombardment since 1932.[22] Throughout these war years, a significant tide of Chinese refugees poured into the interior, though many missionaries remained where they were.[23] By late 1939, only six of the universities, colleges, and vocational schools that had operated in what was then Japan-occupied territory remained.[24] Simultaneously, there were considerable tensions rising between the Nationalists and the Communists within China.[25] In 1942, in view of the occupation of Shanghai by the Japanese, the CIM established a "provisional Headquarters" in Chongqing, which would "begin to function immediately if Shanghai became totally cut off."[26] However, despite the uncertainty, the routine work of administration continued to be carried out at the

---

21. *China's Millions* (1899): 72, 116, 152.
22. *China's Millions* (March 1935): 55.
23. Sih, *Nationalist China*, 373–397. See also Lam Wing Hung 林榮洪, 中華神學五十年 (A Half Century of Chinese Theology), 407–408.
24. Lam, 407–408.
25. Fairbank, *Republican China*, 568.
26. *China's Millions* (1942): 14.

CIM headquarters in Shanghai while Houghton remained as the general director.[27] Out of the 1,300 CIM missionaries, about 1,000 remained in China, including 250 in the Japanese-occupied area.[28] Despite all the uncertainties and war threats, the work of the CIM continued steadily, though it was slow in comparison to the remarkable growth in the number of self-supporting Chinese workers.

Though Hoste had stepped out of leadership, the CIM continued to embrace his vision that the gospel could advance along parallel lines: the Chinese church advancing to be fully independent and CIM missionaries advancing to go into interior China to preach the gospel. In 1935, *China's Millions* reported 1,313 CIM missionary workers in 125 centres in fifteen provinces and 2,350 self-supporting local Chinese workers associated with the CIM. By 1940, there was further growth, with 1,363 CIM missionaries and 2,835 self-supporting local Chinese workers.[29] The growth in the number of local workers far exceeded that of the CIM missionaries.

Thus, nearly 500 new self-supporting local Chinese workers were added within the five-year period between 1935 and 1940. Despite the reported increase in the number of self-supporting workers, very little information is available about them in *China's Millions* or archival materials.[30] The reason for this is not clear. According to Li Nan (李楠), it quite is possible that these records might have been lost when all CIM missionaries had to leave China by 1951 or destroyed during the Cultural Revolution.[31]

Yet there was evidence of growth of the indigenous effort – in varying degrees in different provinces. Below are a few snippets about the growth of the indigenous Chinese church as recorded in *China's Millions* between the years 1935 and 1949.

---

27. *China's Millions* (March–April 1942): 14.

28. *China's Millions* (1942): 14.

29. *China's Millions* (January 1940): 2. From 1941, *China's Millions* stopped reporting the number of workers.

30. The CIM kept a registry of all missionary workers, including their names, their given Chinese names, place of designation, and year of joining. This registry is currently kept at the OMF International Archive Department in Singapore. However, no such registry was kept for Chinese workers. Similarly, no detailed records of the names of these local Chinese workers could be found in the SOAS, University of London Archives, Archives of the Billy Graham Center, Wheaton College, or the Yale University Archives Department.

31. Li Nan, "Retrospect and Prospect: Research on the China Inland Mission in the Past Thirty Years," in *Religious Studies*, Volume 2 (2015): 212–219.

In 1935, Charles. H. Green (1865–1958), the CIM superintendent of Hopei Province (河北, Hebei) reported that though there were sixteen full-time CIM missionaries in six of the sixteen walled county towns, self-supporting Chinese workers were occupying the other ten cities with steady progress towards the objective of establishing self-supporting churches.[32]

In the same year, another report came in from Paoning (保寧, Baoning) in Sichuan by another CIM missionary, R. Victor Bazire (1900–1990), who mentioned a church in the mountainous area "set around in shady trees and standing in the midst of farmlands" that was "going full swing under local leadership."[33]

Another report spoke of a small church becoming self-supporting in Kweiting (貴定, Guiding), Kweichow (貴州, Guizhou), having given $37 to the church for pioneering church planting work during 1937.[34]

In 1942, Leila Cook (1895–1943) reported from Yunnan regarding the work among the Lisu. There was an average attendance of 1,505 local believers at the services in the villages. The local believers made this request of the CIM missionaries: "Please do not send money . . ., for we could not accept it if you did. The work is entirely self-supporting."[35]

In 1942, John Sinton (1882–1960) reported that "scores of the CIM associated churches that are now, to all intents and purposes, independent of foreign mission or missionary control. Many have been self-directing and financially self-supporting for years, but also by self-extension, hence lies the secret of permanence."[36]

In 1948, Herbert Kane (1910–1988), a CIM missionary in Anhui Province, reported that in the district of Fowyang (阜陽, Fuyang) forty local churches with 101 outstations were entirely self-supporting. Church leaders refused to ask the CIM for funds. "If the sum required is particularly large, sometimes letters were sent to other churches in other Districts to get help in this way."[37]

In the same year, A. Bramwell Allen (1898–1992), another CIM missionary, reported "signs of indigenous growth" in East Yunnan. In the absence of

---

32. *China's Millions* (January 1935): 8.
33. *China's Millions* (October 1935): 186.
34. *China's Millions* (July 1937): 135.
35. *China's Millions* (March–April 1942): 17–18.
36. Sinton, "Trends and Tendencies," 50.
37. *CIM Field Bulletin* (1948): 121.

CIM missionaries, the church had gone ahead and rented their own chapel. "Four hundred catties of sugar were put down as a deposit on the chapel, and three hundred catties of sugar paid down as one year's rent."[38]

Also, in 1948, Allan C. W. Crane (1909–1987) reported the development of indigenous churches in the Gansu region, proclaiming that "the Chinese were ahead of the missionaries in this matter!"[39]

Many of these field reports referred back to the Statement of Policy and expressed appreciation for Hoste's vision.[40] The Statement of Policy, which articulated Hoste's plan to establish "self-governing, self-supporting and self-propagating churches," was beginning to bear fruit after an initial slow start. CIM missionaries were beginning to take a secondary role in leading the Chinese church.

Taking a broader view, indigenous movements were already taking place beyond the CIM in different regions in China. In 1931, the *Chinese Recorder* observed that the indigenous revival in Shandong during that year "spread without any direct organizational planning" and was accompanied by "advance in self-support, self-propagation and the development of lay leadership. It is the fruit of the work of indigenous zeal and Chinese zealots"[41] In 1935, the *Chinese Recorder* also noted other indigenous church developments, including the South Fukien Church, one of the oldest indigenous churches in China, which already had forty-four ordained and self-supporting local Chinese ministers, along with twenty thousand members.[42] Other groups – such as the Little Flock Movement led by Watchman Nee, which initially begin in Shanghai in 1928 – also grew rapidly.

---

38. *CIM Field Bulletin* (1948): 126.
39. *CIM Field Bulletin* (1948): 76.
40. See *CIM Field Bulletin* (March 1942): 1; (November 1946): 14; (July 1948): 102.
41. "Indigenous Revival in Shantung," *Chinese Recorder* (December 1931): 767–772.
42. *Chinese Recorder* (1935): 339. See also Leung Ka-lun 梁家麟 *Fulin Zhonghua-Zhongguo jindai jiaohuishi shijiang* 福臨中華—中國近代教會史十講 (Blessing Upon China-Ten Talks on the Contemporary Church History of China), 161–162.

4. Further Development of Hoste's Indigenous Principles by Houghton

On 22 October 1940, Bishop Frank Houghton (1894–1972) became the new general director of the CIM, taking the place of Gibb – who was ill and died shortly after Houghton's appointment.[43] Houghton was born in Stafford, England, in 1894 and had joined the CIM in 1920, initially working in East Szechwan (Sichuan). Returning to England in 1928 because of the Anti-Christian Movement, he served as the editorial secretary of the CIM for nine years. Houghton was known for his prolific writing, including his famous book *China Calling*.[44] He came back to China in 1937 and remained with the CIM even though he had been appointed the first Anglican bishop of East Szechwan (Sichuan).[45] Houghton was one generation younger than Hoste in both age and seniority. In 1923, he married Dorothy – the daughter of William Cassels, who was one of the Cambridge Seven.[46]

Even before Houghton took on the leadership role of general director of the CIM, his view on the indigenous church was very similar to that of his predecessors, Taylor and Hoste. In 1932, looking back on the rising xenophobic tide that had resulted in the massive evacuation of missionaries in 1927, Houghton expressed the opinion that the evacuation of the CIM missionaries was a blessing in disguise as the development of Chinese leaders had "inevitability been arrested by the presence and the competence of their foreign friends." Houghton felt that "God had indeed given gifts to the Chinese church and thus self-government and self-supporting churches should be the foundation of all the CIM policies and not just a goal to be aimed at."[47]

Houghton, therefore, was completely in line with Hoste's indigenous principles. However, he felt the need to address one issue in implementing Hoste's Statement of Policy. In 1943, based on the decisions made at the October China Council meeting, Houghton published an important document that contained a fresh exegesis of the Statement of Policy issued by Hoste back in 1927. Houghton's article, entitled "The Pattern Shewn," was later published in

---

43. *CIM Field Bulletin* (November 1940): 2.
44. Houghton, *China Calling*.
45. *China's Millions* (November 1940): 132.
46. *China's Millions* (September 1940): 131.
47. Broomhall, *Shaping of Modern China*, 770.

1944 in *China's Millions*.⁴⁸ It presents Houghton's fresh understanding of the indigenous process in his current context. While affirming what had already been the direction of the CIM in establishing "self-governing, self-supporting and self-propagating churches," there was a "New Emphasis" on the relationship between the CIM missionaries and the Chinese church.

Houghton puts forward several important arguments. First, while the CIM missionaries tended to "press to an extreme" an important aspect of the Statement of Policy (1928), namely, the release of the Chinese church from missionary control, with "Hands off the Chinese Church" as the slogan of those days, this drastic action had been wrongly interpreted by the church as "an inexplicable aloofness" of CIM missionaries. Thus, the implementation of the Statement of Policy had been received with hesitation by the Chinese church.

Second, while it appeared wise and right for CIM missionaries to refuse to accept leadership responsibility for the church since it ought to be in Chinese hands, their "doctrinaire devotion" to Hoste's Statement of Policy made some Chinese believers wonder why the CIM missionaries had come to China in the first place. What the Chinese church was hoping to see was that the CIM missionaries would "stand shoulder to shoulder" with them rather than standing to the side. According to Houghton, many of those who questioned the intentions of the CIM missionaries were not "merely old-fashioned people of parasitic tendencies" but "solid Chinese believers."⁴⁹

Third, Houghton felt that the metaphor of the scaffolding representing the CIM – as something to be removed as soon as its support is no longer needed – only expressed "a half-truth." Houghton argues that "while it is right that we should think of ourselves as 'advisers' rather than 'rulers' of the church; . . . an adviser may be cold and aloof." Thus, the New Emphasis put forward by Houghton maintained that the CIM must indeed "remove the controlling hand, but at the same time offer the helping hand as well."⁵⁰ Houghton believed that what the Chinese church needed was CIM men and women who, in the warm spirit of fellowship, would stand with the Chinese believers. Houghton says, "the one [thing] which occupied most of

---

48. Houghton, "New Emphasis," Appendix, 1–2.
49. Houghton, 2.
50. Houghton, 3.

our time and thought, should be co-operation with the Chinese church and with Chinese fellow-workers."[51]

Though the Statement of Policy was generally accepted by the Chinese church, it seems from what Houghton writes that many Chinese church leaders had misunderstood the CIM's future commitment to journeying with the many young and emerging Chinese churches. Houghton spoke strongly about the situation, emphasizing the balance of "removing controlling hands and offering the helping hand."

Apart from the "New Emphasis" on "offering helping hands," Houghton also put forward another important emphasis on the way in which evangelization should be carried out. Houghton highlighted that the CIM's policy and strategy in the past had always been to conduct evangelization in the following order of priority: first, CIM missionaries should focus on the unevangelized or unreached areas; then, CIM missionaries could consider working in partially evangelized areas; and only after that should CIM missionaries engage in the "church areas," where churches were already established.

However, Houghton proposed that the CIM should "reverse that order," recognizing that the Chinese church should be "central to the thinking." The CIM was to be "the contribution" to the church in China, and its commission was to "work with, and under, the Church."[52] Houghton highlighted that "it is our business to consider how best we may co-operate with the Church in evangelization."[53]

Hoste's original two-pronged strategy was to have CIM missionaries moving into unevangelized pioneering areas while local leaders led the indigenous churches in already churched areas. What Houghton was proposing was that the CIM would no longer take the initiative to go to pioneering areas but would do so only at the request of the church. Thus, this "reversal of order" was a major shift in the CIM's paradigm of the way evangelization was carried out. The "reversal of order" advocated by Houghton did not actually contradict what Hoste had proposed but, rather, was a natural outcome of Hoste's vision if that vision was to be truly realized. Both Hoste's and Houghton's

---

51. Houghton, 3.

52. "The Pattern Shewn: An Account of the Session of the China Council, held at Mission Headquarters in Chungking, October 18–30, by the General Director, Bishop F. Houghton," *China's Millions* (1944): Appendix, 3.

53. *China's Millions* (1944): 3.

visions coincide, in that they believed that, ultimately, the Chinese church should take the initiative to lead in all the work they believed God had called them to do, whether in churched areas or unchurched areas. This proposal from Houghton was moving one step further in the indigenization process of the Chinese church. Recognizing that some churches might not be ready, Houghton's "New Emphasis" allowed for some exceptions. Houghton mentioned that for churches who remained unresponsive, "we should beg the church to regard us as its representatives, temporarily doing the work until it is strong enough to undertake it."[54] This is very similar to what Hoste had proposed when he introduced the Statement of Policy back in 1928.

Houghton's proposal was "well-received by the CIM missionaries" according to the September 1944 China Council minutes.[55] However, some questions were raised regarding the proposal about "reversing the order," and these were taken up at the China Council meeting in September 1944.

First, since missionaries were being asked to take on a more advisory role rather than direct leadership for the church, there was concern that there would be little scope for the missionary of average gifts and education. Thus, to engage well with Chinese church leaders in the future, a missionary would need not just excellent Chinese language skills but also sufficient theological training.

Second, if the evangelistic aim of the CIM had become obscured by the New Emphasis on cooperation with the local churches, then evangelism would be relegated to second place, which went against the ultimate purpose of the CIM.

Third, if the missionaries' activities were directed by the Chinese, there was danger that their activities might be hampered by the lack of vision of mediocre church leaders.[56]

According to the 1944 and the 1945 *CIM Field Bulletins* and the China Council minutes, further consultations with the CIM Home Councils and field leaders were held. Houghton assured them that the evangelistic aim of the CIM should always continue. At the same time, he emphasized that "the

---

54. *China's Millions* (1944): 3.

55. "China Council Minutes" (4 September 1944).

56. CIM *Field Bulletin* (November 1944): 3; see also "CIM China Council Minutes" (4 September 1944).

CIM aims to build strong living churches, and together for mutual help and fellowship, where it is possible and desirable."[57] The "New Emphasis" was finally accepted, confirmed, and endorsed as the "guiding principle in matters involving the church and its relationship to the missionaries."[58]

This "New Emphasis" by Houghton was also enthusiastically received by Chinese church leaders and led to increased cooperation.[59] One example was the increased cooperation between CIM missionaries and local Chinese churches in South Gansu. A decision was made to merge the CIM "district mission committee," comprising four CIM missionaries overseeing mission matters, with the South Gansu Church Association Executive Committee, comprising thirteen Chinese Church leaders, to oversee church matters. With this merger, the two groups began to work together as one team to plan the annual conferences, provide training materials for believers, and run short-term rural Bible schools. Chinese church leaders commented that the New Emphasis "was remarkable. It is not simply just a paper program."[60] Houghton's concept of removing the "controlling hand" but also offering a "helping hand" reassured Chinese church leaders that the CIM was not in exit mode and that it did not stand "cold and aloof." Thus, the "Statement of Policy" introduced by Hoste in 1928 on the indigenous principles was further developed by Houghton in the new historical context.

5. Hoste's Indigenous Principles and the "CIM" Name Puzzle

By the time Hoste stepped down as the general director, the CIM was already a household name among Chinese churches. Latourette comments that "the CIM was in time to have in China more missionaries than any other single agency, Protestant or Roman Catholic. Its beginnings and its development are in some respect the most remarkable chapter in all the history of Christian

---

57. *CIM Field Bulletin* (August 1944): 5.

58. "China Council Minutes" (January 1947): 6.

59. A Chinese version of Frank Houghton's "Pattern Shewn" was distributed to all CIM-related churches. See "China Council Minutes" (April 1845).

60. *CIM Field Bulletin* (November 1944): 1; see also "China Council Minutes" (September 1994): 2.

missions in China."⁶¹ Yet the CIM was not denominational. In fact, from the start, Taylor had insisted that the CIM should be interdenominational. Thus, it was never the CIM's intention to establish "CIM churches." Whenever CIM referred to churches started by CIM missionaries, these churches were usually referred to by their location – either the name of the village, the city, or the province.⁶² In contrast, the Chinese believers preferred to call these churches "CIM churches" because of their affinity with the CIM.⁶³

The name "CIM churches" had become a subject of debate at the China Council in the 1940s. This problem initially originated from a practical issue relating to the purchase of property for church purposes in the name of the CIM. A new law had been introduced whereby "purchase of property was forbidden to foreigners including any missionary bodies."⁶⁴ Houghton raised this matter at the China Council in May 1941 because it was an issue for which a satisfactory solution had to be found. However, the discussion became broader, and questions were raised about whether the continual use of the name "CIM" for Chinese churches might actually be inappropriate as it could be misinterpreted as meaning foreign control since the name "CIM" represented a foreign mission society established in England. With the implementation of the new law forbidding foreign missionary bodies to purchase property in China, Houghton and the China Council believed that it might be a good opportunity for the CIM, bearing in mind Hoste's indigenous principles, to review the use of the name "CIM" for Chinese churches.⁶⁵

The China Council recognized that the CIM was clearly not a church but a missionary body; therefore, they felt that the designation "CIM" should not be used to describe a church or churches. However, the Council also recognized that many churches already established by the CIM bore the name "Nui Ti Hui" (內地會, Neidihui) – meaning "CIM" – that had been chosen by the local church leaders.⁶⁶ This matter would continue to prove problematic and

---

61. Latourette, *History of Christian Missions*, 382.
62. "China Council Minutes" (May 1941): 8–11.
63. "China Council Minutes" (May 1941): 8–11.
64. "China Council Minutes" (May 1941): 8–11.
65. "China Council Minutes" (May 1941): 8–11.
66. The spelling "Nui Ti Hui" was used in the China Council minutes as an equivalent to 內地會 in Chinese.

would be "a deterrent to the CIM's aim of an autonomous indigenous church," which had been strongly advocated by Hoste.⁶⁷

Even before Houghton, Hoste, using the metaphor of the scaffolding, was upfront in proposing that the CIM should only play a supporting role. Thus, the China Council felt that the continual use of the word "CIM churches" did not align with Hoste's indigenous principles.

As the China Council consulted with Chinese church leaders, it became clear that some of these Chinese church leaders felt strongly – "to the point of great distress" – about the name "Nui Ti Hui," which they had been using for so long, being taken away from them.⁶⁸ Some CIM-established churches, however, had taken the initiative to change to a new name – for example, a church group in South Gansu adopted the name "Chong Hwa Chi Tuh Chiao" (中華基督教, Zhonghua Jidujiao), meaning a Chinese Christian Church.⁶⁹ This may have been motivated partly by a desire to disassociate themselves from the title of a foreign missionary body. However, such changes were not universal among the churches, and many still retained 內地會 as part of the Chinese name of the church.⁷⁰

While the CIM was clearly keen not to use the name "CIM Churches," many Chinese church leaders had already developed an attachment to the name "Nui Ti Hui" (CIM). From the Chinese church leaders' perspective, if the CIM was allowing the Chinese church to be truly self-supporting and self-governing, they should not require that the Chinese church abandon the name "CIM" since these churches should be given the choice to voice their own opinion and make the decision themselves.

After almost year-long discussions, debates, and consultations with Chinese church leaders, the CIM finally came to a decision. They recommended replacing the name "Nui Ti Hui" 內地會 with the Chinese name 基督福音聖教會 (Jidu Fuyin Sheng Jiaohui) – literally the "Holy Church of Christ's Gospel" – with the place or location of the church as a prefix.⁷¹ This

---

67. "China Council Minutes" (May 1941): 8–11.
68. "China Council Minutes" (May 1941): 8–11.
69. "China Council Minutes" (May 1941): 8–11.
70. "China Council Minutes" (May 1941): 9.
71. "China Council Minutes" (March 1942): 4.

name was considered a more neutral name compared to the name "Nui Ti Hui," which had links to a foreign mission agency.

The CIM's recommendation was obviously a long name to adopt. Subsequent China Council meetings revealed that there was no unified agreement among Chinese church leaders about whether or not to adopt this recommended new name. Letters received from many parts of the field also indicated that there was no agreement over a suitable alternative name for those churches related to the CIM. To change to a new title that was twice as long as the original name but had no relationship to its historical roots was not an attractive option. Thus, many Chinese church leaders decided to continue to use the name "CIM Church."[72]

In hindsight, for the CIM to recommend a new name for the Chinese churches could actually be perceived as another way of "controlling." The CIM would have been much more in line with Hoste's indigenous principles if the China Council had recommended that Chinese churches be totally free to choose a suitable name for themselves without the Mission's influence.

Despite the unsatisfactory outcome on the debate over the CIM name, Houghton did bring about some positive changes to the CIM that reflected the Mission's ongoing commitment to Hoste's indigenous principles. One example was the letter Houghton issued to all missionaries in April 1944, informing them that the CIM would no longer use the term "Missionary-in-charge" to refer to missionaries assigned to a specific church or location[73] because he contended that "in-charge" conveyed the idea of controlling.

6. Evolving Relationship between the Chinese Church and the CIM

As mentioned previously, *China's Millions* reported there were 2,350 and 2,835 self-supporting Chinese workers associated with the CIM in 1935 and 1940 respectively.[74] Though there was no comprehensive list of the names of such workers in the CIM records, reports of the work of some of these Chinese

---

72. "China Council Minutes" (October 1942): 5–7.
73. "China Council Minutes" (October 1942): 5–7.
74. *China's Millions* (1935) and (1940): index page.

workers were published in *China's Millions* from time to time.[75] These names were published under the category "Chinese pastors and evangelists."[76] It is noteworthy that the 1946 *China's Millions* published, for the first time, a new section entitled "Chinese Church Leaders," which included the names of some of the well-known Chinese church leaders at that time. These included John Sung (宋尚節, 1901–1944), Marcus Cheng (陳崇桂, 1884–1963), Calvin Chao (趙君影, 1906–1996), Wang Ming-Dao (王明道, 1900–1991), Chia Yu-ming (賈玉銘, Jia Yu-ming 1880–1964), Andrew Gih (計志文, Ji Zhiwen, 1901–1985), David Yang (楊紹唐, Yang Shao-tang 1898–1969), and Chow Tse-Yu (Zhou Zhiyu 1889–1973).[77] The commencement of publication of such a section on "Chinese Church leaders" in *China's Millions* was probably related to the passing away in September 1944 of of John Sung, who was considered one of the most influential evangelists in twentieth-century China.[78]

While these leaders had been working independently, they had often maintained good relationships with many CIM missionaries. They were, in one way or another, leading and influencing the Chinese church significantly, independent of missionary influence. One example was the evangelistic work of John Sung, which led to massive conversions among the Chinese – not only in China but also in Southeast Asia.

Some examples of cooperation were noted. For instance, Calvin Chao (趙君影), who was the general secretary of the China Intervarsity Fellowship (CIVF), asked David Adeney (1911–1994), a CIM missionary, to deputize for him in his absence in 1946.[79] It was no small matter for a Chinese leader working among students and intellectuals to ask a CIM missionary to represent him. This was certainly a reversal of roles, to have the CIM receiving an invitation from a Chinese leader to be involved in their work and not the other way round. This invitation by the Chinese leader also reflected Houghton's "New Emphasis" back in 1944 – removing the "controlling hand" but offering a "helping hand" when asked.

---

75. One such example was in *China's Millions* (1944): 2, 4, 10, 20, 22, 26, 35, 39, 47, with individual names of Chinese workers mentioned – usually, with the surnames only.
76. *China's Millions* (1944): index page.
77. *China's Millions* (1946): iii.
78. *China's Millions* (1946): 20.
79. *China's Millions* (1946): 45.

Another example was the setting up, in 1943, of the Chung King (重慶, Chongqing) Seminary by Marcus Cheng (陳崇桂), who had been encouraged to do so by Houghton and who later became its president. Cheng was already a well-known Chinese leader, who had been converted through the Swedish Lutheran Mission.[80] He approached the CIM to ask if they could supply members who could join the teaching staff and even serve as dean of the seminary.[81] It had always been the aim of the CIM to assist in the setting up of Bible seminaries, but they desired that those seminaries be led by Chinese leaders. The CIM was "prepared to cooperate with them when invited."[82] The CIM regularly reported the work of Marcus Cheng in *China's Millions* between 1945 and 1950. By early 1950, almost all the teaching staff at Chung King Bible Seminary were CIM missionaries.

While there was good cooperation between Chinese church leaders and the CIM missionaries, the CIM was also sensing that the time might be coming when such cooperation would no longer be possible due to political changes.[83] In fact, much earlier, John Sung had predicted that "a great revival was coming [to China]. But all the missionaries would all have to leave first."[84] When Sung made this statement, it was in the context of believing that the growth of the Chinese church was based purely on the work of God rather than on the efforts of the missionaries. Sung had not made a political statement. However, his prediction did eventually come true.

In December 1950, Cheng, who had always worked with the CIM, insisted that "all CIM missionaries be withdrawn completely from his staff in the seminary."[85] According to a report in the 1950 *China's Million's*, Cheng was chosen by the new government authorities to represent the "Religious Bodies" in a representative assembly that would meet to discuss the future of the municipal government in Chongqing.[86] In a similar position to other church leaders, Cheng's explanation to the CIM was that "the missionaries would be an embarrassment to Chinese church leaders – foreigners from imperialist

---

80. *China's Millions* (1944): 11.
81. "China Council Minutes" (April 1944): 3.
82. *CIM Field Bulletin* (June 1945): 12.
83. "China Council Minutes" (January 1947): 2.
84. Shubert, *I Remember John Sung*, 65–66.
85. Thompson, *Reluctant Exodus*, 54.
86. *China's Millions* (1950): 55.

West."87 It was obvious to the CIM that Cheng's reference to the "imperialist West" was driven by politics. Ying Fuk-Tsang explains Cheng's stance: While Cheng lost faith in nationalist rule because he saw rampant corruption and social injustice, at the same time, he did not see that the Christian faith and the atheistic ideology of the Communists were incompatible.88 The days were numbered for the CIM and other mission organizations working in China.

In many ways, the Chinese church associated with the CIM had been getting ready for such a time as this. Hoste's advocacy of the Statement of Policy regarding "self-governing, self-supporting and self-propagating" back in 1928 had caused some churches to misunderstand the CIM's apparent "aloofness," and this had sometimes very nearly wrecked the happy relationship that existed between them. But, as Arnold J. Lea (1907–1992), the CIM deputy China director reported in the 1951 edition of *China's Millions*, it was in hindsight that the CIM realized how infinitely worthwhile it was for the Chinese Church to have reached the stage of independence in financial matters. The CIM was grateful for "the efficacy of that early move advocated by Hoste.

Lea commented that a secular press in Sichuan reported how the CIM churches had become totally financially independent, "while those from other churches [of other mission societies] were listed as still partially, if not wholly, dependent on foreign funds."89 Many church leaders admitted that those who had not received help from foreign organizations "found it a great deal easier when coming under the Communists, to clear themselves from the charge of having been linked up with imperialists."90

Two years earlier, Houghton had written to all CIM missionaries, instructing them to remain in China. That decision had received unanimous support and approval. But by the end of 1950, the situation had changed. Sinton, the China director of the CIM, wrote, "Our presence is making things worse for the very people we most want to help. It is with sorrow of heart that we have reached the conclusion that we must proceed with a planned withdrawal of our missionaries. It will seem to many that this is the beginning of the end."91

---

87. *China's Millions* (1950): 55.
88. Ying Fuk-Tsang "The Praxis and Predicament of a Chinese Fundamentalist," 245.
89. *China's Millions* (May 1951): 50.
90. *CIM Field Bulletin* (September 1952): 7.
91. *CIM Field Bulletin* (September 1952): 7.

7. The "Reluctant Exodus"[92] of CIM missionaries

The year 1949 – when the Chinese Communists took control of the country – marks a turning point in the history of the church in China. By 1950, the National Christian Council (NCC) had adopted the government's new policy of the "Three-Self" formula, which, though not new to the CIM, was given a new twist. At the NCC's fourteenth anniversary conference held in Shanghai on 18 October 1950, the NCC publicly supported the pro-government "Christian Manifesto," also known as the "Three-Self Manifesto."[93]

The main author of the Three-Self Manifesto was Wu Yaozong (吳耀宗, 1893–1979), a progressive Christian leader recruited by the political leader Zhou Enlai (周恩來).[94] Wu was the YMCA secretary, who was later officially appointed as the first chairman of the Chinese Christian Three-Self Patriotic Movement (TSPM) in 1954.[95] In the Christian Manifesto, Wu emphasized the "Direction of Endeavour for Chinese Christianity in the Construction of New China." Wu insisted that that the Chinese church must declare its support for the state and the general policies of the Communist government.[96] The fundamental aim of the Christian church was to make Christians aware of the imperialistic influences within Christianity. All foreign financial assistance must be terminated.

Phyllis Thompson explains the new meaning of "Three-Self" as given by the NCC: "Self-governing meant throwing off the control of the imperialists. Self-supporting meant throwing off the imperialists' money. Self-propagating meant throwing out the poisonous doctrine of the imperialists."[97] Among the many Chinese pastors who refused to sign the Manifesto, Wang Ming-Dao

---

92. Title of the book by Phyllis Thompson.

93. Wan Fulin 萬福林, "Zhongguo Jiaohui zizhi ziyang zichuan yundong de jieshao" 中國教會自治自養自傳運動的介紹 (An Introduction to the Self-government, Self-support and Self-Propagation in the Church in China), *Tian Feng* 天風 23, no. 9 (November, 1950): 2.

94. Wu Yaozong 吳耀宗, "Judujiao gexin yundong de xinjieduan" 基督教革新運動的新階段 (A new milestone in the transforming movement of Christianity), *Tian Feng* 天風 246 (1951): 2.

95. For more details, see Kang, *House Church Christianity*, 3–10.

96. Leung Ka-lun 梁家麟 *Fulin Zhonghua- Zhongguo jindai jiaohuishi shijiang* 福臨中華—中國近代教會史十講, (Blessing Upon China- Ten Talks on the Contemporary Church History of China), (Hong Kong: Tian Dao Publishing, 1988), 182–185. See also So, "Passion for a Greater Vision," 270–273.

97. See Lo, "Three-Self Movement," 17; Phyllis Thompson's book, *The Reluctant Exodus*, Chapter 7. See also Zhang, "Three Self," 175–202.

from Beijing is probably the best known.[98] Wang's decision was not politically driven but was made for theological reasons because he saw the need for the separation of religion and state.[99]

In 1905, it was difficult to accurately assess the status of indigenization among the different churches associated with different mission groups in China. However, an article published in *Tian Feng* (天風) in November 1950 gave an indication of the overall picture.[100] First, the article confirmed that indigenization of the Chinese church – namely, the "Three-Self" movement – was not a new phenomenon but had been in effect during the previous thirty years. However, it acknowledged that what had happened regarding indigenization so far was only a superficial movement without a real, substantive change. It was estimated that only about 30 to 40 percent of all churches had reached the level of "half self-support" and that the majority still relied heavily on mission funds from the West. Thus, it was proposed that the "Three-Self Movement" in 1950 should be called a "New Three-Self Movement" without any foreign influence or control.

The January 1951 issue of *China's Millions* records that

> during the course of its eighty-five years of history, the churches were once few, small, and wholly dependent upon missionary care and enterprise. They have [now] become very numerous, independent, self-supporting, and self-propagating. The passing of the decade has only increased the evidence that fruitfulness of the [indigenous] work has now far exceeded human statistics.[101]

While there is no formal record of how many churches associated with the CIM had become totally self-supporting and self-governing, the report in the 1951 *China's Millions* clearly indicates that such churches were "numerous" in contrast to what is described in *Tian Feng*.[102]

With the announcement of the Three-Self Manifesto, the CIM recognized that the time to exit had come. In the same issue of the 1951 *China's Millions*,

---

98. So, "Passion for a Greater Vision," 293–294.
99. Lam Wing-hung 林榮洪, *Zhonghua shenxue wushinian* 中華神學五十年, 219–222.
100. Wan Fulin 萬福林, "An Introduction to the Self-government, Self-support and Self-Propagation in the Church in China," in *Tian Feng* 23:9 (11 November 1950): 2.
101. *China's Millions* (March 1951): 28.
102. *China's Millions* (1951): 28.

the following statement was published: "As this issue goes to press, cables have been received from the general director indicating the general situation in China. It appears that a fairly widespread withdrawal of missionaries is imminent."[103] Houghton wrote further, specifying the reason for the withdrawal, indicating that in more and more centres and with increasing intensity, the presence of missionaries would "involve the Chinese Christians in difficulty, embarrassment, even danger." The missionaries' ongoing presence would "in fact, be hindering rather than helping."[104]

The decision was made. The reluctant exodus had begun. At the beginning of 1951, the CIM had 518 full members and 119 associate members in China.[105] Obtaining exit permits had become increasingly difficult and the process was subject to delay because Chinese guarantors had to be provided in each case to vouch for the missionary's reputation and financial position.[106]

Arnold Lea (1907–1992), the acting deputy China director of the CIM, who directed the withdrawal of workers from the China inland, wrote these final solemn words in Shanghai in May 1951:

> Self-reliance, which leads to healthy independence, is something to be commended and encouraged. The emergence of a self-contained national church is something in which Christians of other lands should all rejoice even though the accomplishing of such may mean the fading out, temporarily, or even permanently of foreign missionary enterprise. The CIM has been gradually coming to and more recently effecting the healthy independence of the churches. Now in a remarkable way, an atheistic government is completing this movement.[107]

Lea's article very helpfully points out that, since the days of Hoste, the CIM had been trying for many years to bring about "the withdrawal from the churches of missionary control, whether financial or administrative." The widespread withdrawal of missionaries in 1927 resulted in Hoste launching the new Statement of Policy, with "the CIM taking a definitive step to

---

103. *China's Millions* (January 1951): 11.
104. *China's Millions* (January 1951): 13.
105. So, "Passion for a Greater Vision," 266; see also Thompson, *Reluctant Exodus*, 175–180.
106. See *China's Millions* (March 1951): 35.
107. Lea, "Mission and Church," 47–49.

encourage self-support and self-government amongst churches." Even though this had caused misunderstanding between local churches and missionaries, in the end, as Lea points out, some churches expressed their appreciation: "At the time, we could not understand why the Mission asked this. But now the government's insistence on our dispensing with all foreign aid makes no difference to us. We took that step long ago," said one of the Henan church leaders.[108]

Lea also points out that subsequent to Hoste, Houghton launched a second movement with the New Emphasis, "calling for placing in the foreground in all our thinking the essential need of Chinese leaders and control of the church by the Chinese. The insistence by the current government on Chinese leadership is now putting the *finishing touches* to the movement for self-control launched [since the days of Hoste]."[109] It was obvious to the CIM that the new government rejected any foreign influence and control over the Chinese church. In fact, the NCC issued a statement declaring that churches, Christian bodies, and institutions should "show the maximum determination in bringing to completion within five years the movement for self-government, self-support, and self-propagation."[110] However, the CIM had already been implanting such a plan of action since the days of Hoste.

The withdrawal of all CIM missionaries was painfully slow. Distances and ineffective communications complicated the matter. In May 1951, 220 CIM missionaries remained in China.[111] Every missionary needed to obtain an exit visa before they could depart. According to the records, there were eight CIM missionaries still in China in May 1952. By January 1953, there were four left, and by March, only two.[112] The last two CIM missionaries, Rupert Clarke and Arthur Mathews, were finally released. After more than two years of imprisonment, they crossed into Hong Kong via the Kowloon station on 20 July 1953.[113] The withdrawal was complete.

---

108. Lea, 50.
109. Lea, 50. Emphasis added.
110. *CIM Field Bulletin* (1950): 198.
111. *CIM Field Bulletin* (1950): 58.
112. *China's Millions* (May 1953): 39.
113. Thompson, *Reluctant Exodus*, 180.

8. From CIM to Overseas Missionary Fellowship

A special CIM Directors' Conference was held from 10 to 17 February 1951 at Mount Dandenong, near Kalorama in Australia while the withdrawal of the CIM missionaries was underway.[114] One of the main aims of this conference was to address "the immediate future" of the CIM given the rapidly changing situation.[115] Six home directors were present, along with the general director, Frank Houghton.

At this conference, the CIM leaders arrived at a number of decisions. First, they again affirmed that the presence of CIM missionaries in China would be an "embarrassment" to the local Christians and, at times, even a "positive danger" to the Chinese believers. Second, while they recognized that a return to China was not likely for some time to come, they also "steadfastly refuse[d] to relinquish the hope of returning at some later date."[116] However, if the missionaries were to return, they recognized that this had to be by the clear invitation of the Chinese churches and to serve under their direction. Third, in terms of the immediate future, the CIM leaders began to look for new fields under the banner "the Chinese of South-East Asia," which included millions of overseas Chinese in lands such as Thailand, Malaya, Indonesia, and Philippines, not forgetting the Chinese in Western countries.[117] A unanimous decision was made to send survey teams as expeditiously as possible "in order to discover the extent of the unmet needs."[118]

There was one major setback at this conference. Most of those who attended were from the Western home offices. Apart from Houghton, who was the general director and the chair of the conference, no other leaders from the China field were present, which was understandable given the uncertain situation in China at that time. Thus, it was decided that another conference with more comprehensive representation should be arranged soon.

---

114. *China's Millions* (March–April 1951): 35, 38. Those who attended the Directors' Conference included Bishop Houghton, J. R. Sinton (China), Fred Mitchell (England), H. M. Griffin (North America), J. O. Sanders (Australia), J. H. Robinson (South Africa), and H. W. Funnell (New Zealand). Because of its location, this conference was also referred to as the "Kalorama Conference."

115. *China's Millions* (March 1951): 35.

116. *China's Millions* (March 1951): 35–40.

117. *China's Millions* (March 1951): 39.

118. *China's Millions* (March 1951): 39.

In November of the same year, the CIM's future direction was finalized at a conference in Bournemouth, England. Altogether, twenty-four CIM leaders were present, both from the Fields and Homes Offices, and decisions made at this conference were considered "binding."[119]

While there was much discussion about possible future work in East Asia beyond China, one main topic, which touched on the fundamentals and ethos of the CIM, was the "Principles of Indigenous Work Carried Out in the New Era."[120] The CIM recognized that this "was not just a goal to aim for but the foundation on which its policy was based."[121] As they planned to launch into new fields outside China, the CIM leaders reaffirmed the CIM's ongoing commitment to the principle of indigenous work that had been endorsed by Hoste and was part of the general policy of the Mission.[122] The leaders at the conference affirmed that while there would be a need "to adopt new methods: to be less rooted and more mobile; to have fewer and simpler possessions, both of property and personal comforts, an indigenous church should be the aim from the outset, unspoilt by the misuse of money and misapplication of denominational bias."[123]

While the CIM was keen to set up a Bible seminary in both Singapore and Indonesia, it was also decided that indigenous principles should apply – meaning that no regular long-term funding should come from the CIM beyond some initial set-up costs.[124]

A major discussion at the Bournemouth Conference aimed to determine whether the old name "CIM" should be retained as they prepared to launch out into new fields. The CIM leaders recognized that the name CIM carried

---

119. Those present included Bishop Frank Houghton, R. J. R. Butler, M. Griffin, A. J. Lea, F. Mitchell, J. H. M. Robinson, J. O. Sanders, J. R. Sinton, E. Weller, A. J. Broomhall, F. L. Canfield, E. Baumann, G. T. Dunn, C. Faulkner, L. G. Gaussen, E. F. Glasser, E. Keeble, J. B. Kuhn, W. J. Michell, J. M. Rockness, G. M. Steed, L. A. Street, R. E. Toliver, and G. A. Williamson. See *China's Millions* (January 1952): 8. See also "Bournemouth Conference Minutes," 8, available at the OMF International Archives, OMF International headquarters in Singapore

120. "Minutes of the Conference of Mission Leaders of the China Inland Mission held at Bournemouth, England, 16–30 November 1951," 77–78.

121. "Minutes," 78.

122. "Minutes," 78.

123. "Minutes," 78.

124. The CIM agreed to provide funds up to five hundred dollars for the purchase of furniture for the Bible College in Singapore. See "Bournemouth Meeting, 1951, Council Minutes," 108.

strong connotations, recognized by others, of the unwavering commitment to the "planting of indigenous churches and the training of national leaders for these indigenous churches."[125] Thus, the continued use of the old name would convey the assurance that in establishing a work in the new fields, the Mission would still adhere to these principles and objectives.[126]

However, it was finally decided that the name "China Inland Mission" by itself would no longer be sufficient as it no longer truly described the identity of the Mission or its work in the new era.[127] After many rounds of debate, a new name was finally decided upon for the Mission: the name "China Inland Mission – Overseas Missionary Fellowship" for use at the home offices and the name "Overseas Missionary Fellowship" for use in the fields.[128] Thus, on 27 November 1951, the China Inland Mission officially became the Overseas Missionary Fellowship. Despite the change in name, the indigenous principles remained central to the ethos of the the Mission.[129]

9. Conclusion

In 1935, having served as the general director of the CIM for thirty-five years, Hoste stepped down. Though the handover process was not completed as smoothly as he had wished, Hoste remained patient and gracious until a general agreement was reached about his successor. He stayed in China afterwards and was imprisoned by the Japanese army in 1944. After the Second World War ended in 1945, Hoste returned to England, and he passed away during the following year.[130]

Hoste's achievements during his directorship may not be comparable to the founding work of Taylor, but his accomplishments in leading the CIM through a period of turmoil and drastic social and political changes yielded some important results, especially in regard to the growth of Chinese churches under the Mission's continual support over a period of several decades.

---

125. "Minutes of the Conference of Mission Leaders of the China Inland Mission held at Bournemouth, England, 16–30 November 1951," 77–78, 121.
126. "Minutes," 43.
127. "Minutes," 44.
128. "Minutes," 44.
129. This emphasis was reflected in the minutes of the Bournemouth Meeting.
130. Thompson, *Reluctant Exodus*, 151.

Hoste had always advocated that the Chinese church should become indigenous, self-supporting, self-governing, and self-propagating while the CIM missionaries should have fellowship with and extend cooperation to their Chinese colleagues.

When Bishop Frank Houghton took the helm of the CIM in 1940, he continued in the same vein as Hoste, strongly advocating that the Chinese church should be indigenous. Houghton, however, had to correct a misconception held by some Chinese church leaders – namely, that the CIM had become "unsympathetically aloof" – which nearly "wrecked the relationship between the Chinese Church and the CIM."[131] Thus, Houghton put forward "a New Emphasis," insisting that the CIM would remove the "controlling hand," but also offer the "helping hand" when requested.

However, with the rapid political changes, the need for the indigenization of the Chinese church – for which both Hoste and Houghton had advocated – became even more urgent. The Chinese church had to become totally independent of all foreign connections. By the end of 1951, all missionaries had to leave China.

Both CIM leaders and the Chinese church had initially failed to understand why the Statement of Policy Hoste put forward in 1928 had included such stern stipulations. However, in retrospect, they recognized that the indigenous policy introduced by Hoste prepared the Chinese church for the time when all missionaries had to leave China in 1951. As one church leader declared, "Now the government's insistence on our dispensing with all foreign aid makes no difference to us. We took that step long ago."[132] When the NCC declared that all churches, Christian bodies, and institutions should demonstrate the utmost determination to complete "the movement for self-government, self-support, and self-propagation," since Hoste's time, the CIM, despite its slow start, had already been carrying out this task for years.[133]

The exodus of all CIM missionaries signified the end of the CIM in China but not the end of the Chinese church, for whom it actually marked a new beginning. Hoste's vision of seeing indigenous principles carried out, though not groundbreaking, left a special mark on the development of Chinese

---

131. *China's Millions* (1951): 50.
132. *China's Millions* (May 1951): 50.
133. *CIM Field Bulletin* (1950): 198.

Christianity in later decades. This vision also recognized that many indigenous church leaders were already leading the Chinese church with significant impact outside CIM influence, while also maintaining a good cooperative relationship with the Mission.

The political change that took place in the country actually helped to realize Hoste's vision of an indigenous Chinese church. In the years after the exodus of missionaries, the Chinese church, far from diminishing, grew in the absence of missionary influence. As Hoste wrote in 1900, the Chinese church would "come to the front, proving themselves equal to missionaries, facing of danger, bearing of responsibility, and growing into leadership."[134]

---

134. *Chinese Recorder* (1900): 511

Conclusion

1. Overview

As described in the introductory chapter, this research was designed to conduct a full-fledged study of the life and work of Dixon Edward Hoste, especially his leadership of the China Inland Mission in the post-Taylor period and his influence on the development of the indigenous Chinese church in the early twentieth century. This research aims to fill the gap in understanding of the CIM's second-generation leadership during a critical period of the development of the CIM and the Chinese church in the early twentieth century.

Based on various historical sources, particularly those newly discovered in the CIM archives – including the China Council minutes – this thesis presents a comprehensive picture of Hoste. One significant factor, which was largely neglected in previous research, is Hoste's close, ten-year relationship with Pastor Hsi. The fieldwork and experience he gained under the strong character of Pastor Hsi prepared Hoste for his demanding leadership role with the CIM. The research findings also reveal how Hoste, succeeding Taylor, fulfilled his role as a capable leader for the CIM during some of the most challenging periods of the CIM, especially when it was confronted with severe crises such as the Boxer Uprising and the Anti-Christian Movement. Hoste repositioned the CIM in the new era so that its missionaries could offer spiritual guidance to the Chinese church while, at the same time, letting go of control.

Hoste, in the Statement of Policy issued in 1928 and the Forward Movement introduced in 1929, claimed that the CIM should not work alone but should always serve in cooperation with the Chinese church. This resulted in significant growth despite the social turbulence of early twentieth-century

China. Hoste's continuous service as the general director of the CIM for more than three decades proved that he was an able leader, who could effectively operate a large-scale missionary enterprise that had nationwide influence in early modern China. One should also note Hoste's long-term commitment as a faithful friend in developing the indigenous Chinese church during his thirty-five-year period as the leader of the CIM.

In the post-Hoste era of the CIM, Hoste's legacy remained visible under the leadership of Frank Houghton. The indigenous principles Hoste advocated continued to have a positive impact on the CIM and the Chinese church. Hoste's vision of these indigenous principles made a unique contribution and laid a solid foundation for the development of Chinese Christianity, particularly in the formation of self-supporting, self-governing, and self-propagating churches. The steps proposed by Hoste in developing the indigenous Chinese church had been "taken long ago," well before the political Three-Self campaign in the 1950s.[1]

The literature review includes an extensive search of biographical and archival materials on Hoste. One of the most valuable materials was the CIM "China Council Minutes." The 1885–1945 *China's Millions* cover the period when Hoste was in China, providing an in-depth understanding of Hoste's life and leadership. Apart from extensive Western scholarship, the literature review also examines various studies on the CIM and the Chinese church by Chinese scholars of the past few decades. More than sixty theses in Chinese were completed between 2001 and 2015 on various subjects related to the CIM. The literature review shows that while extensive efforts have been made to explore multiple interrelated topics on the history of the CIM, with a special focus on its founder, Hudson Taylor, and his leadership, the life and work of Hoste in the post-Taylor period has received scarce attention.

2. Hoste and His Leadership

With a clear focus on Hoste and his leadership, I conclude this research by highlighting three aspects of the man. First, Hoste was a leader who was open to change and who repositioned the CIM to be fit for its purpose in a new age, guided by a long-term vision. Second, Hoste was a faithful friend to the

---

1. Lea, "Mission and God," 47–49.

indigenous Chinese church, both working under and believing in Chinese leadership. Third, Hoste was an unassuming character, yet to be rediscovered – a man who lived to be forgotten but wanted the Chinese church to be remembered.

2.1. A Visionary Leader Bringing the CIM through Crises and Changes

Hoste, during his leadership, had to handle at least two major crises: the Boxer Uprising in 1900 and the Anti-Christian Movement in the 1920s. Through these difficult events, Hoste was able to see beyond the crises, and he demonstrated courage, wisdom, and determination in bringing about changes to make the CIM fit for its purpose.

When Hoste took the helm of the CIM in 1900, fifty-eight CIM missionaries and twenty-one children had been killed by the Boxers. The indemnity issue was high on the agenda of the foreign powers and many missionary agencies. Yet the CIM, under Hoste's leadership, formally decided "not to enter any claim against the Qing government for lives lost, bodily injury or loss of property, but also to refrain from accepting compensation even if offered."[2] This decision came at a great cost because since the Boxer Uprising, donation income for the CIM had dropped significantly. Although the Mission faced many uncertainties, Hoste never wavered in his determination not to accept compensation.

This research shows that the main difference between Hoste and other mission leaders was not so much in his refusal to accept compensation – since a few other mission groups also took a similar position – but, rather, his understanding of the relationship between the CIM and the indigenous Chinese church. Hoste saw that the Chinese church neither belonged to the Mission nor was in the service of the Mission. Rather, as fellow Christians, Hoste was keen to see the CIM give a helping hand to the Chinese church to recover from the Boxer crisis. Hoste worked closely with over forty Chinese leaders from Shanxi to "superintend the native indemnity." Hoste's major positive impact was his insistence on integrity in ensuring that there must be no "carelessness or overstating"[3] of any claims by the Chinese church.

---

2. Broomhall, *China's Open Century*, 7:724.
3. *China's Millions* 1901, 163.

This impressed not only the Chinese church leaders but also the governor of Shanxi.

This research also reveals that Hoste was able to see beyond the immediate crisis and envision the changes that must take place. Hoste's far-sighted article – "Possible Changes and Developments in the Native Churches Arising out of the Present Crisis" – published in the *Chinese Recorder* in October 1900, soon after the Boxer Uprising, set out Hoste's vision for the Chinese church. In this article, Hoste indicated that the current system employed by the missionaries did not encourage self-government in the native churches. He insisted that control of the indigenous church belonged to the Chinese and that the authority of the missionaries should remain spiritual in nature – so that they were only viewed as guides and exemplars – and advocated that the Chinese church should avoid dependency on missionaries. Sixteen years later, Hoste wrote another article in the *Chinese Recorder*, again reminding those from the West that the Chinese "will prove themselves equal to the task." Hoste's view was very much ahead of his time, and not everyone agreed with his view. Some, particularly those from outside the CIM, felt that what China needed at that time was a "Christianized China" in order to save the nation. Some even claimed that Western missionaries should play the role of "apostles of human rights" and, in this matter, discharge their duty to help China. However, this was never Hoste's focus, and he insisted that "missionaries should exercise much humility and patience in dealing with their self-will and pride." Hoste's agenda was never political.

The emergence of the second crisis – namely, the Anti-Christian Movement in the 1920s and the May Thirtieth Incident in 1925 – led to increasing social unrest and forced the CIM to temporarily evacuate to the coastal area. In response, Hoste felt that the indigenization process was even more urgent and must be accelerated. This research demonstrates that Hoste – who possessed a careful mind and the ability to pay close attention to details – was able to give substantive thought to how the indigenous principles should be implemented. Along the same vein as Taylor, Hoste proposed that foreign missionaries were to be the "scaffolding," while the Chinese church was to be the permanent structure. The two-pronged approach of the Statement of Policy in 1928 and the Forward Movement in 1929 highlighted a vision of a parallel advancement: the Chinese church advancing to be fully independent and the CIM missionaries advancing to the unchurched interior of China where people had not been touched by the word of God. Hoste saw the urgency of the task of repositioning the CIM to limit itself to offering spiritual guidance and to transfer leadership to the Chinese. Two key concepts stand out in Hoste's proposal: "without delay" and "cooperation."

Hoste was also careful to explain, in detail, that the new proposals included in the Statement of Policy were not a diversion from the original direction and purpose of the founder but, rather, "an outgrowth and development of the first principles of the CIM." At the same time, Hoste was a man of action. With the support of the China Council, he gave detailed instructions that all churches established by the CIM should proceed without delay with the nomination, election, and appointment of Chinese church officers in order to carry out the Mission policy of establishing self-supporting, self-governing, and self-propagating churches.

In both crises, Hoste was able to direct the CIM to examine its role in its relationship with the Chinese church. He brought changes in the way the CIM operated to discourage dependency but ignite a self-supporting effort by the Chinese church. He did not avoid the sensitive subject of finances but, tather, openly stated that the local churches should increasingly take on full responsibility for the local Chinese workers, including financial responsibility, and that foreign support should be terminated in the long run. Hoste was able to help the CIM not only to emerge from the crises but also to move ahead. The Forward Movement proposed by Hoste resulted in the recruitment of more than two hundred new workers within three years to work in the unchurched inlands of China. During times of crisis, Hoste gave hope and direction to the Mission under his leadership. By 1935, the year that Hoste stepped down from leadership, the CIM had grown to 1,313 missionaries. More important, there were 2,350 self-supporting Chinese workers associated with the CIM across nineteen provinces in China.[4] The growth of self-supporting workers far exceeded that of the foreign missionaries.

2.2. A Faithful Friend Journeying with the Indigenous Chinese Church

This research presents an extensive discussion on Hoste's relationship and collaborative work with some of the leading Chinese Christians of the time.

---

4. *China's Millions* (1935): 2.

The best example is his long-term friendship with Pastor Hsi. Hsi's hot temper and assertive leadership made some CIM co-workers uncomfortable. Stanley Smith, one of the Cambridge Seven who was also assigned to Hsi's mission, could not work with Hsi and left him within two years to work in another province. Hoste, however, was able to maintain a close relationship with Hsi for ten years, probably because of Hoste's gentle character and submissive manner. Though Hoste was from the British elite ruling class, he showed deep respect for Chinese culture and was willing to work under Hsi's leadership. One can hardly find a better example of collaboration in the early decades of the CIM mission.

The close friendship between Hoste and Hsi may be vividly seen in a personal letter written by Hsi to Hoste's family in 1895. This particular detail has not received much discussion or study in past research. Hsi's letter clearly demonstrates his affection and appreciation for Hoste. Hsi's use of Chinese honorifics not only shows respect and deference to Hoste's father but also indicates that he regarded Hoste as his brother. Hsi also demonstrated his sincere concern for Hoste's father by providing two types of Chinese medicines – both the "red pills and the black pills" – intended to help restore Hoste's father's health. Hsi also acknowledged the pain Hoste's father had to endure because of the loss of one his sons. Though Hsi had never met General Hoste before, there is a tone of intimacy in the letter – like one speaking to a family member. In his letter, Hsi asks for prayer that more missionaries would be able to come to China. This demonstrates a marked change in his attitude towards foreigners, which can probably be attributed to the closeness and authenticity of his relationship with Hoste. In the past, Hsi had had nothing to do with foreigners, but Hoste had proven to him that a trusting relationship could be built between a Westerner and a Chinese.

In response, Hoste paid due respect to Hsi. He saw in Hsi a living example of a confident and able Chinese indigenous leader. There were many occasions when Hoste knew that Hsi had great needs, including financial needs. Despite this, Hoste felt an inner conviction that giving money would not be right as it would only create dependency. Hsi later thanked him, saying that it was a blessing that Hoste had not provided for him since "a gift from a missionary in times of hardship would be a hindrance to the work." Hoste demonstrated how to honour a Chinese leader with respect and dignity.

Though not without faults, Hsi proved to Hoste that the native leaders would "come to the front, and proving themselves equal to the facing of danger and bearing of responsibility, growing into leadership."[5] Even before the arrival of the Cambridge Seven, Hsi had already established eight opium refuges in Shanxi, completely independent of missionary help. Later, his work grew and expanded into the adjacent provinces. Hoste and Hsi's close relationship and collaboration contributed to the conceptualization and consolidation of Hoste's indigenous church principles in later years. This might also have been an important factor that influenced Taylor, the founder of the CIM, to choose Hoste as the next leader of the CIM.

This research also indicates that Hoste attempted to help Western readers appreciate Hsi's work and maintain an open mind regarding his unique spiritual work, including exorcisms. Hoste himself, as a young missionary who had absolutely no experience and had received no teaching on this subject, confessed that the whole question of the devil was naturally perplexing. However, after his experience of ten years of working closely with Hsi, Hoste was willing to take "a cautious and open attitude" on this subject.

This research also confirms that even after Hsi's death in 1896, Hoste continued to maintain a strong relationship with the church leaders in Shanxi. In June 1901, after the Boxer Uprising, he personally visited the Shanxi pastors and encouraged them. He also worked closely with Elders Qü, Xü, and Si – former associates of his – and over forty local Chinese church leaders in Shanxi to ensure that there should be "no overstating or carelessness" in any claim by the Chinese church for the indemnity associated with the Boxer Uprising.[6] Hoste's insistence on integrity made a deep impression on the Chinese church leaders as well as the governor in Shanxi.

As Hoste took the helm of the CIM, he did not just pursue growth in the number of missionary workers. During the first five years of his leadership, there was also significant growth in the number of self-supporting local workers associated with the CIM – a total of 332, compared to 172 prior to the Boxer Uprising.[7]

---

5. *Chinese Recorder* (1900): 511.
6. *China's Millions* (1901): 163.
7. *China's Millions* (1989): 165–168; Broomhall, *Land of Sinim*, 178.

In 1919, with Hoste's encouragement, the Shanxi churches enthusiastically initiated the formation of a Home Missionary Movement for the province.[8] The Chinese church was to be entrusted with responsibility for evangelization across the different *hsien* (縣) districts in Shanxi that had hitherto been largely unreached. This movement became a pilot project for Hoste to experiment with the indigenous process before fully launching the Statement of Policy in 1928. Hoste also introduced a system whereby funds from the CIM and from local churches to support local workers would be pooled and managed by a committee led mainly by local church leaders. It was also anticipated that the proportion of Mission money to Chinese contribution would gradually decrease.

Cheng Jingyi (誠靜怡, 1881–1939) – one of the key Chinese church leaders and secretary of the China Continuation Committee, which had been a follow up from the 1910 Edinburgh World Missionary Conference – affirmed Hoste's view that "foreign missions in China were the scaffolding and the Church the permanent building itself."

While Hoste continued to encourage the Chinese churches to be independent, he also warned the different Mission groups against denominationalism and parochialism. Hoste claimed that denominational distinctions would only be a hindrance to the development of self-supporting, self-governing, and self-propagating Chinese churches.

At the same time, perhaps the biggest challenge Hoste faced in relating to the Chinese church leaders was the severing of the relationship between the CIM and the National Christian Council (NCC). Hoste became increasingly concerned about the liberal theological position adopted by the NCC on the subjects of biblical authority, the deity of Christ, and commitment to the proclamation of the gospel. Increasingly, the NCC had departed from the conservative doctrinal standards to which the CIM held. In 1925, Hoste had to make a difficult decision that led to "the CIM terminating its relationship and fellowship with the NCC."[9] While Hoste distanced himself from the NCC, he openly associated himself with the Bible Union of China, a theologically fundamentalist group to counteract the rampant modernist

---

8. *China's Millions* (1919): 70.
9. *China's Millions* (May 1926): 79.

viewpoints.[10] Thus, while Hoste maintained a strong friendship with the Chinese church, it was not indiscriminate – particularly when Hoste felt that fundamental Christian doctrines were being compromised. Hoste was also a focused man. He was not interested in diverting his attention to endless theological and doctrinal debates with the modernist party.[11] Under Hoste's leadership, the CIM maintained strong friendships with more conservative indigenous church leaders like John Sung (宋尚節), Andrew Gih (計志文), Wang Ming-Dao (王明道), David Yang (楊紹唐), and others.

Although we cannot ascertain Hoste's level of proficiency in Chinese, we can infer, from the records available, that Hoste had a good command of Chinese based on at least two examples of his communication with government officials and Chinese church leaders. The first example is an agreement written in Chinese and signed by Hoste, addressed to the Foreign Affairs Bureau 洋務局 in August 1901.[12] This agreement includes a detailed declaration by the CIM that it would not accept compensation for any damage or lives lost due to the Boxer Uprising. The agreement is written in an official manner in the format of a legal document in Chinese. The second example is a letter written by Hoste in Chinese, in 1926, addressed to the president, Yu Rizhang 余日章 (1882–1936), and the executive director, Luo Bingsheng 羅柄生, of the National Christian Council, setting out the reasons for the CIM's decision to withdraw from the NCC.[13] The letter is firm but cordial, with Hoste expressing his appreciation for the past friendship and collaboration with the NCC. Both letters contain formal and carefully chosen words. Both documents show that Hoste was fluent in Chinese and had a strong command of the language.

---

10. Yao, *Fundamentalist Movement*, 67–70.

11. Yao, 14.

12. "*Beijing Xinwen Huibao* 北京新聞匯報," *Beijing News Report*, August 1901, 2741–2757, accessed June 28, 2022, https://www-cnbksy- com.eproxy.lib.hku.hk/literature/browsePiece?eid=null&bcId=null&pieceId=0eeb1ba2aaacf7132ee96628d9912f81&ltid=7&activeId=62baa84f84b8494a8530c242&downloadSource=GENERALSEARCH,

13. Dixon E. Hoste, *Xinghua* 興華 23, no. 24 (1926): 25–28, accessed June 28, 2022, ,https://www-cnbksy-com.eproxy.lib.hku.hk/literature/browsePiece?eid=null&bcId=null&pieceId=981104b85f41ce7e44b0f5e74d67d734&ltid=7&activeId=62baa84f84b8494a8530c242&downloadSource=GENERALSEARCH

2.3. An Unassuming Character

As indicated earlier, Hoste did not seem to have had the qualities expected of a top leader. In fact, he was the quietest and shyest of the Cambridge Seven and preferred to remain in the background. Even his pastor, Rev. Storrs, considered Hoste "not very enterprising and not fitted for missionary work." Storrs was also concerned about Hoste's high-pitched voice, which did not make him a natural speaker. The records reveal that among the farewell speeches given by the Cambridge Seven in early 1885, before they left for China, Hoste's sharing was rather flat, monotonous, and unimpressive, while Stanley Smith's speech was the most colourful. Nevertheless, Hoste always spoke with sincerity.

Hoste's military training at the Royal Military Academy prepared him for the rough conditions and challenges he had to face when he arrived in China. Even though Hoste was not physically strong, he was the longest surviving member of the Cambridge Seven for all other members of the group had died by 1939. As shown in this research, apart from the strict training of a disciplined life at the Military Academy, "with all the luxuries removed," precision was also a hallmark of Hoste's training, which had focused on mathematics and the scientific principles of gunnery and fortification. Exactness and accuracy were important to Hoste. We see this value demonstrated in the way he advised the Chinese church leaders regarding making indemnity claims after the Boxer Uprising, emphasizing that there should be "no carelessness and overstating" and that every claim submitted should be carefully examined.

Stemming from his military training, Hoste was also known to pay great attention to detail. When he introduced the Statement of Policy in 1928 to show how the CIM should operate to establish indigenous churches, he articulated this in great detail. For example, he proposed that none of the missionary residence properties should be purchased but only rented to enable missionaries to remain mobile and free to move on to other places once the church was established. While Hoste was a man of great vision, who was often ahead of his time, he was also a man who had his feet firmly planted on the ground in a way that ensured his plans would succeed.

While Hoste was from an elite background and a member of the upper class, he was gentle and humble by nature. In his first encounter with Taylor in 1883, when applying to join the CIM, Hoste was told to wait and "to mature as a Christian first." Phyllis Thompson records that, surprisingly, Hoste "walked away from that interview feeling encouraged. His enthusiasm had been quickened rather than dampened by what he had heard. Hoste was not a person who easily gave up."

By 1885, with the Cambridge Seven's arrival in China, both Stanley Smith and Hoste were assigned to work under Pastor Hsi. More than fifty years later, in *China's Millions*, Hoste confessed the tension he experienced in working with Stanley Smith. Smith felt that one of them should be recognized as the missionary-in-charge and that he should be that person.[14] As they had come out to China as members of the same party and were of the same age, initially, Hoste was not prepared to accept this arrangement. However, soon afterwards, Hoste felt in his conscience that his refusal was not due to a pure desire for God's will and glory but, rather, because of his unwillingness to humble himself and take a lower place. He also admitted that Smith – particularly due to his gifts as a speaker, his resourcefulness, and his quickness in current affairs – was better qualified to lead. In the end, Hoste told Smith that he welcomed the proposal and accepted a junior role by submitting to Smith's leadership. In his testimony, Hoste affirmed that relationships with fellow workers can only be "perfect in the sight of God through the working of death to self."[15]

In 1900, when Taylor was ill and decided on the surprising appointment of Hoste as his successor, Hoste initially declined, feeling strongly that John Stevenson, the China director at the time and a more senior leader, should take up the role. In the end, after months of waiting, he sought Stevenson's blessing and his wholehearted acceptance of Taylor's proposal, indicating that if Stevenson did not agree to the appointment, he would readily let it go. Hoste later wrote to Taylor, mentioning Stevenson's "eminently Christian spirit and largeness of mind" in the course of their conversation. Clearly, Hoste was a man of compassion.

As Phyllis Thompson points out, Hoste likened himself to a coxswain – a little man "to sort of steer" at the back of the boat – while Hsi or another Chinese leader could be the pacesetter – the leader who strokes the boat.[16] Hoste's leadership style was one of journeying with others while not imposing

---

14. *China's Millions* (1940): 99–101.
15. *China's Millions* (1940): 99.
16. Thompson, *Prince with God*, 62.

his own views. This is evident in the way he supported Pastor Hsi in times of crisis, particularly when Hsi was opposed by his enemies in the opium refuge work. Mrs. Howard Taylor points out that Hsi discovered a rich treasure of sympathy and friendship with Hoste, a deep friendship such as was rarely known between a Westerner and a Chinese during that time. Nevertheless, despite his deepest appreciation of Hsi's character and work, Hoste was not blind to his friend's faults. Yet he stood by him as few others could have done even among his own CIM colleagues.[17] Hoste admitted that a great deal of patience and humility were required to work with a man who had such a dominating personality as Hsi. In some ways, "it would have been easier to strike out alone, build up on his own work, on his own lines rather than cooperate with Hsi."[18] Yet Hoste concluded that "had he done so, he would have missed what later proved to be the best training in real life." Hoste's friendship with Hsi deepened as the years passed and these two friends journeyed together, but their relationship was cut short when Hsi died in 1896. Examining the records, it would also be fair to say that among the many Chinese church leaders Hoste interacted with over his thirty-five years of leadership, there was not another like Hsi with whom he had journeyed so closely.

Throughout the history of the CIM, the general director's authority was paramount. The *Principles and Practice*, which was essentially the constitution of the CIM, stipulated that the China Council – which was composed of the superintendents of all the provincial districts, who in turn directed the operation of each province – advised the general director.[19] The CIM was set up in such a way that it was administered by a general director who was "in full control and whose power was final."[20] The "fount of authority rests in the General Director."[21] Under Taylor's leadership, decision-making within the CIM was much more centralized and directive. However, during Hoste's leadership, even though he had to make many critical decisions, his style was mostly consensual rather than directive. He made every effort to seek

---

17. Taylor, *Pastor Hsi*, 239.

18. Thompson, *Prince with God*, 62.

19. *Principles and Practice of the China Inland Mission*, 1914, 1.

20. See Minutes of the "Conference of Mission Leaders of the China Inland Mission held at Bournemouth, England," 16–30 November 1951," 123, 127.

21. Minutes of the "Conference of Mission Leaders of the China Inland Mission held at Bournemouth, England,"., 125.

the "intelligent and cordial concurrence of all those concerned," as evident in the following two examples.

First, as previously mentioned, Hoste had to make the painful decision to withdraw from the NCC because of its liberal stance, a decision Hoste considered "extremely undesirable." Before a final decision was made, Hoste consulted with a number of Chinese church leaders, which included making a special trip to Hangzhou to consult with Pastor Ren Chengyuan (任樨園,1852–1929), a senior Chinese leader who was also a member of the NCC. While expressing regret over the possible severance of CIM's relationship with the NCC, Ren concurred with Hoste. Thus, in March 1926, Hoste, representing the CIM, officially withdrew from the NCC.

A second example of a significant consensus-building exercise by Hoste was the implementation of the Statement of Policy in 1928. Three special consultations were arranged in Yantai, Tianjin, and Shanghai, where Hoste met with more than four hundred CIM missionaries from fourteen provinces to hear their concerns and receive their input. That same year, Hoste also sent Gibb, the deputy director in China at that time, on a special trip to England and America to consult with the Home Councils on the Statement of Policy. While Hoste saw the urgent need to implement changes within the CIM to enhance the indigenous process, he also took great care to consult extensively among his own troops.

Although Hoste exercised leadership responsibility for the CIM, he was also a private man. Phyllis Thompson highlights how challenging it was to write a biographical sketch of Hoste. He was so different from Taylor, his predecessor, as no diaries and very few personal letters of Hoste can be found. Thus, it is difficult to present a complete picture of the man. There was little record of his inner conflicts or the joy and sorrows he experienced during his years of leadership. "With almost startling suddenness a curtain seems to have been drawn across the sanctuary of his personal life. If he kept a private diary, it has never come to light."[22] Much of Hoste's work and contribution remains unwritten and unknown.

Despite his contributions to the CIM and to the development of the indigenous Chinese church, Hoste's accomplishments are usually viewed as a

---

22. Thompson, *Prince with God*, 103.

"hidden ministry."²³ Hoste, unlike his predecessor, was never a public man. According to Phyllis Thompson, his clarity of thought and expression were seen to better advantage when he was in the council chamber than on the platform. Many in the CIM would consider that Hoste's most effective service was his private, unremitting, watchful prayer that did not fluctuate or slacken.

Not only did Hoste adopt a low-key posture, he also desired the same for the CIM. In 1905, in an address to a group of CIM supporters in London, he said,

> I asked for your prayers and your continued prayers that we may be guided in regard to these three things: first that we may, as a Mission, retain the spirit of willingness to be small, to be despised, to be poor, to suffer hardness . . . no work of God is done easily, and no work is done without real sacrifice, real suffering, real loss, and real shame and contempt in the doing it. Let us make up our minds to that.²⁴

In Hoste's vision of the development of the indigenous Chinese church, he always saw the CIM as being only a small part of a far-reaching movement.

Hoste's unassuming leadership does not imply weakness. On the contrary, Hoste did not yield to pressure when he realized that the truth was being comprised. During his negotiations with the Qing authorities in the aftermath of the Boxer Uprising, the circuit intendant (Daotai) asked to first subtract 20 or 30 percent from whatever was claimed by the Chinese church leaders as it was a customary practice to always ask for more and expect a reduction later. Hoste refused to comply since to accept the reduction was a virtual admission that the Christians had been dishonest in their estimates. Hoste upheld integrity throughout the negotiation process.

Wu Yaqun (吳亞群) in his study on Hoste, comments that Hoste rarely interacted with the intellectuals of his time, whether Christians or non-Christians.²⁵ It would be correct to say that the CIM's focus had always been the urgent spreading of the gospel in the inlands of China, particularly among

---

23. Thompson, 103.

24. *China's Millions* (1906): 6.

25. Wu Yaqun 吳亞群, "A study on Dixon Edward Hoste, the second General Director of the CIM," 32.

the peasants.²⁶ Throughout the 1920s and the early 1930s, under Hoste's leadership, the CIM's focus on evangelization never diminished, particularly in relation to the rural inlands of China. Thus, as some scholars suggest, the CIM seemed to "ignore the ethical and theological issues [and debates] about which other Protestants earnestly contended."²⁷ As mentioned earlier, Hoste did not allow his attention to be diverted from evangelism to the endless doctrinal controversies that were possible with the liberal, modernist camp. Yet, Yao rightly points out that Hoste, along with other CIM leaders, still remained actively and extensively engaged in the fundamentalist cause, challenging the liberal intellectuals, though he did so individually – through publications, the Bible Union, and other fundamentalist enterprises in China.²⁸ It would be fair to say that Hoste did not engage adequately with the modernists on key contextualization issues related to Christianity in China, in order to help the Chinese church to find its own cultural identity when embracing the Christian faith.²⁹

After Hoste stepped down from leadership in 1935, he and his wife continued to stay at the CIM headquarters compound in Shanghai. In 1941, however, with the Japanese occupation, they were ordered to leave the place that had been their home for more than forty years. Although exempted from internment because of age, they were housed, together with other foreigners, in a crowded place. In April 1944, Hoste's wife died after a short illness. Hoste was eighty-three years old at that time. Two months later, he had to move again because the temporary exemption was cancelled, and he was required to go to an internment camp along with three hundred others. Though Hoste was growing weaker, what brought him most joy was when someone would come to his room and pray with him.³⁰ In October 1945, when the war was over, he was carried on board the *Oxfordshire* and sailed to England for the last time.

---

26. So, "Passion for a Greater Vision," 85.
27. Stauffer, *Christian Occupation*, 371–373.
28. Yao, *Fundamentalist Movement*, 14.
29. Lam Wing Hung 林榮洪, *Fengchaozhong fenqi de Zhongguo jiaohui* 風潮中奮起的中國教會 (Chinese Theology in Construction), 138–145.
30. Thompson, *Prince with God*, 148–149.

Hoste first arrived in China in 1885 and, having spent nearly sixty years in the country, finally left China in 1945. He passed away on 11 May 1946. In part, his eulogy stated that

> the Boxer crisis was a God-given opportunity for placing greater responsibility upon the Chinese Church and its leaders. In this Mr. Hoste, no doubt, profiting by the lessons he had learned in his labors with Pastor Hsi. However, I fear his words were not given the consideration they deserved, because the vast majority of missionaries felt at that time that the Chinese Church and its leaders were not yet ready for such a move. It took another upheaval – that of the Communist Movement to make men realize that the time had come.[31]

3. Lessons for Today

The life and leadership of Hoste teaches several lessons. First, when Hoste took on the leadership of the CIM, he specifically asked people to pray for him for three things: a spirit of willingness to be small, to be despised, and to be poor.[32] These are not usually the aspirations of modern leaders, among whom the norm tends to be elevating charisma and celebrity status. However, we see that Hoste exemplified a model of servanthood, submitting to the Father with a secure and clear sense of identity in Jesus Christ. Hoste willingly served under a Christian Chinese leader, Pastor Hsi, for ten years, with deep loyalty and without exerting control.

In his recent book, *Leadership or Servanthood?: Walking in the Steps of Jesus*, Hwa Yung argues that the key emphasis in the Bible's teaching is that we are called first and foremost to be servants, not leaders.[33] He points out that the New Testament is rather sparing in its use of words for leadership that carry the idea of positional status and authority over others. Instead, the two words for "servant" – *diakonos*, meaning household servants, and *doulos*, usually meaning slaves – along with their related verbs, are used about fifty

---

31. Folder 56, Box 4, Collection #215, CIM Philadelphia Archives, Archives of the Billy Graham Center, Wheaton.
32. *China's Millions* (1906): 6.
33. Hwa Yung, *Leadership or Servanthood?*, 5.

times in the New Testament to describe service to God and to the church. Thus, "the New Testament makes it abundantly clear that the fundamental nature of ministry and leadership to which they are called is defined by servanthood, and not by position, status, and power."[34] We often think that being small means being weak, and we wonder how such a person can possess the authority and power to effectively and faithfully carry out the ministry that God has entrusted to them. However, as we have seen in the example of Hoste, he demonstrated the courage and the spiritual authority to contend for the faith and speak up strongly when the truth was compromised. Although the decision that the CIM should withdraw from the NCC in 1926 was a painful decision, Hoste never regretted it. He spoke strongly:

> It is my conviction that the Modernist movement, as a whole, is a departure from the Christian faith – revealed in the Bible. Observation of its past and present processes makes me fear that, in the future, its phases will increasingly develop into avowed unbelief in the Bible and its doctrinal teachings. Many connected with the Modernist movement are active in spreading its views, and, in so doing, ignore or deny what I believe to be divinely revealed truth . . . [I need to] identify myself by voice and by pen, to restore those who have departed from those doctrines, and safeguard others from such departure.[35]

Being willing to be small, to be despised, and to suffer for the Lord also means being willing to stand up for the truth, willing to defend the faith, and willing to face rejection by those who depart from the faith.

Second, from the first day he took on leadership as the general director of the CIM to the time he stepped down, Hoste believed that the Chinese church should be led by the Chinese. Hoste was convinced that those "whose very force and independence of character unfitted them for office under the old regime, will come to the front; and proving themselves equal to the facing of danger and bearing of responsibilities, growing into leadership."[36] Peter Rowan, a missiologist from the UK, asks a pertinent question given our

---

34. Hwa Yung, 11.
35. Hoste, "Bible Union," 469–472.
36. *Chinese Recorder* (1900): 511.

current mission landscape: "Should White People Be Missionaries Overseas?" His answer is "No" if we think mission is about taking our theological categories and church structures and transplanting them somewhere else – with the underlying notion that our theology and church structures are "normative" and that, therefore, we need to teach new Christians how to adopt them. His answer is "Yes" if we understand the contextual nature of theological reflection and appreciate that understanding the gospel, expressions of faith, and the emergence of Christlike communities will take a different shape in different parts of the world and that, by reading the Bible with the other, we will ourselves be transformed.[37] Local believers must have the space to read Scripture so that localized faith emerges in ways that connect with the lived reality of their daily experience as a community. Local churches have the "freedom to theologize and express their experience of God in ways that may not look orthodox to outsiders."[38] Thus, we must embrace a posture of humility. Hoste's reference to Pastor Hsi's casting out of evil spirits in answer to prayer might raise scepticism among Western readers. However, Hoste urged his readers to maintain an open mind even though he himself did not grow up as a Christian with that understanding or experience. A willingness to listen with "learning, unlearning and relearning" is critical in global mission leadership.[39]

Third, with the Boxer Uprising, Hoste believed that more significant changes would certainly take place with the absence of missionaries "in whom the centre of gravity of power, influence, and initiative had rested."[40] Hoste was not assuming that the very fact of the Boxer Uprising would automatically produce strong, mature, and influential native leaders of the Chinese church. However, he believed there must be a new rearrangement in the relationship between the missionaries and the native leaders by increasing trust. The CIM missionaries had to let go of control so that the Chinese church could become truly indigenous – that is, self-supporting, self-governing, and self-propagating. Hoste introduced the concept of the "Statement of Policy" in 1928,

---

37. Peter Rowan, "Should White People Be Missionaries Overseas? Absurd Question or Pathway to Reimagining Missional Faithfulness in a Postcolonial World?" (paper presented at the OMF International Mission Research Consultation, May 2023).

38. Rowan, 7.

39. Rowan, 9

40. Broomhall, *Martyred Missionaries*, 280.

repositioning the CIM to let go of positional authority in the Chinese church and serve only as advisers with spiritual influence. This was the practice that Hoste had adopted since the days he served with Pastor Hsi. Letting go of control does not mean abdicating responsibilities. A truly biblical indigenous movement will not only move from dependence to independence but also towards interdependence. We are called to collaboration for the sake of God's kingdom. We have seen enormous changes in the mission landscape over the past one hundred years, especially since the 1910 Edinburgh Conference.[41] During the last decade, many have written on the concept of "Polycentric Mission Leadership". Paul Woods comments on today's new mission dynamic:

> We can see a rainbow around the table- whether the table actually is round is another matter. Today we can rub shoulders with brothers and sisters from many different continents in a polycentric world, different backgrounds, North and South, East and West. Rather than passing the mission baton from the Western world to the majority world Church, God is adding more hands to it.[42]

One of the best definitions of polycentrism in the context of world mission is by Kirk Franklin:

> The concept of polycentrism is an outcome of globalization and glocalization and it provides a deliberate movement away from established centers of power, so that leadership takes place among and within a community that learns together. Polycentrism assumes self-regulating centers of influence within a given structure. This occurs when there are many centers of power or importance within a political, cultural, or socio-economic system. The multiple centers may be of leadership, power, authority, ideology, or importance within a larger political boundary.[43]

---

41. The 1,215 official delegates were predominantly British and American, with a small minority coming from the non-Western churches – nine Indians (including one Eurasian Methodist woman from Madras), four Japanese, three Chinese, one Korean, one Burmese, one Anatolian, and a Europeanized Black African.
42. Woods, "Perichoresis and Koinonia," 4–5.
43. Kirk Franklin, "Polycentrism in the Missio Dei," 1.

Professor Andrew Walls insightfully highlights the concept of polycentrism in global mission: "The riches of a hundred places learning from each other." He believes that there is no one single centre of Christianity or one single centre of missionary activity and says that one necessitates the other.[44] Each centre enriches the others, and each of them needs one another. In our global family, some will bring quite different gifts. Some will model faithfulness in the face of suffering and persecution and show us a vital element of authentic gospel living. Some will bring years of experience of commending the Lord Jesus Christ in the context of another world faith. Some will show how to live with shining trust in God despite poverty or injustice. Others will bring deep traditions of believing prayer. The body of Christ needs all of these and much more; and in true partnership, we shall each bring what we have, not what we don't have, to bless the world church in its mission. And we will respect and rejoice in diversity, rather than impose on others just one way of doing mission. Thus, Bishop Frank Houghton, Hoste's successor, was correct when he emphasized that we not only let go of "controlling hands," but we offer our "helping hands" for the work of the kingdom.

4. Concluding Remarks

This research fills a gap in what has been lacking in past scholarship on CIM leadership after Taylor. Hoste, succeeding Taylor, fulfilled his role as a capable leader over a thirty-five-year period during some of the most challenging periods of the Mission. The findings of this research demonstrate that Hoste was a leader who embraced change, repositioning the CIM to offer spiritual guidance and letting go of control over the Chinese church in the new era. In his faithful friendship and continuous support, he went a step further than his predecessors and contemporaries. Therefore, the committed work of Hoste should be duly recognized as an integral part of the indigenous movement of modern Chinese Christianity. However, because of his low-key character, much of Hoste's contribution to the CIM and the indigenous Chinese church have remained hidden. Hoste was a man who lived to be forgotten so that Christ might be remembered.

---

44. "Andrew Walls: Historian Ahead of His Time," *Christianity Today*, February 2007.

Bibliography

Archives

CIM London Archives. School of Oriental and African Studies, University of London.

Collection #215. CIM Philadelphia Archives. Archives of the Billy Graham Center, Wheaton College.

Collection AR 6.1.4, Box 1. CIM Singapore Archives. OMF International, Singapore.

China's Millions. London: China Inland Mission, 1875–1951.

"China Inland Mission China Council Minutes, 1897–1947."

CIM Field Bulletin. Shanghai: China Inland Mission, 1939–1952.

Chinese Recorder. Shanghai: American Presbyterian Press, 1869–1936.

Books and theses

Austin, Alvyn. *China's Millions: The China Inland Mission and Late Qing Society, 1832–1905*. Grand Rapids: Eerdmans, 2007.

Baller, F. W. *A Primer in the Mandarin Dialect Containing Lessons and Vocabularies, and Notes on Chinese Constructions and Idioms*. Shanghai: China Inland Mission; American Presbyterian Mission Press, 1887.

Bickers, Robert. "Introduction." In *The Boxers, China, and the World*, edited by Robert Bickers and R. G. Tiedemann. Plymouth: Rowman & Littlefield, 2007.

Boynton, Charles Luther, and Charles Dozier Boynton. *1936 Handbook of the Christian Movement in China under Protestant Auspices*. Shanghai: Kwang Hsueh, 1936.

Brandt, Nat. *Massacre in Shansi*. Lincoln: Excel, 1999.

Broomhall, A. J. *Hudson Taylor and China's Open Century*. 7 vols. London: Hodder & Stoughton; OMF Books, 1981–1989.

———. *The Shaping of Modern China: Hudson Taylor's Life and Legacy*. 2 vols. Carlisle: Piquant, 2005.

Broomhall, Marshall. *The Chinese Empire: A General and Missionary Survey*. London: Morgan & Scott; CIM, 1907.

———. *Days of Blessing in Inland China*. London: Morgan & Scott, 1887.

———. *The Jubilee Story of the China Inland Mission*. London: China Inland Mission, 1915.

———. *The Land of Sinim: An Illustrated Report of the China Inland Mission*. London: China Inland Mission, 1905.

———. *Martyred Missionaries of the China Inland Mission: With a Record of the Perils and Sufferings of Some Who Escaped*. London: Morgan & Scott, 1901.

Cairns, Earle E., and J. D. Douglas. *The New International Dictionary of the Christian Church*. Grand Rapids: Zondervan, 1978.

Chao, Jonathan Tien-en. "The Chinese Indigenous Church Movement, 1919–1927: A Protestant Response to the Anti-Christian Movements in Modern China." PhD diss., University of Pennsylvania, 1986.

Chang, Irene, ed. *Christ Alone: A Pictorial Presentation of Hudson Taylor's Life and Legacy*. Hong Kong: OMF Hong Kong, 2005. c

Choi, Kamto 蔡錦圖. *Daidesheng yu Zhongguo Neidihui, 1832–1953* 戴德生與中國內地會, 1832–1953 (Hudson Taylor and the China Inland Mission, 1832–1953). Hong Kong: Jiandao Shengxueyuan Jidujiao yu Zhongguo Wenhua Zhongxin, 1988.

Chow, Tse-tsung. *The May Fourth Movement: Intellectual Revolution in Modern China*. Stanford: Stanford University Press, 1967.

CIM, *The Principles and Practice of the China Inland Mission*. Shanghai: China Inland Mission, 1886.

Clark, Anthony E. *Heaven in Conflict: Franciscans and the Boxer Uprising in Shanxi*. Seattle: University of Washington Press, 2015.

Cohen, Paul. *History in Three Keys: The Boxers as Event, Experience and Myth*. New York: Columbia University Press, 1997.

Edwards, Ebenezer Henry. *Fire and Sword in Shansi: The Story of the Martyrdom of Foreigners and Chinese Christians*. Edinburgh: Oliphant, Anderson & Ferrier, 1900.

Esherick, Joseph. *The Origin of the Boxer Uprising*. Berkeley: University of California Press, 1988.

Fung, Patrick. *Changjiang Xinglin* 長江杏林 (Medical Missionaries of the China Inland Mission). Hong Kong: OMF Hong Kong, 2007.

———. *Live to Be Forgotten*. Hong Kong: OMF Hong Kong, 2008.

Griffiths, Valerie. *Not Less Than Everything*, Oxford: Monarch Books, 2004.

Grubb, Norman P. *C. T. Studd: Athlete and Pioneer*. Grand Rapids: Zondervan, 1937.

Bibliography

Guggisberg, F. G. *"The Shop": The Story of the Royal Military Academy*. London: Cassell, 1900.

Hamrin, Carol Lee, and Stacey Bieler, eds. *Salt and Light, Volume 3: More Lives of Faith That Shaped Modern China (Studies in Chinese Christianity)*. Eugene: Pickwick, 2011.

Harrison, Henrietta. *The Missionary's Curse and Other Tales from a Chinese Catholic Village*. Berkeley: University of California Press, 2013.

Houghton, Frank. *China Calling*. London: China Inland Mission, 1937.

Huang, Dashou 黃大受, *Zhongguo Jindai Shi* 中國近代史 (*China Contemporary History*). Taipei: Dazhongguo tushu, 1954.

Inglis, Brian. *The Opium War*. London: Hodder & Stoughton, 1976.

Kaiser, Andrew T. *The Rushing On of the Purposes of God: Christian Missions in Shanxi since 1876*. Eugene: Pickwick, 2016.

Kang, Jie. *House Church Christianity in China: From Rural Preachers to City Pastors*. Switzerland: Springer, 2016.

Kepler, A. R. "Movements for Christian Unity." In *The China Christian Yearbook*, edited by Frank Rawlinson, Section VIII p. 73–89. Shanghai: Christian Literature Society, 1928.

Lam, Wing Hung 林榮洪. *Fengchaozhong fenqi de Zhongguo Jiaohui* 風潮中奮起的中國教會 (Chinese Theology in Construction). Hong Kong: Tien Dao, 1980.

———. *Zhonghua shenxue wushinian* 中華神學五十年 (A Half Century of Chinese Theology). Hong Kong: China Graduate School of Theology, 1998.

Latourette, Kenneth Scott. *A History of Christian Missions in China*. London: SPCK, 1929.

Leung, Ka-lun 梁家麟. *Fulin Zhonghua- Zhongguo jindai jiaohuishi shijiang* 福臨中華—中國近代教會史十講 (Blessing Upon China: Ten Talks on the Contemporary Chinese Church History). Hong Kong: Tian Dao, 1988.

Lin, Zhiping 林治平, and Wu Yoxing 吳昶興, eds. *Kuayue san ge shiji de chuanjiao yundong, 1865–2015: Neidihui laihua yibaiwushi nian xuanjiao lunwenji* 跨越三個世紀的傳教運動, 1865-2015: 內地會來華一百五十年宣教論文集 (Christian Missions Spanning Three Centuries: Essays on the 150th Anniversary of CIM-OMF Work in China). Taiwan: Yuzhouguang, 2016.

Liu, Tianlu 劉天路, ed. *Shenti, linghun, ziran: Zhongguo Jidujiao yu yiliao, shehui shiye yanjiu* 身體、靈魂、自然:中國基督教與醫療、社會事業研究 (Body, Soul, and Nature: Chinese Christianity and Medical Service). Shanghai: Shanghai Renmin Chubanshe, 2010.

Lutz, Jessie Gregory. *Chinese Politics and Christian Missions: The Anti-Christian Movement of 1920-1928*. Notre Dame: Cross Cultural Publications, 1988.

Lyall, Leslie. *A Passion for the Impossible: The China Inland Mission, 1865–1965*. London: Hodder & Stoughton, 1965.

Miner, Luella. *China's Book of Martyrs: A Record of Heroic Martyrdoms and Marvellous Deliverances of Chinese Christians During the Summer of 1900.* New York: Pilgrim, 1903.

Phillips, Richard T. *China since 1911.* New York: St. Martin's, 1996.

Pollock, John C. *A Cambridge Movement.* London: Marshall, Morgan & Scott, 1953.

———. *Cambridge Seven.* London: Christian Focus, 2006.

Puncher, Sebastian Alexander George. "The Victorian Army and the Cadet Colleges, Woolwich and Sandhurst, c. 1840–1902." PhD diss., University of Kent, 2019.

Qiao, Zhiqiang 喬志強, ed. *Yihetuan zai Shanxi diqu shiliou* 義和團在山西地區史料 (Historical Materials Concerning the Boxer Movement in Shanxi). Taiyuan: Shanxi Renmin, 1982.

Shubert, William E. *I Remember John Sung.* Singapore: Far East Bible College Press, 1976.

Sih, Paul K. T. *Nationalist China during the Sino-Japanese War, 1937–1945.* Hicksville: Exposition Press, 1977.

So, Wingyui 蘇穎睿. "A Passion for a Greater Vision: The Role of Leslie T. Lyall in the History of the China Inland Mission/Overseas Missionary Fellowship." PhD diss., The University of Hong Kong, 2016.

Stauffer, Milton. ed. *The Christian Occupation of China.* Shanghai: China Continuation Committee, 1922.

Sung, John. *The Diaries of John Sung: An Autobiography.* Translated by Stephen L. Sheng and Luke H. Sheng. Brighton: 1995.

Tao, Fei Ya 陶飛亞. *Bianyuan de lishi- Jidujiao yu jindai Zhongguo* 邊緣的歷史- 基督教與近代中國 (Marginal History: Christianity and Contemporary China). Shanghai: Shanghai Guji Chubanshe, 2005.

Taylor, F. Howard, and Mrs. Howard Taylor (née Geraldine Guinness). *Hudson Taylor and the China Inland Mission: The Growth of a Work of God.* London: Morgan & Scott, 1995.

———. *Hudson Taylor in Early Years: The Growth of a Soul.* London: Morgan & Scott, 1911.

Taylor, Mrs. Howard (nèe Geraldine Guinness). *One of China's Scholars: Pastor Hsi.* London: Morgan & Scott, 1900.

———. *Pastor Hsi (of North China): One of China's Christians.* London: Morgan & Scott, 1903.

Taylor, James Hudson. *China: Its Spiritual Need and Claims.* London: China Inland Mission, 1865.

Thompson, Phyllis. *China: The Reluctant Exodus.* London: Hodder & Stoughton, 1979.

———. *D. E. Hoste: A Prince with God.* London: China Inland Mission, 1947.

Thompson, Roger R. "Reporting the Taiyuan Massacre: Culture and Politics in the China War of 1900." In *The Boxers, China, and the World*, edited by Robert Bickers and R. G. Tiedemann, 66–92. Plymouth: Rowman & Littlefield, 2007.

———. "Twilight of the Gods in the Countryside: Christians, Confucians, and the Modernizing State 1861–1911." In *Christianity in China: From the Eighteenth Century to the Present*, edited by Daniel H. Bays, 53–72. Stanford: Stanford University Press, 1966.

Tiedemann, R. G., ed. *Handbook of Christianity in China: Volume Two: 1800 – Present*. Leiden: Brill, 2010.

Twitchett, Denis, and John Fairbank, eds. *Republican China, 1912–1949*. Volume 12 in *The Cambridge History of China*. Cambridge: Cambridge University Press, 1983.

Wong, Sik Pui 黃錫培. *In Remembrance of Martyrs a Century Ago*. Petaluma: CCM USA and OMF Hong Kong, 2010.

Woodcock, George. *The British in the Far East*. London: George Weidenfeld & Nicholson, 1969.

Wu, Jingheng 吳敬恒, and Cai, Yuanpei 蔡元培, eds. *Yihetuan yundongshi* 義和團運動史 (History of the Boxer Movement). Shanghai: Shangwu, 1931.

Wu, Yaqun 吳亞群. "Zhongguo Neidihui dierdai zongzhuren He Side yanjiu" 中國內地會第二代總主任何斯德研究 (A Study on Dixon Edward Hoste, the Second General Director of the CIM). Master's thesis, Zhejiang University, 2016.

Yao, Kevin Xiyi. *The Fundamentalist Movement among Protestant Missionaries in China, 1920–1937*. Lanham: University Press of America, 2003.

Yuan, Sylvia Y. 袁暘. "Zhongguo zhihou hechuqu? Zhongguo Neidihui/Haiwaijidushituan (CIM/OMF) guoji chuanjiao yundong zhi quanqiu diyuhua jincheng" 中國之後何處去? 中國內地會/海外基督使團 (CIM/OMF) 國際傳教運動之全球地域化進程 (After China, What?: The Glocalization of the International Missionary Movement of the China Inland Mission/Overseas Missionary Fellowship – CIM/OMF). PhD diss., Fudan University, 2012.

Yung, Hwa. *Leadership or Servanthood?: Walking in the Steps of Jesus*. Carlisle: Langham Global Library, 2021.

Zhao, Tian En 趙天恩. *Zhongguo jiaohuishi lunwenji* 中國教會史論文集 (Essays on China Church History). Taipei: Yuzhouguang, 2006.

Articles

朱金甫, *Qingmo jiaoan* 清末教案 (Late Qing Incidents), Volume III (Beijing: Zhonghua Shuju, 1998), 187–208.

Clements, K. W., and J. A. Frenkel. "Exchange Rates, Money, and Relative Prices: The Dollar-Pound in the 1920s." *Journal of International Economics* (1980): 249–262.

Federal Reserve Bulletin (January 1920): 49–51, 111–112.

Franklin, Kirk, and Niemandt, Nelus. "Polycentrism in the Missio Dei." *HTS Teologiese Studies*. Vol 72, No 1 (2007): 1–9.

Hodgkin, Henry T. "National Christian Council in 1927." *China Christian Yearbook 1928* (1928): 67–69.

Hoste, Dixon E. "Possible Changes and Developments in the Native Churches Arising out of the Present Crisis." *Chinese Recorder* (October 1900): 509–512.

———. "Preparing for a Great Advance: A Letter from the General Director of the Mission to the Friends and Supporters of the Mission in Great Britain." *China's Millions* (February 1929): 22.

———. "Why I Have Joined the Bible Union of China." *Chinese Recorder* (1921): 469–472.

Houghton, Frank. "A New Emphasis." *China's Millions* (1944): Appendix 1, p1–2.

Lea, Arnold. "Mission and Church." *China's Millions* (May 1951): 47.

Li, Nan 李楠. "Huigu yu qianzhan: Sanshi nianlai Zhongguo Neiduhui shiyanjiu" 回顧與前瞻 三十年來中國內地會史研究 (Retrospect and Prospect: Research on the China Inland Mission in the Past Thirty Years). *Religious Studies* 宗教學研究, 2 (2015): 212–219.

Lo, C. L. "The Origin and Development of the Three-Self Movement." *Ching Feng* 71 (September 1982): 17

Mingnan, Ding. "Some Questions Concerning the Appraisal of the Boxer Movement." *Chinese Studies in History* 20, no. 3–4 (1987): 24–41.

Ng, Peter Tze Ming. "Cheng Jingyi: Prophet of His Time." *International Bulletin of Missionary Research* 36, no. 1 (January 2012): 14–16.

Shenk, Wilbert R. "Rufus Anderson and Henry Venn: A Special Relationship?" *International Bulletin of Missionary Research* 5, vol. 4 (October 1981): 168–172.

Sinton, John R. "Trends and Tendencies." *China's Millions* (November–December 1942): 50–51.

Tao, Feiya 陶飛亞, and Dai Wanqi 戴婉琦. "Jinnianlai dalu Zhonghua Neidihui yanjiu shuping" 近年來大陸中華內地會研究述評 (Recent Survey of Studies in Mainland China on the China Inland Mission). *Jinan Daxue Xuebao* 濟南大學學報6 (2016): 69–77.

Wan, Fulin 萬福林. "Zhongguo jiaohui zizhi ziyang zichuan yundong de jieshao" 中國教會自治自養自傳運動的介紹 (An Introduction to the Self-Government, Self-Support and Self-Propagation in the Church in China). *Tian Feng* 天風 23, no. 9 (November 1950): 2.

Woods, Paul. "Perichoresis and Koinonia: Implications of Our Fellowship with God for the Changing Missionary Endeavour." *Mission Round Table* 10, no. 1 (January 2015): 4–5.

Wu, Yaozong 吳耀宗, "Judujiao gexin yundong de xinjieduan" 基督教革新運動的新階段 (A new milestone in the transforming movement of Christianity), *Tian Feng* 天風 246 (1951): 2.

Ying, Fuk-Tsang 邢福增, "Zhongguo jiyao zhuyizhe de Shijian yu kunjing: Chen chonggui de shenxue sixiang yu shidaii" 中國基要主義者的實踐與困境: 陳崇桂的神學思想與時代 (The Praxis and Predicament of a Chinese Fundamentalist: Chen Chonggui's Theological Thought and His Time). *Jian Dao Shenxueyuan* 建道神學院, (2001): 245.

Zhang, Liang 張靚. "Zhongguo Neidihui zaoqi xuanjiao shiyele de Zhongguo tonggong" 中國內地會早期宣教運動事業裏的中國同工 (Chinese Workers of the Early China Inland Mission). *Shi Lin* 史林, no. 4 (2015): 119–126.

Zhang, Richard. "The Origin of the 'Three Self'." *Jian Dao: A Journal of Bible and Theology* 5 (January 1996): 175–202.

Langham Literature, with its publishing work, is a ministry of Langham Partnership.

Langham Partnership is a global fellowship working in pursuit of the vision God entrusted to its founder John Stott –

> *to facilitate the growth of the church in maturity and Christ-likeness through raising the standards of biblical preaching and teaching.*

Our vision is to see churches in the Majority World equipped for mission and growing to maturity in Christ through the ministry of pastors and leaders who believe, teach and live by the word of God.

Our mission is to strengthen the ministry of the word of God through:
- nurturing national movements for biblical preaching
- fostering the creation and distribution of evangelical literature
- enhancing evangelical theological education

especially in countries where churches are under-resourced.

Our ministry

Langham Preaching partners with national leaders to nurture indigenous biblical preaching movements for pastors and lay preachers all around the world. With the support of a team of trainers from many countries, a multi-level programme of seminars provides practical training, and is followed by a programme for training local facilitators. Local preachers' groups and national and regional networks ensure continuity and ongoing development, seeking to build vigorous movements committed to Bible exposition.

Langham Literature provides Majority World preachers, scholars and seminary libraries with evangelical books and electronic resources through publishing and distribution, grants and discounts. The programme also fosters the creation of indigenous evangelical books in many languages, through writer's grants, strengthening local evangelical publishing houses, and investment in major regional literature projects, such as one volume Bible commentaries like the Africa Bible Commentary and the South Asia Bible Commentary.

Langham Scholars provides financial support for evangelical doctoral students from the Majority World so that, when they return home, they may train pastors and other Christian leaders with sound, biblical and theological teaching. This programme equips those who equip others. Langham Scholars also works in partnership with Majority World seminaries in strengthening evangelical theological education. A growing number of Langham Scholars study in high quality doctoral programmes in the Majority World itself. As well as teaching the next generation of pastors, graduated Langham Scholars exercise significant influence through their writing and leadership.

To learn more about Langham Partnership and the work we do visit langham.org

www.ingramcontent.com/pod-product-compliance
Lightning Source LLC
Chambersburg PA
CBHW051541230426
43669CB00015B/2677